T0370128

A Timeless Script From a 1st Century Doctor

ADVENT THROUGH THE EYES OF DR. LUKE

RICK FARMER

WESTBOW
PRESS®
A DIVISION OF THOMAS NELSON
& ZONDERVAN

WestBow Press books may be ordered through booksellers or by contacting:

WestBow Press
A Division of Thomas Nelson & Zondervan
1663 Liberty Drive
Bloomington, IN 47403
www.westbowpress.com
844-714-3454

ISBN: 979-8-3850-2819-1 (sc)
ISBN: 979-8-3850-2820-7 (hc)
ISBN: 979-8-3850-2821-4 (e)

Library of Congress Control Number: 2024912637

Print information available on the last page.

WestBow Press rev. date: 09/11/2024

About The Author

"Being in a Dr. Farmer's class is being in the presence of someone who genuinely cares about you and wants to do everything they can to help you succeed. He always has so many things to teach you that you did not even know you would be getting into when you signed up for the class." (Kathryn Inman, Flagler College Student)

"Being in Dr. Farmers' class is very educational and interesting. Students learn more about psychology than one would expect from an intro class. This is one of the best classes I have ever taken. I highly recommend Dr. Farmer and his book because it is great." (Alexis Gifford, Flagler College Student)

"Having Dr. Farmer as a teacher means having a class to look forward to. He teaches in a way where I can understand the material at a fast pace and never fails to make me laugh." (Gia Venetucci, Flagler College Student)

"What it is like to have class with Dr. Farmer? Since the first day of class, Dr. Farmer'ss' captivating attitude has encouraged a two-way conversation with us students. His unique, knowledgeable, and engaging approach gives room for open, yet respectful class discussions. It is an honor to be part of his class." (Karla J. Lopez, Flagler College Student)

"Being enrolled in a class with Dr. Farmer is a change of pace I had to get used to. Through the eyes of a Fine Art major, adjusting to Dr. Farmer's class style would not have come easy on my own. Dr. Farmer has a unique way of adapting his teaching style to fit each of his different class groups. The first week of class he stated, " If you are not having a good time at Flagler, come stop by my office and I will make sure I change that." Dr. Farmer leads an open and honest classroom, always engaging his students, incorporating different teaching methods throughout the course. I really enjoy Dr. Farmer as a teacher and having a mutual comfortability to share personal stories and laughs." (Jordan Outland, Flagler College Student)

"Dr. Farmer has been one of the most welcoming professors I have had since entering Flagler College. His class is always so warm, fun, and lighthearted. His class is one I always look forward to, even on days when I would usually rather be lying in bed. He has helped me prepare for my college career more than I ever could have expected, and I am profoundly grateful that I decided to take his class." (Cosette Bryndal, Flagler College Student)

"To have Dr. Farmer as a teacher is a breath of fresh air. Someone who can be honest and give all perspectives is very refreshing in many ways. He explains controversial topics in a way that is digestible. It is extremely refreshing to have someone you can trust to tell you the truth. He has broadened my view of the world in many positive ways and for that I will forever appreciate his point of view." (Evie Schmidt, Flagler College Student)

(All words printed with permission from each student)

Contents

Thank you, Professor Massey

As a formal Psychology Professor at Bluefield University, I was touched by many colleagues. I will mention some of them below. However, one person who preceded me at this great institution of learning was retired English Professor Wayne Massey. Though I had heard of him from other members of BU Faculty, I had never had the privilege of meeting him in person. With a single phone call, I got to know him for the first time. He willingly took upon himself the task of doing a final edit of this manuscript. His amazing effort left me speechless. Not only did he take the time to read the entire manuscript in a few short days, but he responded quickly with advice, comments, corrections, and above all, amazing encouragement. I wanted to share some of the things he garnered from the reading of this book. My hope is that his words might encourage you to participate in what follows with enthusiastic attention and a genuine pursuit of knowledge about what I believe to be the most important event in human history, the birth of Jesus of Nazareth. (RF)

This is what Professor Massey wrote:

"Rick, I want to thank you for allowing me to read and offer my suggestions regarding your manuscript, A *Timeless Script from a 1ˢᵗ Century Doctor.* You are to be commended. This is more than first century. It is first class! Thank you for the privilege. I am most grateful.

May I say, too, that your writing style is appealing. You have blended excellent research with brilliance of thought, and your readers will quickly discover your perceptions to be worth their serious consideration. The blend continues: humor, anecdotal enrichment and local arrangement, work together to enhance a serious study and analysis of a most important subject.

Yes, you've done what you set out to do. You have written conclusively and convincingly. Your readers will not forget the experience of learning that you have offered them.

Finally, Rick, I praise our Lord for this effort of love for Him" (Wayne Massey).

Acknowledgements

Thirteen years ago, I began the concerted effort of organizing my thoughts around Luke's Gospel, chapters 1- 2, and Advent in general. This has been a process of tremendous growth and powerful transformation. There is no way I make it to this point in my thinking without the incredible contributions of the following people. I always hesitate to express public appreciation, for inevitably I leave someone out who certainly ought to be mentioned. I make the effort here, nonetheless.

For guiding my theological journey from day one of my academic experiences I express my sincere appreciation for Dr. Ed Jacobs and Dr. Art Lindsley. For inspiration to keep writing I express great thanks to Mrs. Owens, my 8th grade English Teacher, and several of my colleagues who pushed me forward in this adventure – Teanna Crockett and Henry Clary especially. For holding before me the challenge of speaking the Truth of Scripture into the *real world* I must acknowledge Dr. Mark Piacentini and Dr. Kelley from Pittsburgh Theological Seminary, two of the greatest bridge builders from Scripture to the real world I know. Taking courses from Al Wolters and Eugene Peterson challenged me to dig deeply, speak passionately, and impact powerfully when teaching and preaching. Thank you, Margeret (Peggar) Dixon, Ruth Paul, Dennis Amrine, and Michael Farhart, who spent countless hours helping me hone my thoughts in conversation in my campus ministry days. All of these profoundly impacted both my thinking and my teaching style. Thank you, Dr. Steve Willis, and Scott Weibling, for your consistent advice throughout this project. Finally, thank you Dr. Wayne Massey for the tireless effort you put into weeding through this document as my primary Editor. Your skill and passion for this task is inspirational.

I would not have been able to organize these thoughts had it not been for my son Josh asking me the right questions and listening to endless musings from the day he began speaking. My wife Kim freed me for countless hours of study, writing, and verbalizing with compassion, patience, and outstanding insight. For all the loving parishioners who voluntarily listened as I weekly preached the Gospel, I cannot express enough thanks to you. I especially acknowledge Fred Price (who asked the best questions), Dane Moore (who constantly pushed me toward Truth), Willis Thomas (who fixed my Bible more than once), and Willy Parker (who supported my teaching ministry vehemently) for these opportunities. Most of all, thank you to all my students, who challenged me with powerful insight, incredible questions, challenging push back, beautifully written essays, interesting class discussions, and tremendous attention and energy. Thank you beyond measure BCM Students at WVU, Bluefield University Psychology Students, and Flagler College Students. You are the best! For helping me with the cover you see for this book I say thank you to the talented and gracious Kate Inman. For those students who took time to write a couple sentences for me, your input was invaluable. I wish I could name you all. Finally, thank you Jesus Christ for becoming the source of Life that so many of us reflect upon and write about. You are our Inspiration and our Guide as we try to encourage those around us and impact people during our search for Truth.

Foreword

I first met Rick Farmer the summer before my first year of college. He was a counselor at a Christian camp I had attended since childhood and was the newly hired collegiate minister at First Baptist Church, Morgantown, WV. Having just graduated from a small coal-mining town in a modest senior class of 250 students, my upcoming matriculation into a university of 20,000+ was a matter of concern for both me and my family. Neither my parents nor grandparents had gone off to college and the questions surrounding my future were many: How would I fare socially and academically? Would I deal with homesickness? Might I find good friends? Could my faith stand the test of being immersed into what Playboy Magazine deemed the "#1 party school in the nation"?

Knowing I was headed to his campus, Rick took me under his wing and guided me through the culture shock that ensued. In my four years in Morgantown, we watched his collegiate ministry grow from around a dozen students to nearly a hundred weekly. I think it grew, in large part, due to Rick's unique style of teaching. Coming from a small country church, I had never heard a man integrate the truth of the gospel with the historical context of the Ancient Near East in quite the manner Rick did. He had a gift that enabled him to communicate biblical truth in a way that combined social justice and academics that led to college students synthesizing our faith with the secular education we were receiving at the state university.

Three decades later, Rick continues to inspire students through similar means of integration of faith and the social sciences. He has always had a heart and passion for reaching the intellectual skeptic, the lost and the hurting, both the addict and the erudite alike. In this present work, *A Timeless Script from a 1ˢᵗ Century Doctor*, Professor Farmer does what he has always done, he takes a story that has been told a thousand times before and delivers it in a way that is fresh and inspiring.

So, as you gather around the glow of the Christmas lights, and warm yourself by the hearth in your living rooms, I encourage you to enjoy Rick's take on the yuletide stories through the eyes of a first-century physician and historian. I expect this devotional will act as a source of comfort, inspiration, and intellectual stimulation. Dive into the pages within, and may these words and reflections bring you peace, comfort, and connection with the Prince of Peace at a time when peace is most needed.

(Rev. Stephen R. Willis, Ph.D.; Author of Bestseller *Winning the Food Fight,* published by Regal from Gospel Light. Senior Pastor, One Church, Murfreesboro, TN)

"Therefore, the Lord will give you a sign:
The Virgin will conceive and give birth to a son,
and will call Him Immanuel" (Isaiah 7:14) [1]

Immanuel [2] or "God with Us," is one of the most powerful
names in Human History. Just entertaining the idea that God
has come to us, has walked among us, has so identified with
us that we are able to speak His Name among the people,
is both a Supreme Opportunity and the Most Serious of
Responsibilities, regardless of what a person believes about
Jesus of Nazareth. The mere possibility must be investigated.
May the words which follow invite us into the Advent Story
in such a way that we might explore afresh the Greatest
Opportunity of all - "God With Us," *Immanuel* to All!!!

---

[1] All Biblical passages throughout this document are quoted using the NIV, or
New International Version, except where otherwise noted.
[2] For a great discussion of *Immanuel* please refer to : Benjamin Johnson: *Is he called*
Jesus or Immanuel? January 29, 2023. Longview News Journal. News-journal.com

Note for the Reader

This book can be used as a *Preparation Event for Advent*, reading each labeled day one day at a time as you make your way toward December 25th. You might also choose to read during the calendar year, as you keep alive the Spirit of Advent throughout all months, "Living Advent Every Day." Or you might choose to read any time at your own pace as you treat each day as a separate *Thought-provoking Essay*. Under each day you will find a discussion of an interesting idea that will "set the stage" and correlate with the reading for that day. I have included various pieces of background information that will help you journey back in time as we attempt to apply long-standing truths which might help us live life to the fullest in our time. I will sometimes break out into thought and reflection about a particular idea for some deeper thinking, a peek inside the author's mind, if you will. I will also include some humor which relates, some of my own poetry which hopefully inspires, and quotes that lend wisdom. I hope you find these materials as interesting and inspirational as I did when researching them. My desire is that every part of this document will stimulate thought, create a desire to learn, and challenge the thinking person to reconsider a two-century old Story as a *Timeless Script* which speaks to our Day. This "Script" is to be administered in 28 doses, a Lunar month. I have called them "days" .... days as in *Yom* (The Hebrew word for "Day" in Genesis 1 and 2, which can often mean a time or a season as well as 24 hours). [3] I invite you to use twenty-eight *Yom* to study Luke's Advent Story, and you get to define the *Yom*. Please pick the pace you want to read, but by the end of the journey my hope is that you find yourself challenged to read Luke's Gospel in its entirety, inspired to deeply consider the Jesus Luke wrote about, and that you might find yourself more equipped to face the challenges we inherit as 21st century world citizens.

Blessings, Dr. Rick Farmer

---

[3] Although *yom* is commonly rendered as day in English translations, the word *yom* can be used in different ways to refer to different time spans. For example, it can mean a point of time (a specific day), a time period of a whole or half a day as in the period the sun is shining (since *Yom* literally means "warm" or "period of warmth"), a period of light (as contrasted with the period of darkness), sunrise to sunset, 24 hours, or it can mean a long time period in which certain conditions are met like the " day" of Creation or the "day" of the Romans or the "day" of Revolution. All these meanings are used in the Old Testament.

Introduction

Traveling Through the Mind of DR. LUKE
– We need this Word today…

"Indeed, if things don't improve, today's unprecedented
levels of loneliness, depression, and suicide will prove
to be only a preview of greater tragedies to come. When
life hits the fan, people young an old will discover
too late that their unexamined worldviews are empty,
toxic, and even deadly." [4] (Michael Guillen)

The Gospel of Luke is a unique telling of the Good News of the
Coming, Life, Death, and Resurrection of Jesus of Nazareth.
Luke wrote for common folk, men and women who come from
the other side of the tracks. In Luke's Gospel we see women
highlighted in a way that would be deemed scandalous in his day.
Women simply did not garner the respect due them. However,
because they were so important in the telling of the story of
Jesus, they were very much "prime time" with Dr. Luke. Luke
alone highlighted some very prominent women we would know
little to nothing about if not for Luke: *Mary and Elizabeth* (Luke

---

[4] For a brillant discussion of how what we believe ultimately impacts what we see or
don't see, hear or don't hear, please take the time to read: Michael Guilen, "Believing
is Seeing: A Physicist Explains How Science Shattered His Atheism and Revealed the
Necessity of Faith", 2021. Tyndale House Publishers, Carol Stream, IL.

1 and 2); *Anna* (Luke 2;3); *The Widow of Nain* who had lost everything (Luke 7:11-17); The desperate woman of the streets who anointed Jesus' feet at a Pharisee's house (Luke 7:36-50); Two of Jesus' closest friends named *Mary and Martha* (Luke 10:38), who occupied a luxurious home always open to Jesus; And of course *Mary Magdeline*, redeemed woman of ill repute who was a traveling companion of Jesus and one of the first witnesses to The Empty Tomb.

For any gifted 1st century historian to highlight women in such a way would be quite uncommon. This is recognized as a major piece of evidence in support of the truth of his words, given that women would have given extraordinarily little credence to his Gospel in Luke's day. Why include so many, if not speaking truth? He would only have highlighted them had they been an especially important and trustworthy part of the story he is telling in his Gospel.

Luke also made it clear for all who read that this Gospel is a Universal Gospel. "All the barriers are down; Jesus Christ is for all people without distinction." [5] He gave us a variety of hints throughout. First, we see this in the stories Luke alone chooses to highlight. We are made aware of some parables no other Gospel includes: The Good Samaritan in Luke 10; The Prodigal Son in Luke 15; The Parable of the Tax Collector and the Persistent Widow in Luke 18; the list is long. These stories involved a half-breed Jewish Samaritan, a lost and wandering son, a "can't touch this" Tax Collector, and a Widow thought out of favor with God. Luke wrote a Universal Gospel with a Timeless Message for all categories of people. Luke's primary intent was to speak to the

---

[5] Willian Barclay, *The Gospel of Luke*, *(1953, 1956)*. The Saint Andrew Press, Edinburgh, Scotland. Published in the United States by The Westminster Press, Philadelphia. The quote used is from page xvii.

Gentile,[6] a huge category of people which included anyone not a Jew.

Secondly, Luke highlighted the people's response to Jesus' universal mission beyond that of any other Gospel writer. In Luke chapter 4 he recounted the story of Jesus returning home to Nazareth after beginning his public work as Healer and Teacher. Jesus is given the honor of reading the text for the day and speaking to the people about the text. After announcing he had come in fulfillment to Isaiah's promise (Isaiah 61:1,2) through his reading, proclaiming deliverance and Jubilee [7] for all the world (Luke 4:18,19), He then intentionally highlighted two Old Testament characters - The Widow of Sidon and Naaman the Syrian (See Luke 4:25 and following, I Kings 17:8-16, and 2 Kings 5:1 for context). These two were Gentiles, and Jesus was announcing that He has come for all people of all races, all nations, all sexes, all

---

[6] "Gentile" is a descriptive term meant to refer to any group of people who were not part of the Jewish Faith. These people were typically referred to as "The Nations" in the Old Testament. A "Gentile" was a person belonging to "The Nations." The first Gentile on record to hear and embrace the Gospel Jesus proclaimed was a man named *Cornelius* in Acts 11:19. We might also make a valid case that *Theophilus*, mentioned in Luke's Introduction, was a Gentile Convert. I will discuss *"Theo"* in more detail.

[7] "The concept of the Jubilee, or the collective forgiveness of all debts and debtor/ slaves, had its origins in the Ancient Near East where it was a secular practice of kings. It came into the Bible originally also as a secular practice of kings but then became the province of priests and a calendar observance to be celebrated every 50 years. It was finally understood in the Dead Sea Scrolls and the New Testament to rest in the hands of God alone, an eschatological concept of the forgiveness of all debts/sins and the redemption of all human sins, or debts to God, that became the very basis of the theological history of Luke/Acts. The principal legislation in the Bible on Jubilee is in Leviticus 25. The three salient obligations are a) release of slaves, b) forgiveness of debts, and c) repatriation of property, in the Jubilee year. The primary theological base of the legislation is that the land and the people belong to God. That is the fundamental key to understanding the Biblical concept of Jubilee." (James A Sanders) For further study see especially Jubilee in the Bible, James A Sanders, February 2, 2020. Sage Journals, Biblical Theology Bulletin: Journal of Bible and Culture. Journals.sagepub.com

orientations, all lifestyles, and all anything we can think of that separates us from one another. This pronouncement angered the people of his hometown, as they instantly tried to throw Him from a cliff. Considering the ethnic and religious separation in our world today, the reader of Luke will instantly see the relevance of Luke's Gospel. He left for us a "We Are the World" Gospel, written for everyone, women and men, rich and poor, young and old. He realized other Gospels had a Jewish agenda written for Jewish audiences by Jewish authors. In fact, Luke was the only Greek Author included in the New Testament. His goal was to speak to the rest of the world, to paint an accurate picture of Jesus of Nazareth for the Non-Jew so that the entire World might know and understand that Messiah had come for all people across all nations.

Thirdly, this *Timeless* Gospel may be *timelier* in our *time* than any other *time* in human history. In 2023 around 32% of all adults, and 50% of adults ages 18-24, reported symptoms of depression. These numbers exceed the 20-25% depression rates reported during the Great Depression years of the 1930's, the highest numbers recorded in the 20th century. Though reports of depression are down a bit from the early months of 2021, having peaked during and right after Covid lockdowns, depression and suicide rates remain at all-time highs. In contrast, depression symptoms reported averages around 8-10 % in 2003, 5.7 % in 1992, and around 5.3 % in 1970, according to Statistica, Jama, and Science Direct.[8]

As a Professional Counselor I have learned depression is a dominant diagnosis in our society. The alarming rates reported in the last decade are frightening. We live in unprecedented times, as

---

[8] Statistics based on these articles: 1. Changes in the global burden of depression from 1990 to 2017: Findings from the Global Burden of Disease study, Journal of Psychiatric Research.Volume 126, July 2020, Pages 134-140. 2. Depression in the U.S. - Statistics & Facts, Published by John Elflein,Aug 31, 2023. Statistica. Statistica.com

depression and suicide ideation have risen to epidemic proportions. This is amplified during the winter months. The American Psychological Association found that 38% experience an increase in stress and depression levels in the months of November and December.[9] Some of this is no doubt related to seasonal depression, but much is connected to the stressors associated with the Holiday Season. What was once a tremendous time of joy is becoming for many a time of dread.

The News for younger Generations is worse the deeper we look. It seems that kids and youth in America, and other places in the West, are not doing well. Consider the evidence highlighted by "The Annual World Happiness Report," published by the Wellbeing Research Centre at the University of Oxford.[10] The United States is in 23rd place as of 2023 on the World Happiness Scale. This is the first time our country ever finished out of the top twenty (Finland is number One, btw, a study worth pursuing in and of itself). "In the under-30 category, the US dropped into 62nd place, behind countries including Saudi Arabia and Guatemala."[11] Considering the technological, educational, and economic advantages we enjoy, this drop is amazing. Jan-Emmanuel De Neve, Oxford Business Professor, and editor of this publication, is noted for declaring that American youth had "fallen off a cliff" since 2012. He attributed a loneliness epidemic, social media, and political division as the primary culprits. Dr. Luke would add an even deeper reason. We are suffering a time of extreme spiritual crisis in America, similar to what was occurring throughout the Roman Empire when Jesus arrived. Whereas American Families used to intentionally expose their children to traditional values as espoused by religious

[9] Health Partners Home/Blog/Mental health/Dealing With depression during the holidays/2023
[10] *US Happiness Ranking Plummets as One Group Struggles Most,* Beatrice Nolan, March 21, 2024. Science Alert, Health. www.sciencealert.com
[11] *US Happiness Ranking Plummets as One Group Struggles Most,* Beatrice Nolan, March 21, 2024. Science Alert, Health. www.sciencealert.com

experiences, this pattern has been all but eradicated from normal family practice. Without childhood exposure to the possibilities of faith, adults seldom return. To such a world Dr. Luke offers a prescription, what I am calling "A Timeless Script From a 1st Century Doctor." Dr. Luke is giving us opportunity to enter the Greatest Story ever told.

These current trends in the USA follow the overall trends in other countries. Depression is the most common mental illness worldwide.[12] In 2022 more than 49,500 people committed suicide in the USA, the highest number ever recorded (According to the CDC). Into this arena of depression enters a "Timeless Prescription" from Dr. Luke. He wrote this "Script" some two millennia ago, yet we find it is sorely needed in our time. He introduced us to a vaccine and a cure, for our depressive tendencies are not simply psychosocial issues, but spiritual issues as well. We have reached a pivotal point in human history. Those of us who suffer through depression need this "Script," and those of us who do not experience depression to such a degree will find his words a powerful vaccine.

I realize that the spiritual issues associated with depression are not at the forefront of scientific investigation. However, we have come to a place where answers are needed, and it is high time to expand our thinking for the sake of mental health. It is time to incorporate profound thinking from beyond our time. Dr. Luke has a Word to share. Considering our present mental health concerns, I suggest we reexamine a Gospel specifically addressed to the likes of us.

In addition to mental health concerns, the rejection of a Judeo-Christian Ethic in the West is having traumatic consequences throughout the everyday lives of our citizenry. I find myself conflicted, believing that the foundations of our country are the

---

[12] Journal of Psychiatric Research, "Changes in the global burden of depression from 1990 to 2017: Findings from the Global Burden of Disease study," July 2020. Science Direct, Volume 126, pages 134-140. sciencedirect.com

greatest set of principles and the most powerful ideology in the history of the world. However, I do not believe this means America is guaranteed a future or a free pass on the world stage. In other words, the State is not God. We are a society built through meritocracy, but we cannot stand on the accomplishments of our past. Our system has created a history which is full of the most progressive, fundamentally innovative, and exceptionally compassionate contributions to humanity the world has ever known. But none of these surpass the birth of Jesus in terms of importance for humanity. Though America has profoundly impacted the cause of good in ways that can never be underestimated or fully comprehended, we are still an Experiment in the works, and it is my belief that without the *Foundation of Faith* we will ultimately fail. We have already begun to see the consequences of some of this suppression of foundational values and the sense of cosmic purpose. As I write and teach, I believe Generation Z may be the most important Generation in the history of our nation. I consistently remind my students of this belief.

The last half century has led to a regression in our Land which is alarming to see. A country built on a unique combination of Faith and Science, autonomy and community, Church and State, academics and hard work, equality and capitalism, freedom and responsibility, morality and mercy, and a willingness to sacrifice self for the sake of the many, has slowly but surely begun a migration away from our historical national psyche. We have decided to pick and choose, rejecting elements of the foundation of our "house" (our country), while focusing instead on window dressing in the form of political ideology, both right and left. We have even chosen to so rewrite our history that we are in denial of any good because of the bad. I do not believe we will survive on this road, and the fall of Rome offers historical precedence for this view. Cultural progress has always been a combination of things we celebrate and things we learn from. We have always celebrated the importance of Faith. This is a primary principle that makes us unique in the world. Advent is not a "holiday." Advent is a World Transforming Event.

Without a deeply rooted understanding of history, a passionate celebration of Faith, an unwavering commitment to Family, and a truly open-minded exploration of Metaphysical Truth in our Academic arenas, we will eventually lose sight of the very principles that made us a great nation. We will become something else entirely, and I am not certain this something else will be a step forward for our children and grandchildren. The American Experiment is built upon the institutions of Freedom, Family, Faith, hard work, equality, and an ever-present commitment to the pursuit of Truth, among other easily identifiable values. It is quite apparent that we have shown ourselves willing to sacrifice many of these foundational values for the sake of individual autonomy and personal preference. This is a natural consequence of Worldview transformation, but it is in our best interests to evaluate these changes.

I fear we are becoming a Land that cares more about our own personal point of view (though often disguised as "group think") than we do about building a future that will forever transform the Human condition for good. I watch protests where some do not even know what they march for, Congressmen and women who speak over top of the witnesses they interview without any concern for actual testimony, political accusations and policies that clearly have only the goal of gaining votes and holding onto power, business practices with a goal of wealth with little intention of serving the public, sexual freedom with no sense of consequences, ideologies dominating education over and above the teaching of critical thinking skills, condemnation of marginalized groups in the name of religion, and a denial of Ultimate Truth in the name of Existential truth. We have lost our way. We are becoming a nation prioritizing personal fulfillment while rewriting and suppressing our history, content to risk our future for our pursuit of happiness.

My grandfather taught me, "happiness is overrated, and those who seek it will seldom find it." As a Professional Counselor I have found he was wise beyond his time. In my view, Americans once focused on meaning, purpose, value, and faith, where-by happiness was often a fortunate by-product of such a life. Modern America has flipped the script, as personal fulfillment seems the supreme goal of most. Can we survive this transition?

Into this environment I hold forth a vaccine - The story of Advent as recorded by Dr. Luke. There was a "Timeless Script" gifted all people some 2,000 years ago in the first two chapters of the Gospel of Luke. I understand there are existing debates about the relevance of Gospel content for our time. It is not my purpose to address these thoroughly in this document, other than to demonstrate the powerful dialogue Luke creates when his Gospel is applied to our time (I have listed many references in case you choose to investigate this issue further). However, I am suggesting to you that Objective Truth is not synonymous with Scientific Truth. I am suggesting that those who lived and wrote in pre-scientific days have much to offer us, and many have suppressed an important quest for knowledge in areas of significance, if we are to truly be Truth seekers. A thing can be true, even if we cannot prove said thing in a Laboratory. The entire desire of the Scientist ought to be to explain reality, not to suppress information before we even pause to investigate. Though a Scientist might often pretend to come at her investigation form a value-free position, the impossibility of such a task is obvious. "At the frontier of research, scientists do have to make complex decisions whether to commit themselves to a new line of enquiry... They must make value judgments in the light of a vision of the purpose of scientific activity.... And the Scientist is sustained in the intense mental struggle by a passionate concern to solve the problem she has decided to tackle. His enterprise is not value-free: it is impregnated through and through by commitment to a purpose." The folk concept often quoted within the scientific community, that there exists a world of "facts" and a world of "values," and never the two shall meet within Scientific Enquiry, "is denied by the actual practice of science."[13] Into this environment I hold forth a vaccine - The story of Advent as recorded by Dr. Luke. There was a "Timeless Script" gifted all people some 2,000 years ago in the first two chapters of the Gospel of Luke. I understand there are existing debates about the relevance of Gospel content for our time. It is not my purpose to address these in this document, other than to demonstrate the powerful dialogue Luke creates when his Gospel is applied to our time.

There is one objection, however, I would like to highlight. One of the most common objections people levy against the Gospel Accounts, including but not limited to Luke's testimony, is that Gospel writers spoke with a bias. When an author has a bias, these critics argue, the resulting work amounts to nothing more than propaganda. These are often true observations, which on the surface would seem to negate the value of their work. But does it? Do we make our choices about truth based on the evidence and the argument, or based on whether there is a bias on the part of the author? I maintain that a person with a bias can still speak truth. I would also maintain that a person without a bias, as if such a thing is possible, can still be wrong.

In His book "The God Delusion,"[14] Richard Dawkins concludes "the biblical Yahweh is 'psychotic,' Aquinas's proofs of God's existence are 'fatuous' and religion generally is 'nonsense.'" Though He critiques the Gospels as propaganda spurred by the obvious bias

---

[13] Leslie Newbigin, "Foolishness to the Greeks: The Gospel and Western Culture," 1986, 1988. William B. Eerdmans Publishing Company, Grand Rapids, Michigan. Page 77.

[14] Richard Dawkins, *The God Delusion* (January 2008). Mariner Books. In the seminal text on atheism in the twenty-first century, renowned scientist Richard Dawkins examines the irrationality of believing in God and the grievous harm religion has inflicted on society.

of attempting to display the Divinity and Unique Personhood of Jesus, he does so by profoundly proliferating his own personal bias, and therefore his own propaganda, against the personal existence of God. The simple truth is we all bring our bias to the story. Yes, even Luke. But this has no necessary bearing on the Truth being proclaimed. Bias does not necessitate false information any more than objective observation guarantees truth. I admit my bias in the words which follow. I choose to believe that Luke was a master historian who worked diligently to research and preserve the truth about Jesus. I believe this for good reason. It is not blind faith, as you will see in the words which follow. Luke wrote these words after he became Jesus' follower, and most certainly set out to give us a detailed rendering of what he discovered during his investigation. He wholeheartedly believed Jesus had answers we all need for everyday life. He wrote as a physician who cared for people's health and future.

Luke vehemently believed that Jesus was and is the Son of God and that he was born under miraculous circumstances as the long-awaited Messiah. The evidence Luke gathered and presented overwhelmingly supported the premise of his work. His argument transcended his bias, for Truth has a way of breaking through. I invite you: Let us explore Luke's mind together during a time of tremendous human need, in his day and in ours.

Leslie Newborn further reminds us: "The authority of Jesus cannot be validated by reference to some other authority that is already accepted, because the gospel is a new starting point, a new lens to see the world by. When Jesus' disciples are challenged with the question, 'By what power or by what name did you do this?' Their only answer was 'in the name of Jesus Christ of Nazareth' (Acts 4:7-10). This Lordship extends to all things and because the authority of Jesus is ultimate, the recognition of it involves a commitment that replaces all other commitments." First century Christians lived a perpetual faith that refused to "bow the knee" to anyone other than Christ, even if this meant starvation, bodily harm, risking of family, and even death. The question of Authority was not a political matter in as much as it was a matter of "A Living Faith," which had a beginning point in the birth of a Child-King some two centuries in our past. Advent is the most powerful reminder in human history that The One who made us has not abandoned us, and never will. Jesus is truly *Immanuel*,[15] "God with us."

First Century proponents of the concept of *Immanuel,* "God with us," of which Luke was chief among them, were so completely transformed by the Advent Event that the entire direction of human history was transformed by the birth of this One Child in Bethlehem. Regarding these earlier followers Rev. Frederick Buechner wrote: "Somewhere along the line something deep in them split star wise and they became not simply followers of Christ but bearers of His Life. A birth of grace and truth took place within them scarcely less miraculous in its way than the one the Magi traveled all those miles to kneel before" (*Immanuel*).........." The Child is born, and history itself falls in two at the Star. Whether you believe or do not believe, you date your letters and checks and income tax forms with a maunder representing how many years have gone by since what happened. The world of A.D. is one world, and the world of B.C. is another".[16]

Under the heading of thirty distinct discussions (symbolizing twenty-nine to thirty days of Advent), we will attempt to investigate what Luke was proclaiming in his time and how this Word continues to speak to the 21st century mind. We will sneak a peek inside the message of a Timeless 1st Century Gospel and attempt

---

[15] For a great presentation on the name "Immanuel" see: Michael Card, Immanuel: Professions on the Life of Christ, 1981. BILLY GRAHAM SPECIAL EDITION. 1990 THOMAS NELSON trade paperback

[16] "Weekly Sermon Illustration: Immanuel," Rev. Frederick Buechner, December 16, 2013. The Rev. Frederick Buechner Organization, Denomination: Presbyterian Church (USA).

to discern what Luke's message meant for the 1st century listener, those who had longed for His arrival for centuries. We will also investigate what Luke has to say to the postmodern and post-truth mind of our time. In fact, we are *Theophilus*. We are the intended audience. Luke lays down this account for the non-Jew, the people who received a gift dropped at our door from an unknown uncle we had no idea was our uncle. Luke becomes this uncle for us, and we are the Gentile World.

"Did you hear about the dyslexic, agnostic insomniac who stays up all night wondering if there really is a Dog?"[17] (Anon)

"Historians generally assume that an author's intent is to write history if it appears he or she is trying to write history. And while we may judge this history reliable or unreliable, depending on what the evidence dictates, we in general trust the account unless we have reasons not to do so."[18] (C. J. Reiner)

"The accuracy of Luke as a historian was confirmed by the famous historian, A. N. Sherwin-White, who carefully examined his references in Luke/Acts to 32 countries, 54 cities, and nine islands, finding not a single mistake."[19] (Eddie Hyatt)

---

[17] Unless otherwise indicated, all short quotes used between daily Essays included in this document come from "The Friars' Club Encyclopedia of Jokes", compiled by H. Aaron Cohl, 1997. Black Dog & Leventhal Publishers, Inc. and Workman Publishing Company, both located in NY, New York.

[18] 18 Gregory A. Boyd who is quoting G. J. Reiner in "Sonic, Sage, or Son of God: Recovering the Real Jesus in an Age of Revisionist Replies, 1985. A Bridgepoint Book by Victor Books, Wheaton, IL.

[19] Compelling Historical Evidence for the Virgin Birth of Jesus Christ, Eddie Hyatt, 12/9/2015. Charisma News, charismanews.com/culture/53743

Prelude

Jesus through the eyes of His early followers

If a person shows up at a Bar to buy a drink, she needs proper age-appropriate credentials. If a person is coming to watch a play, he would need a ticket for admission. If a person is boarding a plane for a foreign land, she needs a ticket and a passport to get through customs *(Unless it is the U. S. Southern Border, of course.)* Anywhere we go in life we must be able to prove we are who we say we are to be granted the rights and privileges of the event or location. Advent is no exception. To start the party of God's Visitation we need someone who had the right papers, who fit the bill, whose ID said "Godchild," whose passport was stamped by an angel, whose personality and mission fit the bill of the One who was to come. It needs to be a Person who does not just bring the wine to the party but can turn water into wine so a new party can begin. Luke believed there was only One Person born in recorded history who had Messiah type credentials, who could claim: "I am the Word who was made Flesh" (John 1:14).

If Messiah were to come to us, would it be surprising that this Person would be predicted and recognizable? Reason would dictate that we would be able to know this Person, if such a Person existed. This is precisely the reasonable conclusion Luke claimed to reach.

Paul (Luke's Mentor) called Him "the *morpha* of God," the very species or stuff of God. (Greek translation of Philippians 1:6). Luke called Him "Jesus *Sotiras*," or Savior (John 2:11). His BFF John called Him "The *Logos*," the Word in human flesh (John 1:14). Those who placed their trust in Jesus in the early days of Christianity were not putting their trust in One they believed to simply be a good guy with a new plan. They believed they were trusting in a visitation of God to the earth. You might be one who chooses not to believe this, but it is exceedingly difficult to conclude His earliest followers did not believe that He was indeed the Son of God visiting our planet. They believed they were walking through The Door, following the Good Shepherd, learning from The Teacher, hearing firsthand Universal Truth, and worshipping the long-awaited Messiah. This is a worldview we sorely need to grapple with in our time, for if these claims are valid, the entire landscape of this discussion changes for everyone everywhere. It would be as if we had been plugged into the Matrix, having a false reality pulled over our eyes, until *The One* set us free to see reality anew as it is truly meant to be experienced.[20]

I admit to you, one of the most difficult things to buy about Jesus is that He is somehow a unique combination of God and human, that He is somehow The Creator but was also born a human being. Luke made a stunning case for His Divinity throughout his Gospel. He knew full well that this was the stance of the early Church, especially his mentor the Apostle Paul, whose letters predate Luke's Gospel. For instance, Paul often took Old Testament Passages that spoke of *Yahweh* (One of God's Old Testament Names) and applied them to Jesus. It was clear Paul believed he was discussing the same God. He gave long discourses in several places which highlighted

---

[20] For a fantastic discussion of the philosophy of the Matrix, a film with a fantastic philosophical commentary of our day, please see https://www.reddit.com/r/matrix/comments/rxwukw/spoiler_is_the_matrix_really_so_philosophical/ and https://www.livereal.com/movies/whatisthematrix/ for a deeper look into this philosophical flick and its commentary on our time.

Jesus as our Creator, our Eternal Creator. The best example of this was Colossians 1, where Paul declared, "The Son is the image of the invisible God, The Firstborn over all Creation. For in Him all things were created; things in heaven and earth, visible and invisible, whether thrones of powers, rulers, or authorities, all things have been created through Him and for Him. He is before all things, and in Him all things hold together" (Col. 1: 15-17).

Unless Paul believed in two Creators, which no orthodox Jew would, he most certainly believed Jesus was The Divine Creator and somehow part of the One God. We are left to contemplate whether we agree with him, but what Paul believed is undeniable. And by extension, what his student Luke believed. The question before us is not about what Luke believed as he wrote his account of Jesus. It is rather - "Does he make his case?" Logic says of this same Jesus - A thing is either a created thing or not. And if a thing is not created, then it is by nature eternal. Luke believed this about Jesus.

The Bible, from front to cover, declares eternity an attribute of One Being and One Being alone - God. All three major world religions and many smaller religions proclaim this. If Jesus is in fact eternal, as his early followers declared, we are left with but one conclusion. And if Jesus is not eternal, then He is created or part of an evolving species, and could not have created "all things," for Jesus would be part of "The All." How would one create themself? This would be much like the Sun existing before stars existed, or the moon choosing to "be" without dependance upon our planet earth, or celebrating a honeymoon before marriage is a thing, or having a birthday party for a child not yet conceived, or authoring a poem without language, or singing a song without the existence of music. In other words, a Person who did not exist before Creation cannot be The Creator, for the Creator of necessity comes before the Creation itself, and cannot itself be a created thing, for non-being cannot create Being. "Out of Nothing, nothing comes" (R. C. Sproul).

For something to come from nothing, it must, at the same time and in the same relationship, "be" and "not be." It must create itself. You are no doubt already thinking of the absurdity of such a claim. This is like saying – "We created ourselves from nothing before we ever existed as something." Not only does this take our biological parents out of the equation, but it makes a Creator unnecessary. It assumes the existence of "chance," or a force in the universe that lives outside the realm of cause and effect, which cannot be, even though Science presently surrenders to this non-existent thing called "chance." Chance is nothing. Chance is *no thing*.

The problem with the concept of creating oneself from nothing is that it cannot be true, in this or any universe. "Self-creation is a logical and rational impossibility."[21] Hamlet proclaimed, "to be, or not to be, that is the question." Though existing outside a strictly scientific worldview, Hamlet understood that one could not do both at the same time and in the same relationship. If I am correct, and self-creation is an impossibility, we have an alarming trend being normalized in our postmodern world - Self-Identity which involves Self-creation. The trend to re-create ourselves in our own image is a social contagion which will not take us anywhere, other than a confusing and empty interaction with self and reality. My belief is that our recent cultural trend toward depression is directly linked to this phenomenon.

The philosophers of old debated the concept of "Being." "Being" is not a synonym for "existence." We do not refer to God as the "Supreme Existing One." We call God "Supreme Being." Even the term "higher power" does not cut it when describing the likes of God, if in fact God is out there (here, there, anywhere and everywhere). As human creatures (*created being as opposed to Eternal Being*), we derive our existence from a source outside ourselves. We all admit this in some way. Therefore, every worldview must grapple with

---

[21] R. C. Sproul, *Not a Chance: The Myth of Chance in Modern Science and Cosmology*, 1994. Baker Academics, Grand Rapids, Michigan. Chap.1

the question of *being* - "Where did we come from and why are we here?" These two questions are at the core of why the Gospels were written. They are not scientific documents proving the unique nature of Jesus. They are theological documents, written during a time of openness to Metaphysical Truth which is Truth of a different sort. They are Truth based on Divine Revelation of *how* and *why* we exist gifted by a Source beyond our Existential reality. The Creator spoke to the creature, according to Luke. But we must remember, being a Theological Document does not mean it is not based on historical accuracy. History is recorded in a variety of ways, but it is history, nonetheless.

The Early History of the Church is recorded for us through four primary written forms. First came letters, written by early church Apostles and Leaders to congregations which were under their care. Secondly, we were gifted four Gospels, written by four different authors intended for four distinct audiences. In this manuscript I will focus on the Gospel according to Luke, written primarily with a Greek speaking audience in mind. A third form of early church history is found in sermons written and circulated through various 1st century congregations. These include books like James and Hebrews, the clearest of this format being found in the Sermon/Letter given to the Hebrews. A final form of early church history is found in the Apocalyptic Book of Revelation and is unique compared to all other New Testament Books. It includes vivid imagery and symbolic representation of both historical events and predictive elements of future events the followers of Jesus were meant to prepare for. This book is clearly tied to the 1st century relationship between Jesus followers and The Roman Empire.

From these historical documents we are privileged to be able to systematically develop a history of 1st century Christianity. There are things which rise to the top like cream in my coffee this morning. Luke focuses on at least three of these: The miraculous nature of Jesus' birth (which prepares us for the miraculous events surrounding his death and Resurrection); The clear understanding of early Christians pertaining to the Divine Nature of the man we know as Jesus of Nazareth; The wise and creative teachings of Jesus that Luke, beyond any New Testament Author, records in the form of parables connecting with the real life events of 1st century people. My choice to focus on Advent highlights the first of these three. The Author of the Sermon gifted to the Hebrews said it succinctly:

"Yet at present we do not see everything subject to them. But we do see Jesus, who was made lower than the angels for a little while, now crowned with glory and honor because he suffered death, so that by the grace of God he might taste death for everyone. In bringing many sons and daughters to glory, it was fitting that God, for whom and through whom everything exists, should make the pioneer of their salvation perfect through what he suffered. Both the one who makes people holy and those who are made holy are of the same family. So, Jesus is not ashamed to call them brothers and sisters. He says,

"I will declare your name to my brothers and sisters; in the assembly I will sing your praises."

And again, "I will put my trust in him."

And again, he says, "Here am I, and the children God has given me."

Since the children have flesh and blood, he too shared in their humanity so that by his death he might break the power of him who holds the power of death—that is, the devil - and free those who all their lives were held in slavery by their fear of death. For surely it is not angels he helps, but Abraham's descendants. For this reason, he had to be made like them, fully human in every way, in order that he might become a merciful and faithful high priest in service to God, and that he might make atonement for the sins of the people. Because he suffered when he was tempted, he can help those being tempted" (Hebrews 2: 8-18).

The Gospel of Luke will focus on several elements of what Hebrews introduces. By all accounts, Hebrews was written anywhere from 45 A.D. to 59 A.D... Luke's Gospel was probably written shortly after the book of Hebrews. Part of Luke's goal is to describe the events that led to the theology of the early church we find in this portion of Hebrews. Luke will describe why Jesus is believed to be God incarnate, the beginning of a new family, under the care of angels, fully human yet fully divine, the beginning point of a New Kingdom which battles and conquers the enemies of God, God's solution for fear and death, why Jesus voluntarily suffers for the sake of others, why Jesus came among us to fulfill an already announced purpose, and many other elements of the theology which were circulating within 15 years of Jesus' death. The Gospels gave us the historical context for the message about Jesus that was already invading the Roman Empire. Gospel is both history and hope, Word and Wisdom, discussion and detail, testimony and truth. Gospel is a Genre unparalleled in world history and cannot be appreciated without a genuine commitment to both context and culture. I will offer both as I write. [22]

The Gospels are the Poet's poem, the Song Writer's lyric, the Inventor's gadget, the Professor's presentation, the dad's son and the mother's daughter, coming to us as Personal Revelation from one we cannot know otherwise. The Gospels are God's explanation of the *how* and the *why* of our human *being* as revealed via The Supreme *Being* given through a chosen author. These are more than mere human documents, and anyone who has tested this claim will discover what I already believe to be true as I write. Luke

---

[22] "What is the Gospel?" written by Chelsea Kight, cru.org. In this article we are exposed to a thorough discussion of Luke's Gospel, largely garnered and comparable to the Gospel Paul introduced to the Roman World. I suggest you might also consult "The Genre of the Gospels," written by Phillip J. Long, Sep 2, 2015: ReadingActs.com

has given us a "Timeless Script for the 21st Century," for we are all searching for answers to the *How* and *Why* questions, even if we do not admit we are. (For a great discussion of such things, I leave you a few references in the footnote below.)[23]

I would offer one caution as you ponder His identity. If there is in fact a God, as so many of us believe, would this not make the Incarnation of God a possibility? Could a God we cannot fathom do such a thing? I say, "of course God could." Why call God "God" if God is to be judged by what we deem possible? The readings which follow are a brief Journey through what Luke believed to be the Visitation of God to our planet. Each day, beginning with Day 1 of your choosing, we will travel through a small portion of the story. My hope is that this will add to your Advent celebration, spur you toward thought and contemplation, and help you discover answers for today through some of what is written about the Unique Personhood of Jesus of Nazareth. My hope is that you will choose to hear from those who claimed to have known Him, to test your deepest beliefs about Him, and to reexamine the event, especially if you are one of those who treat Advent with indifference or disdain.

---

[23] "R.C. Sproul Proves that God Does Not Exist", R. C. Sproul, May 29, 2014. Ligonier Updates: In this excerpt from his Foundations teaching series, R.C. Sproul proves that God does not exist. Ligonier.org.
The following list of books are not quoted directly in the section you are now reading. However, these have together shaped my thinking in profound ways and are considered classics when considering the Meaning and Purpose question pertaining to our Existence. They are: "Not a Chance" by R. C. Sproul, "Foolishness to Greeks" by Lesslie Newbigin, "The Invisible Religion" by Thomas Luckman, and of primary interest is "Man's Search for Meaning" by Victor E. Frankl

"Human Beings are pretty smart, but where does human knowledge come from? It comes from God." (Liza Lentini)[24]

"Our fate is transformed into our destiny; that is, we are given the means of love and service to our neighbor. We are contingent beings whose meaning and significance is determined by something, someone other than ourselves. True freedom arises, not in our assertion of our individual independence, but in our being linked to a True Story, which enables us to say yes and no. Our worst sins arise as our response to our innate fear that we are nobody." (Hauerwas and Willimon)[25]

---

[24] How Was the Bible Written, Liza Lenten, 2015. Engaged Media, Inc. Yorba Linda, CA. Page 66. www.engagedmediamags.com
[25] Stanley Hauerwas and William H. Willimon, "Resident Aliens: Life in the Christian Colony," 1989. Abingdon Press, Nashville, TN. Page 67.

Our constant challenge is to remain faithful to the
historical material, allowing our present perspective
to enrich, but not distort, the various ideas and
world views we examine. (Richard Tarnas)[26]

"To evaluate one thing as 'better' than another assumes
the existence of an absolute good with which the two
relative goods can be compared." (Socrates)

---

[26] Richard Tarnas, *The Passion of the Western Mind: Understanding the idea that have shaped our Worldview*, 1991. Harmony Books, NY, NY, Introduction.

Preparation

Toward a Diagnosis and Trusting the Doctor

The Question we are about to entertain is this: "*Can we trust the Postmodern (or Post-Truth) paradigm when it comes to understanding Jesus?*" I am suggesting that since this Gospel was written during a time different than our own, having survived practical application during a time of tremendous political turmoil, and having been a primary part of cultural transformation for those who followed Luke's guidance toward understanding and following Jesus, that we might open our minds further to the possibility that Luke gave us a thoroughly investigated, expertly written accounting of Jesus' beginning. I am enthusiastically suggesting we would be wise to explore Luke's Gospel in our time. Because The Gospels specifically, and Christianity in general, are built upon revelation, namely the revelation about who God is and the identity of God's Son, it is founded on a different kind of Truth. It is not scientific truth, although it certainly complements much of what we discover through science. It is Public Truth, embraced by people groups for 2,000 years because of the powerful testimony and amazingly preserved written records of hundreds of eyewitnesses. That which Luke wrote can be and is trusted by millions and cannot be dismissed simply because it was written during a pre-scientific age. In fact, the pre-scientific writing of Luke's Gospel ought to make it even more appealing to the postmodern mind, to any young person who is reading this today.

I often hear something like - "It's all a matter of interpretation, when it comes to the stories about Jesus." This is an interesting statement for a couple of reasons. First, what does this mean? Does this statement affirm a belief that one person's interpretation is just as valid as another person's interpretation when it comes to the Gospels? I would suggest that we simply do not believe this, for any persons who say this are trying at the same time to communicate an idea that they expect the listener to understand and acknowledge, and to some degree agree with. We all speak in such a way as to attempt to clearly communicate ideas from our own mind, and we do not simply accept the premise that people can interpret our comments however they choose to. I appreciate the postmodern adaptation whereby we elevate the importance of every person's point of view. We must certainly value those brave people who desire to express their opinions about important, even controversial, matters. However, we must never lose sight that some people's opinions are superior to ours in terms of interpreting Truth. Though the worth of the person is not in question, the value of our opinions is. This is why I take my car to a mechanic when it does not work, go to the Doctor when I am sick, look for an IT Specialist when my computer is out of whack, and ask my son when trying to understand Rap Music. I can offer opinions about these things, but I am likely to be "wrong." When it comes to the Gospels, considering now the Gospel of Luke, our interpretation of the text cannot bypass the Author's agenda when he wrote and the theologian's expertise when it comes to discerning what he was trying to say to us. It is not just a matter of anyone's interpretation. Luke knew more about Advent than any of us. His interpretation is a priority simply because of his proximity to the events, his preparation and status as writer/historian, and his quality care for relaying accurate information. Luke knew those who knew Him.

For example, If I say to my wife, "You look fantastic today. I love your hair like that," I would not feel particularly good if she replied, "I want a divorce since you think I'm fat." Her interpretation of my words is not valid, even if she sincerely believes this is what I meant. We cannot survive as a culture if people have the right to turn our words into whatever they desire our words to mean. She may choose not to believe what I am saying, but to do so she must judge my motives for speaking, and this is vastly different than her believing she has the right to transform the meaning of my words into something else entirely. We say what we say because we want to be understood for what we are saying. Even those who make comments like "It's all a matter of interpretation" when speaking of religious issues themselves want to be clearly understood when they speak, without being subject to constant scrutiny and inaccurate interpretation. Luke was trying to speak the Truth, and he knew exactly what he was trying to say.

I will suggest in the words that follow that the Church has been gifted an incredible opportunity during these challenging times. Around 12 years ago I grew convinced of this after reading a smallish book (compared to the size of this one) of incredible insight into the heart and lives of the students I teach. The Book was called "unfashionable," written by gillian tchividjian (use of small letters was his choice). This book was written especially for people within the church who are growing tired of business as usual, a constant effort on the part of the Church to become both relevant and contemporary. Tchividjian believes such a strategy will not work, and that churches are "losing their distinctiveness by accommodating to culture." [27] By the time I finished reading chapter 2 of this book I was climbing into transformation of thought. Tchividjian touched a nerve in me, and since the day I picked up this author's work I have been searching for application of this

---

[27] Tullian Tchividjian, "unfashionable: making a difference in the world by being different (sic)", 2009. Multinomah Books, Colorado Springs, Colorado. Chapter 1.

transformation within my life and my classroom. Foundational to my thinking these words became - "According to Jesus, Christianity is not cool…. I will even go a step further: if what's fashionable in our society interests you, then true Christianity will not. It is that simple."[28] The simple impact of this author upon my life was to stop reading the Bible through the eyes of my culture, but instead learn to read the Bible through the eyes of the Author of the Text itself. Specifically, to read the Advent Story from the perspective of those who lived through the 1st century and gifted us this story. This is a correction The Church needs to embrace. "Unfashionable" challenged my fashionability, which you will discover as you read.

Secondly, the most important consideration when reading any book - text, novel, non-fiction, or bible - is to strive to understand the intent of the author. The best interpretation always involves getting inside the mind of the author. We owe the author an attempt toward understanding what she is trying to say, rather than to interpret her words however we wish to interpret them. Why write anything if the best interpretation is up to the reader, and the author's intent is irrelevant and unimportant as we read? Luke had an intent for investigating, writing, sculpting, confirming, and gifting the world with his Gospel. He was not simply interpreting Jesus; he was testifying to that which he believed to be true. Yes, he had Theological reasons for doing so, but Theology does not exclude historical accuracy. And Theological reflection is not inherently dishonest or meant to be broadly interpreted. In Luke's case, his Theology flows from his accounting of history. He was writing history as he understood it. We must deal with his Truth claims if we are to call ourselves open-minded thinking people, not dismiss them simply because our worldview does not embrace the concept of the miraculous. We owe it to any author to consider his claims. His words were meant to be interpreted in a way that

---

[28] Tullian Tchividjian, "unfashionable", page 19.

faithfully considers what he was trying to say, even if we must challenge our 21st century worldview to peek inside his words. So, let us peek.[29]

"The supernatural Jesus of (the) Gospels, of course, is difficult for many (twenty first - century) people to accept. It is not the kind of portrait a modern could be expected to accept *were there not good evidence in its favor.* But the evidence is there. And rather than adjusting the evidence to make this Jesus more palatable to (modern) sensibilities, it seems more reasonable to leave it intact and simply to allow the enigma of the first-century Jew to confront our (modern) sensibilities. It just may be that history is, after all, not a closed continuum!"[30] (Gregory A. Boyd)

"People in today's world are desperately reaching, not just upward, but backward. They yearn for a day gone by when things seemed more constant and less shallow. They want to tap into treasures of the past as they search for a staying power that seems unattainable in the present" (Tullian Tchividjian, page 13 of "unfashionable").

---

[29] Sir **Willian M. Ramsay** spent decades investigating the New Testament because he was initially a skeptic. However, in time he began to discover the honesty and accuracy of the authors, the truthfulness of the information, and the trustworthiness of the NT. In fact, Ramsay concluded: "Luke is a historian of the first rank: not merely are his statements of fact trustworthy, he is possessed of the true historic sense . . . This author should be placed along with the very greatest of historians." In Ramsay's book Trustworthiness of the New Testament, he provides us with much valuable material showing that the NT is authentic and true. His book is a faith builder for us and an apologetic tool to share with skeptics and those who may have begun to doubt. You can read this book yourself for quality research on the historicity of Luke's Gospel: William Ramsay, *The Bearing of Recent Discovery on the Trustworthiness of the New Testament, 2nd Edition,* 2021. Christian Publishing House, Cambridge, Ohio. (This information was taken from the introduction to this book on amazon.com)
[30] Gregory A. Boyd, "Cynic Sage or Son of God", 1995. Victor Books/SP Publications, Inc., Wheaton, IL. Page 243

Day 1

"The events that have been fulfilled among us" ...Luke 1:1

Setting the Stage: The Expectation is Undeniable

There are at least forty obvious Messianic prophecies commonly identified throughout the Old Testament which relate to the person we call Messiah. Luke claimed these prophecies directly connect us to Jesus of Nazareth (Luke 24:25-27). According to Luke and other Gospel writers, these prophecies linked the life of Jesus to some pretty amazing predictions, which included things like The Resurrection, the beginning of a New Covenant, the fact Messiah would be forsaken and pierced, Messiah would be rejected by His own people, Messiah would be born of a Virgin, Messiah would die for human sin, Messiah would suffer a horrible death, Messiah would be in the grave three days, and many others. (For an excellent discussion of many of these prophecies you can follow this footnote)[31]

The Prophetic Voice which overwhelmingly points toward Messiah separated the Hebrews from all other ancient people groups. "In the darkest hour of adversity, the prophets did not

---

[31] It is not my purpose to discuss these Messianic Prophecies here, though I will discuss some throughout this document. However, if this is a praticualar interest of yours you can consult: "The top 40 Messianic Prophecies", Rich Robinson, August 4, 2020. https://jewsforjesus.org/learn/top-40-most-helpful-messianic-prophecies

despair of Israel. When Jerusalem was desolate, the people were in captivity, and national existence and been crushed, the voice of prophecy speaks out the more confidently. It points us toward to the Divine guidance that had watched over the race, and tells of the mighty destiny that was in store for Israel"[32] The prophecies form a unique combination of declarations for the King, a Word for the people, warning to Israel and the nations around them, celebrations of historical events, even amazing predictions for the future. Of all the words the prophets proclaimed, the ones connected to Messianic expectations are the most profound of all.

For example, crucifixion was predicted in Psalm 22, before it ever existed. It is depicted in one of the most powerful Old Testament Messianic prophesies. According to Gospel writers, Jesus quoted Psalm 22:1 from the cross: "My God, my God, why have you forsaken me: Why are you so far from saving me, so far from my cries of anguish?" This is a clear reference to the humanity of Messiah as He suffers and dies, what early followers believed to be His atoning death for all humanity. How do we know this? Firstly, Jesus quotes this Psalm from the cross. Mathew 27:46 records these words as: "*Eli, Eli, lama sabachthani?*" This is the original Hebrew for the phrase we translate as "My God, my God, why have you forsaken me?" Mark also includes this phrase coming from Jesus on the cross (Mark 15:34).

Additionally, Jesus' use of this Psalm pointed to a powerful moment of self-identification with the words of Psalm 22. Jesus clearly related intimately to the words of the Prophet amid his suffering. His use of the first person singular as He cried out to His God revealed a deeply rooted belief on the part of Jesus that these words were specially made for his experience on the cross, his sense of abandonment, and the overwhelming flood of isolation which transcended the physical experience itself.

---

[32] Arthur W. Kac, "The Messianic Hope: A Divine Solution for the Human Problem", 1975. Baker Book House, Grand Rapids, Michigan. Page 3

Finally, there is the rest of the Psalm: "I am a worm and not a man, scorned by everyone, despised by the people. All who see me mock me; they hurl insults at me, shaking their heads. 'He trusts in the Lord,' they say, 'let the Lord rescue him. Let him deliver him, since he delights in him'" (Psalm 22:6-8). These are the exact words recorded as coming from those who are crucified with Jesus and those who witness his death. The exact words! We were also given details of death by crucifixion in 1st century Rome: "Dogs surround me, a pack of villains encircles me; they pierce my hands and my feet. All my bones are on display; people stare and gloat over me. They divide my clothing among them and cast lots for my garment" (Psalm 22:16-18).[33]

At a time when crucifixion was not practiced, it was clearly defined in detail in Psalm 22. I have yet to discover an adequate explanation as to how the Psalmist could be writing about crucifixion before it was a form of punishment commonly used. This was a noticeably clear prediction of the experience of Messiah's death described with precision a millennia before it happened! The number of prophesies that are fulfilled through the birth, life, death, and resurrection of Jesus numbers above three hundred, according to many Old Testament Scholars.[34] Psalm 22 stands out among them and remains, along with Isaiah 53, one of the most difficult for doubters to explain. These two passages only touch the surface of the power of Messianic Prophecy throughout the Old Testament narrative. Jesus came to His people within a powerful context of hope and expectation created through the words of the Prophets.

"Fulfilled among us" ...

[33] See Matthew 27 and Mark 15 for a precise description of the things predicted in Psalm 22. This is indeed a Messianic Psalm of unparalleled precision.
[34] For a list of Old Testament Prophecies, you might look at List of Old Testament prophecies fulfilled by Jesus (about-jesus.org)

In 1985 Marty McFly journeyed into the future. Thirty years into the future to be precise. He ventured into a time of flying cars, hoverboards, giant television screens on every street corner, and soda without calories. As far as I can tell much of what Marty saw was "misguided prophecy," for so little of what he encountered made it into 2015. One thing which stood out to me, as Marty looked around in awe at a day and time he did not fully comprehend, was the fact that the Chicago Cubs had just won the World Series!! The Headlines declared the impossible!!

Not only did the writers of Back to the Future II correctly predict that from 1985 until 2015 the Cubs would not win a world series (bold prediction indeed, ha ha), but they understood the miraculous nature of such a thing happening for these "lovable losers." Maybe the creators of "Back to the Future II" were simply tortured Cub fans. Personally, I could not wait for 2015 to arrive, and as you read this you now know "Back to the Future II" got it wrong, by one year. For those of us who rooted for the Cubs in the 7th game victory in the 2016 World Series we are willing to give Marty a break.

However, when it comes to Old Testament prophecy, missing the date by one year or one detail is a mistake. Just imagine it had been 2015, and this scene in "Back to the Future II" had been precise beyond explanation. It is amazing when a prediction comes to fulfillment when a thing longed for finally arrives. But history teaches us this is most often not the case. This movie got it wrong, to be precise. What could have been a momentous day for the modern prophet barely missed. As of now we simply consider it a good guess, but science fiction all the same.

Some apply the term science fiction to Luke's Gospel as well. My challenge is that you consider the question further, for good reason, beginning with the recognition that Jesus of Nazareth has become the most famous and well-known individual on the planet. Napoleon is a distant second, yet we teach his history as truth. Historical Science includes the study of both. Let Us Study Together.

Luke tells us that the coming of the Messiah was a precise "fulfillment" of something longed for. We might even call it – "The Fulfillment." for the Hebrew people. If I were a Jew in the first century AD, I would have been taught my entire life that one day, someday, something so incredible, so amazing, so absolutely mind blowing was going to happen that it would change the world forever. Life on this planet would never be the same. I would have been led to believe that the possibility of His arrival might even take place in my lifetime, that I could easily be the generation to see something so far beyond a Cub World Series Victory that it would be like comparing a moon walk to riding the Star Ship Enterprise. The arrival of the Messiah had been anticipated since the birth of Isaac, yea, since the promise of God in Genesis that one day, someday, the "Seed of the Woman" (Genesis 3:15) would completely crush the head of the "Serpent." How awesome to believe that first century Jews were a part of a blessed generation like none before or since this time. Luke, writing to his friend *Theophilus* (at least many believe him a friend), wants him to understand that the event hundreds of prophecies pointed to, which spanned more than 2,000 years, had finally become reality. The future longed for was at last an *existential experience*, now having become a *transformative historical event*. This is Luke's belief about Advent.

Luke's view on this event is incredibly relevant for us as we consider the similarities between Luke's time and our own.[35] From a society which gained wealth by building on the backs of slaves, to the three branches of Government we employ, to the tremendous

---

[35] For a powerful discussion of these similarities, if this topic is of interest to you, I suggest you read this book: Cullen Murphy, "Are We Rome: The Fall of an Empire and the Fate of America" (2007). First Marinar Books, Houghton Mifflin Company, Boston & New York.

opportunities for wealth and business, to advancements in science and technology, to the common community gathering spots, to the emphasis on family life, to the massive gap between the rich and the poor, to the Judicial system designed to protect its citizens, to the freedom to practice a variety of religions, to the growth and impact of Art and Literature, to the prioritizing of public games and leisure activities, to the honoring of State and history, to the celebration of national holidays, to the breakfast on the run culture, and even the gift of our alphabet, the similarities between the 21st century America and 1st century Rome are both striking and undeniable. Are we repeating history? If so, I suggest Luke's Gospel has never been more relevant than it is in our time.

Luke, a Greek Roman Citizen, wrote within the context of a culture he understood. "The community that confesses Jesus is Lord has been, from the beginning, a movement launched into the public life of humankind. The Greco-Roman world in which the New Testament was written was full of societies which offered those who wished to join a way of personal salvation through religious teaching and practice. There were several commonly used Greek words for such societies. At no time did the early church use any of these names for itself. The church was not and could not be a society offering 'personal salvation' for anyone." [36] Luke did not espouse mere "personal salvation." The phrase "personal relationship with Jesus" is a recent creation, rooted in Western autonomy. The New Testament does not use such a phrase, not once, but the Romans certainly embraced it, as we do in Modern Western Culture. Instead, what Luke offered was incorporation into the Life of a Divine Human Being, who then shapes and molds us into a new Temple where God chooses to live. Jesus creates a New Community, a New Family, a New People.

Postmodern Worldview has created an environment where

---

[36] Lesslie Newbigin, *The Open Secret, p.16 (1995). Wm B. Eerdmans Publishing Co., Grand Rapids, Michigan 49505.* www.eerdmans.com

community is often neglected and undervalued. "I must be true to myself, free of my parents, children, spouse, duties, the freer we will be to be 'ourselves,' to flow, to lay hold of new and exciting possibilities." [37] We convince ourselves we cannot discover such freedom inside the barriers and restraints others try to place on us. This is the postmodern argument. *"But what if our true selves are made from the materials of our communal life? Where is there some 'self' which has not been communally created? What if by cutting back our attachments and commitments the self shrinks rather than grows?"*[38]

Christians frequently died at Roman hands toward the end of the first century precisely because they made faith the center of corporate, political, and daily life.   They could not help but go public! They would not "bow the knee" to Rome, as Luke highlighted. For Luke and other followers of Jesus there was a King who rose above the authority of the Roman Empire. Today, we understand Luke as a Gospel addressed to all who are trying to tiptoe their way through a society that demands political allegiance over and above the Authority of Christ. It is a "prescription" written for us by a 1st Century Doctor, that we might be empowered to confidently speak and live Truth in the public arenas of life - politically, vocationally, socially, communally - as we share the surest cure known to humanity for modern ailments in our land. This Gospel is both relevant and transformative pertaining to our modern predicament. As a recent trend in commercials declares: "He gets us." [39]

One example of Roman and Modern Western parallels is our approach toward citizenry. Romans used the word *ecclesia* when speaking of the "assembly of their citizens." The *ecclesia* dealt with the public affairs of the city. The one requirement for all

---

[37] Hauerwas and Willimon, "Resident Aliens", page 65.
[38] Hauerwas and Willimon, "Resident Aliens", page 65.
[39] For the complete collection of "He Gets Us" commercials see Hegetsus.com

members of the *ecclesia* was their allegiance to The State. They were free to pursue "personal salvation" of their souls through the multitude of religions they allowed, including Judaism. But not if it interfered with personal allegiance to The State. The problem with Judaism under Roman rule, and soon after Christianity, was that quite often members of this faith found themselves standing in opposition to the *ecclesia*. One's religious beliefs could not compromise one's "worship" of The State. When Jews did this, Jews were persecuted and silenced. The State allowed religion, but one's ultimate allegiance must be to Rome. Sound familiar?[40]

Those of us who presently practice religion in the U.S. are encouraged to do so in the private sectors of life, without push-back. "Research shows that Black Protestants are the only Christian group in which a majority — 63% — believes that congregations should get involved in social issues even if doing so means having difficult conversations.[41] For the most part, the instant we step outside our lane, whether it be to insist on the value of the traditional family or to take a stand about the "transition of children" or to speak our faith into the public arenas of life, we are silenced, censored, even persecuted. We are allowed freedom of religion, but we are not allowed to exercise this freedom in opposition to what our Culture deems "political correctness." It is perfectly acceptable to publicly celebrate atheism, but we are often criticized in the public arena if we want to discuss Jesus. The consequences in our society may not be as harsh as they were under Roman rule, for we are a bit more sophisticated in our censorship, but the expectations we

---

[40] For a vivid illustration of Religion vs. State Allegiance in 1st Century Rome read and study Revelation chapter 13. This chapter was a warning for 1st century churches who were about to face the wrath of Rome for their religious beliefs. See also Ray Summers, Worthy is the Lamb. Broadman and Holman Publishers, Nashville. 1951.

[41] "The importance of religion in the lives of Americans is shrinking," Jason DeRose (May 16, 2023). NPR, WJCT News. npr.org

place on people and the response to public demonstrations of faith are rooted in political agendas, just like Rome.

I want you to begin to understand the time in which Luke wrote. It was a time of political correctness, oppression of those who opposed the State, emphasis on personal salvation, and religious diversity under the umbrella of unique journeys toward personal salvation. These are the consequences of Roman nationalism and Modern Western Postmodern thought, deeply rooted in a 20th century resurrection of "Gnosticism."[42] Grasping what is at stake in this discussion is long overdue for the postmodern theologian. However, into the theological void of their time and our time, Luke speaks.

The fulfillment of prophecy our ancestors often misunderstood is misunderstood today as well, often the result of simple indifference. Luke has given us a "Timeless Gift," but we cannot find this gift under our Christmas tree. Instead, we are transported to a time and a place we seldom pause to ponder, for we are citizens of the contemporary. We Gentiles, who trust in armies and governments and philosophy and science and education and power and money and various other empty gods to bring us personal salvation, are now transported into a world we do not understand and could not have imagined.... just like Marty

---

[42] For a great discussion of the similarities there are few resources better than one I read in college: "Ancient Rome and Modern America Reconsidered" written by Mason Hammon. Proceedings of the Massachusetts Historical Society. Third Series, Vol. 73 (1961), pp. 3-17 (15 pages). Published By: Massachusetts Historical Society.
"Gnosticism" is defined as a prominent heretical movement of the 2nd-century Christian Church, partly of pre-Christian origin. Gnostic doctrine taught that the world was created and ruled by a lesser divinity, the demiurge, and that Christ was an emissary of the remote supreme divine being, esoteric knowledge ("gnosis") of whom enabled the redemption of the human spirit.
"Postmodernism" is discussed and explored in detail within: "Postmodernism" (First published Friday, Sep 30, 2005; substantive revision Thu Feb 5, 2015), written by Gary Aylesworth. Stanford Encyclopedia of Philosophy. plato.standford.edu

McFly. We must go back to face our future. And we discover that the underdog Won! A Humble Unexpected Rabbi born in a cave has become Champion for all underdogs everywhere and for every time. This includes me and you.

(LAUGH WITH ME...)

A Baptist and a Presbyterian are walking down the road. As the rain begins the Presbyterian grabs the Baptist's umbrella and protects himself from the rain. The Baptist gets drenched. Once they find shelter the sopping wet Baptist says, "You Presbyterians are all about predestination. It seems to me that you are walking without an umbrella, which means God ordained that you get wet. Why not just take your drenching like a faithful servant?" To which the Presbyterian replies. "God warned me it was going to rain. Why do you think I was walking beside someone who had an umbrella?"[43]

---

[43] Humor is a distinct human quality, and often is used in order to better deal with the disappointments and tragedies of life. Humor is at the heart of what it means to be "semi-transcendent," a phrase coined by John Warnick Montgomery in his book "The Suicide of Christian Theology," 1975. Bethany Fellowship, Inc., Minneapolis. See The chapter titled "Is Man His Own God," page 258 and following, for this discussion. Without humor, there is no true humanity. Without humor, Advent cannot be fully appreciated. Humor originates with our Creator and connects the human being to the very source of Joy, Irony, Surprise, and Transcendent Being itself. Humor includes irony, and the one thing that is consistently evident from Luke's account of the birth of Jesus is the irony of it all, the birth of a King out of wedlock from a peasant girl with nothing special to offer in terms of royalty in a town almost unknown except for ties to a shepherd king named David. Yes, we will laugh throughout this book, celebrating throughout the tremendous gift of humor as we set the stage for universal celebration and joy.

Day 2

"From the first were eyewitnesses and
servants of the Word" …Luke 1:2

"Eyewitness Testimony is often not reliable, unless" ……..
supported by other forms of evidence and enhanced by
similar eyewitness accounts. In other words, the more people
who saw it, the more reliable this testimony becomes."[44]

---

[44] "Bria 13 3 c How Reliable Are Eyewitness", Teach Democracy (formerly
Constitutional Rights Foundation) 2023. crf-usa.org

Setting the Stage: *What did you see?*

IF YOU REPORT A UFO TO THE U.S. GOVERNMENT, YOU WILL BE informed that the Air Force conducted a 22-year investigation which ended in 1969 and concluded that UFOs are not a threat to national security and are of no scientific interest. They recently affirmed these findings. This is the official Government position. However, we live in a day of unprecedented mistrust for official Government positions. It is one thing to discredit a thing because it has no basis. It is quite another thing to develop a policy based on the principle introduced by Jack Nicholson in "A Few Good Men": "You can't handle the truth!" Truth covered up does not make a thing less true if it is true. Although eyewitness testimony is not an overly trusted method for getting at reality, if confirmed by other eyewitness testimony, which is also supported by other forms of evidence, it will make for a very solid case.

It is seldom that we can ever know a thing for certain, but it is wise to follow the evidence to a probable conclusion. As far as UFOs are concerned, we have claims of Alien-Human Encounters, the Abduction Phenomenon, Military Witnesses, Pilot Sightings, Scientist Testimony, Police Testimony, and a myriad of other areas of investigation that are considered evidence for exploration. The bottom line - we simply do not know for sure. How can we know there is no threat to National Security? We cannot. If you are a skeptic regarding Jesus, this is the approach I encourage you to take to Luke's Gospel, especially when we consider the sheer importance of the question before us - Is Jesus the Son of God, the Messiah centuries longed for?

Healthy Skepticism is a good thing. I am convinced that few of us grow and prosper as personal thinkers without the practice of skepticism. It is obvious that every culture in human history benefits from healthy skepticism. However, before the printing press came along in the middle of the 2nd Millennium people carried forth truth through oral tradition. People repeated the stories that had been passed down from generation to generation, told repeatedly by those who inherited this task via popular choice from their own communities. The Oral Tradition was a uniquely effective way of transferring truth for further review as brilliant minds began to ask the right questions about the truth being carried forward.

The oral traditions and expressions domain encompassed an enormous variety of spoken forms including proverbs, riddles, tales, nursery rhymes, legends, myths, epic songs and poems, charms, prayers, chants, songs, dramatic performances and more. Oral tradition and expression were used to pass on knowledge, cultural and social values, and collective memory. They played a crucial part in keeping cultures alive.[45] This can be a difficult form of relaying truth for the scientific and the postmodern mind. We have learned not to trust what people express orally as truth. We seek evidence, replication, validation, and evidential support for eyewitness testimony. Wisely so. But we need to understand that the oral tradition of the 1st century was a vastly different animal than oral tradition in the 21st century.

For example, there are those who doubt the reliability of Scripture because they evaluate the Bible through the lens of tremendous skepticism. As I mentioned, healthy skepticism can be a healthy thing. However, skepticism for skepticism's sake can take these benefits past the place of advantage. I have witnessed this working with college students, who will often offer their rejection of the Bible as a relevant book for today without ever having interacted with The Book itself. "Personally, I have never read the Bible, but I have heard it is full of contradictions and outdated." I have heard something like this frequently.

---

[45] "Oral Traditions and Expressions......", UNESCO Intangible Cultural Heritage. 20th Anniversary of the Convention, 3/25/2006. https://ich.unesco.org/en/oral-traditions-and-expressions-00053

Skepticism without evaluation is never a wise course of action, if in fact we intend to discover "True Truth." I took a personal journey into the Bible with my skeptics' hat on, and what I found surprised me. One author succinctly describes what I found to be true: "It is not too much to say that it was the rise of the science of archeology that broke the deadlock between historians and the orthodox Christian. Little by little, one city after another, one civilization after another, one culture after another, whose memories were enshrined only in the Bible, were restored to their proper places in ancient history by the studies of archaeologists... The over-all result is indisputable. Forgotten cities have been found, the handiwork of vanished peoples has reappeared, contemporary records of Biblical events have been unearthed and the uniqueness of Biblical revelation has been emphasized by contrast and comparison to the newly understood religions of ancient peoples. Nowhere has archeological discovery refuted the Bible as history."[46] (John Elder," *Prophets, Idols, and Diggers,"* *1960.* Bobbs-Merrill Co., p. 18). Simply stated, the Bible is a highly trustworthy document, flowing from an oral culture that took great care in preserving tradition and truth, and passing the modern tests of skepticism and scrutiny like no other Book written in all human history. These eyewitnesses are well worth our consideration, for they speak of things that surpass the importance of the UFO phenomenon.

(If you would like to begin such a journey yourself, I recommend the following article as a great starting point, then follow the references you find here: THE BIBLE'S HISTORICAL PRECISION, DON Stewart. Ten Reasons to Trust the Bible. BlueLetterBible.org)

The First Eyewitnesses...

[46] John Elder, *"Prophets, Idols, and Diggers",* 1960. Bobbs-Merrill, Co., p. 18

When I was around 11 years old, I witnessed something which to this day remains a mystery in my mind. I was with a friend who saw the same thing I saw, so if this was indeed a hallucination, we both experienced it. As we gazed over a mountain peak in southern West Virginia we saw a strange light. It was stationary, except for an occasional 90 degree turn up and to the side, then retracing back its original spot. We stood with our mouths open, without a single word passing between us for what seemed like an hour. (I am sure it was more like 10 minutes.) We spoke little of the event after, and even today the memory causes me to internally investigate my sanity. Even as I type this memory for you, I realize I do not really know what I saw and would doubt I ever saw it at all were it not for my friend by my side. Since that time, I have had a particular interest in what scientists call UFOs, or unidentified flying objects. Whenever I watch an investigation of such an event, I notice that what people want to know, what they want to hear about, are eyewitness testimonials. The most compelling evidence is what people see with their own eyes, especially if they can get it on film of some sort. I have no evidence of what I saw beyond my memory and my friend. Many would say this is a very weak case, given there were only two of us and both 11 years old.

In contrast, Luke wanted *Theophilus* to understand that his accounting of events was based on the best possible evidence he could find through thorough investigation – eyewitness testimony affirmed and confirmed by other eyewitnesses, tied to dates of actual verifiable historical events attested to by authors other than Luke. Luke did not claim he was one of these eyewitnesses to Jesus. In fact, he said the opposite. Whatever Luke wrote he wanted his readers to know that he had traveled all over Judea to interview those who had seen, those who had witnessed, those who had firsthand knowledge of the events he described. You cannot know what I saw as an 11-year-old, nor are you able to tell me if there was something there. Why not? Because you did not see. You were not there. The absolute best you can do is tell this story to someone else as something Rick claims to have witnessed.

Our opinion about events witnessed by others is of secondhand importance when it comes to eyewitness testimony. Therefore, my testimony carries more weight than those who were not with me, though two witnesses does not erase all doubt. Luke understood this. He knew his word could not stand on its own. So, Luke goes to the best possible place – he talked to those who were there to see, who witnessed the events in question. And he did not write without substantiating their testimony.

As his Gospel unfolds, we discover he did this job very well. He talked to Jesus' Mom, His Aunt, His Uncle, His disciples, His followers, His enemies, those who had been healed, those who heard Him preach, those who could not believe their eyes, those whose lives had been transformed, those who had been imprisoned, and on and on the list goes. Luke, as educated as they come into the world of this time, was a gifted and trained historian/philosopher/doctor who set out to investigate the most important event the world had ever experienced. He knew how transformative his subject matter was to become, for it had already transformed so many in his viewing. So, he based his testimony on those who had witnessed these events, firsthand. He made sure to get it right. Whatever we may say about Jesus today, we must admit there are those who knew Him, witnessed Him, followed Him, and loved Him.

Two specific pieces of evidence stand strongly behind a belief in the historical accuracy of Luke's writings. First, his recorded history in both Luke and Acts are highly collaborated by other 1st century historical authors. Though I will not take the time to point out all the collaborations here, I point you toward an exceptionally reliable source for this evidence. It seems that trusted historians and discoveries from the first century confirm Luke's writings, such as Josephus; the discovery inscriptions at Delphi; the writings of Suetonius, Tacitus, and others, who quite often recorded history identical to events and locations Luke wrote about in Luke/Acts. We would expect this from someone who carefully investigated the "facts."[47] Luke's knowledge of details of this time points to both his trustworthiness and his passion for accuracy.

Second, Luke displays an incredible accuracy for "Titles, Geography and Customs." "The officials with whom Paul and his companions brought in contact are those who would be there. Every person is found, just where he ought to be: proconsuls in senatorial provinces, *asiarchs* in Ephesus, *strategoi* in Philippi, *politarchs* in *Thessalonica,* magicians, and soothsayers everywhere."[48] When one takes time to consider the overwhelming evidence of the historicity of Luke, one is left with little conclusion other than a belief that Luke recorded a faithful representation of eyewitness testimony regarding the Jesus event - His Birth, Life, Death, Resurrection, Ascension, and early Church presence. We have no good reason to doubt Luke, unless we first decide said doubt is what we will find before we begin considering the evidence.

When we read such testimony, we are left with a choice – believe or not believe, embrace or dismiss. But honest consideration must be our goal. Thanks to Luke, we have the privilege of learning what early followers believed about Jesus, and we also get to evaluate his understanding of what it all means. As far as lights in the sky are concerned, you have one example from me and my friend, 11-year-old though we were. You are left to interpret our testimony. I have since learned that the early 70's was a period of an influx of reported UFO sightings in the region of the country in which I lived.[49] Although this does not prove my story, it does indicate

---

[47] Gregory A. Boyd, "Cynic Sage of Son of God?".......page 257

[48] Gregory A Boyd quoting *The Bearing of Recent Discovery on the Trustworthiness of the New Testament,* 1915. Hodder and Stoughton, New York. Pages 96,97

[49] See especially the Documentary series produced by IMDb, "UFOs of the 70's, 2007. https://www.imdb.com/title/tt1172468/

that others were seeing the same sort of phenomenon around the time I saw mine. This fact alone raises our level of consideration.

In Luke's case, we have hundreds of people who witnessed God's Gift to us. At the least, we should be willing to lean in and listen, unless we have already decided that Luke's accounting is not worth listening to, which is not wise given the situation in the 21st century. I reason this extensive list of eyewitnesses and the care Luke took to give us their story would at least warrant a few moments of our time.

Luke's Gospel is unique in its perspective. It resembles the other synoptics[50] in its treatment of the life of Jesus, but it goes beyond them in narrating the ministry of Jesus, widening its perspective to consider God's overall historical purpose and the place of the Church within it. Luke, and its companion book "Acts of the Apostles," portrayed the church as God's instrument of redemption on Earth in the interim between the death of Christ and the second coming. The two books combined provide the

---

[50] Luke is one of the Synoptic Gospels, along with Mark and Matthew. These Gospels focus more on the details surrounding Jesus' life, gives a vailed understanding of Jesus' identity, displays Jesus' teaching in parables, focuses on the details of Advent and His human beginnings, and shares common stories shared by all three of the Authors. John is not a Synoptic Gospel. It is more forthright and clearer about Jesus' identity, assumes readers to be familiar with the stories so focuses on direct meaning of Jesus' words, and begins telling the story from the perspective of the Eternal Beginnings of Jesus. "Matthew, Mark, and Luke seem to be on the same page about the coming Kingdom of God, but in John, there is no mention of the coming Kingdom. John focuses readers on Jesus as one being sent by God. The use of metaphor and mystical language is rampant in the Gospel of John whereas the Synoptic Gospels tell stories that sound more historical in nature. *Jesus according to John is a cosmic force in the world, sent by God to love, forgive, and empower people through his presence.* The other three Gospels leave much more meaning unpacked as readers are plunged into narratives that are anything but explicit." For a thorough discussion of Synoptic vs. John see especially Bart Ehrman Teachings, Article by Keith Long, "THE SYNOPTIC GOSPELS & THE GOSPEL OF JOHN: 7 KEY DIFFERENCES" (Dec. 18, 2023). Bartehrman.com

first Christian history, outlining God's purpose through three historical epochs: the epoch of the Law and the prophets, which lasted from ancient Israel to the time of St. John the Baptist; the epoch of Jesus' ministry; and the epoch of the Church's mission, from the Ascension to the return of Christ.

"The author of Luke had a cultivated literary background and wrote in good idiomatic Greek, written by the lone Greek author of a New Testament book. Luke/Acts were composed during or shortly after the Jewish revolt (66–73 AD) … "Jesus' parting words, 'It is not for you to know times [of the consummation of this age] …but you will receive power…and you will be my witnesses…' (parts of Acts 1:7,8), provide a guideline for Luke's theology. He called the Church back from overeager speculation about the precise time of the Lord's return and the end of the age to its proper task of faithful mission in the lengthening interim. By the selection and interpretation of his sources, he charted the path by which the church would understand both its own uniqueness in the world and its continuing relationship. This is a primary reason Luke is so important for us in our time."[51]

To a large degree, we have lost our sense of purpose, we have forfeited our status as truth tellers, we have compromised our message to such a degree that it no longer connects with the needs of people or the existential problems of our day. Just as Luke's readers, we are so consumed with the return of Jesus that we have voluntarily exited the conversation when it comes to meeting the psychological and physical needs of the people around us.

Just this past Sunday I tuned into five separate sermons on You Tube - one about Israel as God's chosen people, two about God's timetable for the 2nd coming and the imminent Rapture, and two about the fulfillment of prophecy in the Middle East.

[51] "History and Society: St. Luke", E. Earle Ellis, Last Updated: Sep 20, 2023. Britannica, britannica.com

During my brief search, I could not find a single sermon about how to live a meaningful life as a follower of Jesus in service to others. I recognize this is a small sample size, but this theme is pervasive any given Sunday. It is to this Church Luke wrote, then and now. Jesus himself taught His followers to curb their preoccupation with such things when he said, "But concerning that day and hour no one knows, not even the angels of heaven, nor the Son......" (Matthew 24:36, 37) Luke is pleading with us to fade our preoccupation with the return of Jesus in order that we might renew a concerted effort toward being the disciples of Jesus for people in need all around us.[52] It is to this end Luke's Gospel became *A Timeless Script from a 1ˢᵗ Century Doctor.*

"We should be careful to get out of an experience only the wisdom that is in it - and stop there, lest we be like the cat that sits down on a hot stove lid. She will never sit down on a hot stove lid again - and that is well, but also she will never sit down on a cold one anymore." (Mark Twain)

"New developments in physics and cosmology open the way for the real dialogue between believer and scientists such as was impossible when the mechanistic model dominated physics…. this is rendered more difficult by the fact that

---

[52] A growing number of church members in America are preoccupied with end times theology, and a higher percentage of these folk come from impoverished and minority populations. Simply put, suffering breeds a desire for His return, which in turn highlights the failure of the Church to reach people with Good News for today. For a couple examples of a lack of preoccupation with end time theology please see: "Why I'm Not Obsessed with End-Times Theology", Carolyn Moore (June 29, 2018). Artofholiness.com and "About four-in-ten U.S. adults believe humanity is 'living in the end times' ", Jeff Diamant (DECEMBER 8, 2022), Pew Research Center, PewResearch.org.

other branches of science are still so largely controlled by mechanistic (Naturalistic) models."[53] (Lesslie Newbigin)

Dr. Luke searched the Roman Empire for The Truth...

Then shared it with those who would listen...

[53] Lesslie Newbigin, "Foolishness to the Greeks: The Gospel and Western Culture," 1986, 1988. Eeardmans Publishing Company, Grand Rapids, Michigan. Page 73

Day 3

"Since I myself have carefully investigated
everything from the very first" ...Luke 1:3

Setting the Stage: Luke's Gospel is Volume 1 of 2

LUKE IS THE AUTHOR OF LUKE/ACTS, A TWO-VOLUME SET WHICH
highlighted the life and teachings of Jesus from birth through
the arrival of the Gospel of Christ to the streets of Rome itself.
Luke was a close colleague of the apostle Paul, meaning we can
assume much of what he wrote was heavily impacted by the most
influential voice in the New Testament. "He traveled with Paul
from Troas to Philippi on Paul's second missionary journey (notice
the "we" in Acts 16:11ff), remained there for a few years, rejoined
Paul at the end of the third missionary journey (Acts 20:5-6),
and stayed with him over the next four years while Paul was in
prison."[54]

Luke was a physician by trade, which would mean he was
among the educated elite of his time. His Gospel is a "Prescription"
written for an entire population living through a time of ever-
growing spiritual hunger. He was precisely the physician needed
for such a remedy. Physicians were trained in all major academia
of the time, which included medicines, history, philosophy, and
the arts. Galen drafted a short essay called "The Best Doctor Is

---

[54] John Whittaker, *New Testament Writers: Who Were They?* https://renew.org/
new-testament-writers

Also a Philosopher," where he wrote that a physician needs to be knowledgeable about not just the physical, but additionally logical and ethical philosophy. He writes that a physician "must be skilled at reasoning about the problems presented to him, must understand the nature and function of the body within the physician's world, and must practice temperance and despise all money. The ideal physician treats both the poor and elite fairly, is a student of all that affects health."[55]

There is little doubt that Luke was of unique intelligence and processed a sophisticated writing ability, given his status as Physician. It makes perfect sense that this Gospel would be a supreme example of the Life of Jesus for the Greek thinking world, for Greeks have always been those who search for increased knowledge. Luke was the perfect author for them, which makes him the perfect author for us as well. Indeed, we are a Greek thinking people in the West today.

"Modern Greeks often allude to their ancestors. The culture of ancient Greece is still alive and kicking, centuries later. Their language and literature are still used to teach and express fundamental ideals. The writings of Plato and Aristotle (among many others) are the foundation for much of Western thought, while their art remains an inspiration for modern artistic creation."[56] From the time of Christ, and leaking forward into our day, we find at least 6 principles that were embraced by Luke in his time, and by Western Culture throughout the last two centuries: 1. Greeks celebrated arduous work and held a strong work ethic. Rest assured that Luke used all his energy to investigate the testimony he gave us. It was their practice. 2. Greeks valued as supreme education and academia. Luke would have been one

[55] Scott, William (1955). "The practice of medication in Ancient Rome". *Canadian Anesthetists Society Journal.* **2**: 281–290. doi:10.1007/BF03016172. S2CID 71952217
[56] The Top Ten Facts About Greek Culture, Vangelis Kotselas, Social Media Manager for Study in Greece, November 7, 2021. StudyInGreece.edu.gr

of those minds trained in all available avenues of discerning truth since the time he was a noticeably young boy. 3. Greeks were a very family-oriented people, which could be the reason family is central to Luke's telling of Advent, more so than any other Gospel. 4. Greek women were fierce and influential, so Luke fills the pages of Luke's Gospel in a way that was ahead of his time when it comes to highlighting the lives of women. This fact alone is a powerful piece of evidence for the validity of Luke's Gospel, for it would not be a popular move for a writer of his time to make women so prominent, unless of course you are simply relaying what took place. 5. Mathematics and Philosophy both came from Ancient Greece, giving us one clue as to why Luke focused intently and precisely on details, dates, and numbers. 6. The Greeks were the first society to practice democracy, meaning a government ruled by the people. The word "democracy" comes from two Greek words that mean people *(demos)* and rule *(kratos)*. Whatever we believe about Luke, we can be certain that he wrote to appeal to the masses in a cultural context that resembles our own Western Worldview in many ways.

Luke desires to break through the cultural barriers we might set up to protect ourselves from challenge and change. Gen Z, he is speaking to you, for you are the generation in a position to transform the future of Western Culture. You have already decided to "push back" when given a cause. You have already learned to question the status quo. You have been given a voice. Every day I speak to college students about this pivotal time. Every day Luke speaks to us about what remains the most important event in human history, A Visitation from the Divine. There is no way we can adequately speak to the future without remembering the significance of the past. The easiest way to destroy a people is to rewrite or forget their history. Might we give history a chance to provide insight into a truly transcendent future? This was always Luke's goal, Greek scholar that he was.

Luke gave us a detailed account, which came from those who knew Him best as Jesus walked among humanity. Luke presented this Man in such a way that Jesus would have no doubt created scandal in his day, which led to his death. It is hard to imagine that some of the things Luke claimed Jesus said and did could be made up stories by even the most creative mind, especially if the goal was to have people believe and follow. Let's take a glimpse into a two century old story and discover what Dr. Luke left us pertaining to this "Jesus of Nazareth," as he interviewed John, Mary, his disciples, his friends, his family, and a myriad of other people who were there to witness his deeds, listen to his stories, and witness the timeless miracle of Advent unfold before their very eyes. The Advent Event has the power to transform individual lives, unite families, and reform entire cultures in the 21st century and beyond.

(LAUGH WITH ME...) COLLEGE STUDENTS SET THE PACE.

Ten ways the Bible would be different had
it been written by college students:

1. The Last Supper would have been eaten the next morning -- cold.
2. The Ten Commandments would have been only five. They would have been double-spaced and written in a large font.
3. The Bible would have come out in a new edition every two years in order to limit re-selling.
4. The reason the forbidden fruit would have been eaten was that it wasn't cafeteria food.
5. Paul's letter to the Romans would become Paul's e-mail to abuse@romans.gov.

6. The reason Cain would have killed Abel: They were roommates.
7. The place where the end of the world occurs: Finals, not Armageddon.
8. Out go the mules; in come the mountain bikes.
9. The reason Moses and those following him would have wandered in the desert for 40 years: They did not want to ask directions and look like first-year students.
10. Instead of God creating everything in six days and resting on the seventh, He would have put it off until the night before it was due and then pulled an all-nighter.[57]

"I have carefully investigated everything" ... Luke 1:3

One of the most watched television shows of our time is CSI. In every episode you can expect at least three things to occur: A crime or event to be investigated; A gathering of evidence that will lead the team toward solving the crime; An outcome to the investigation as the evidence is pieced together to get at the truth. I find myself wondering why these shows in their various forms - CSI, NCSI, CSI WV, CSI Cub Fans, CSI Who Cares, or Way Too Much CSI - are so popular among modern TV Viewers. Could it be that we all love a good mystery? Could it be that we love watching those with special investigative skills following the evidence as they piece together amazing truth from tiny details?

This is most certainly one reason I love Luke's Gospel. You see, Luke was an investigator of facts so that he might discern Truth. He came to the evidence with eyes open, ears focused, and mind engaged, as he began to piece together the testimony of the events surrounding the life of Jesus. He certainly had the training, the

---

[57] Humor is one thing that goes most unappreciated when we consider the life of Jesus. Joy and laughter go together like sunshine and flowers, like dogs and their tails, like coffee and doughnuts. For a great discussion on this topic see: Elton Trueblood, "The Humor of Christ", 1964. Harper and Row Publishers, New York City.

expertise, and the mind for the task. We get glimpses of this all through the Gospel of Luke. We see how he organizes his material, with the expertise of a remarkable historian and a gifted poet. One clear example is found in Luke 15, where Luke strung together three stories with the same theme, all building on the other as he helped us to understand how Jesus used parables to answer his opponents. The stories themselves reflect the incredible teaching talents that we might expect from the Son of God. The position Luke placed them shows us an unbelievable understanding of Jesus' relationship to the Pharisees and his method of apologetics. Seeing that Luke is the only Gospel writer who gave us the parable of The Prodigal (Luke 15), he pointed us to a piece of evidence, CSI agents among us. Luke's investigation opened for him stories and parables that others either did not remember, did not deem important per their themes, or did not possess the same investigative talents toward discovery.

Luke's Gospel takes us deep into the heart of God. Luke was a Profiler, of sorts, as he allows us to peek inside the very heart of Jesus to his passions, his priorities, and his people skills. In Luke 15 Jesus spoke of a son who squandered his father's wealth, much the way the people of God have often squandered the incredible blessings of God. It is quite easy to understand that Jesus used the younger son to point to the outcasts who were flocking to Him for grace, mercy, and forgiveness. They were "coming to their senses;" they were returning home.

However, in this portion of Luke's Gospel (Luke 15) he was dealing with an even deeper problem, a more elusive sinner. We were introduced to a religious elite who did not agree with Jesus' tactics, especially as it related to the company he kept. The Pharisees, with their moral law and their extreme code of conduct, understood Jesus an enemy of the religious establishment, a defiler of the Temple, and most certainly not a brother to the True People of Israel. In Jesus' story they were the elder brother, standing outside the feast, refusing to enter for fear of being defiled by their defamed younger brother. They had redefined family. They had rejected the Father and His Son. Luke went to great lengths to highlight the failure of the religious establishment of the day toward recognizing genuine human need. Sound familiar?

Let us consider the progress of our investigation. We determined the crime, and we have seen the evidence. Jesus came to throw a feast in honor of the lost sheep of Israel. The evidence was overwhelming, as he healed the sick, cleansed the leper, loved the Romans, and shared numerous meals with Tax Collectors. The Feast was to be all inclusive. *Theo* himself was to be in attendance, Roman Centurion that he was. The so called "good people" would never attend such a Feast, represented by the elder brother. They were left to mutter, complain, and begrudge the father for such an outlandish denial of the faith. This was indeed the twist. The unexpected culprit. The surprising crime. Those who had longed for the Messiah their entire lives, taught of his coming in the synagogues, are the very people who will reject him upon arrival.

If you love a good mystery, you must love the Gospel of Luke. The outcome of Luke's investigation will prove to be shocking. He has pieced together the evidence, he has found the perpetrator, and he has highlighted both villain and hero. No one expected the Pharisees to be identified as the conspirators. No one expected the "low lives" to become the Beloved. How could we predict the Romans would react so harshly? How could Luke have formed such a surprising conclusion if not for the facts leading him there?

The answer is obvious. He would not have. If we follow the evidence, the entire premise of CSI investigations, we find a very conclusive case for the truth of Luke's testimony. People who refuse to embrace Advent do so without thorough investigation. Often, those who reject Jesus' self-proclamation passed down from Luke's witnesses to our ears have done so without truly considering His claim. Luke took more than a decade to investigate this material. He risked his life to transfer his investigation into a written document. And He left us with one of the most powerful biographies ever written. He purposely invited his readers to challenge the facts by placing so much public information inside his Gospel account. No matter where you are in your investigation of the content, there is no denying the enormous importance of the claims we find in the first two chapters of Luke. Enter the Laboratory, follow the evidence, and you will end up where I find myself - in awe of Jesus.

Do You Hear Them?[58]

Do you hear them as they call to us from
the drugged streets of our Land?

Or the baby as she vainly sucks from the dry breast in her hand?

The Refugee at the brink of death in a country far away?

Or the child who has lost her legs to beg on Tourist Day?

The mother who must watch her child all too slowly die?

A child who has not yet learned to ask her mother why?

The elderly who must make their choice -
starve or freeze to death?

Or the Fetus who was not allowed her first unassisted breath?

---

[58] From the Journal of Dr. Rick Farmer, https://www.youtube.com/watch?v=oYj 80enx-x8

Day 4

Theophilus, please consider "An account of the things that have been fulfilled" ...Luke 1:1

Setting the Stage: "Consider This" ...Riding the Ideological Tide of our Time

PURE AND SIMPLE, THE COMING OF JESUS IS A STORY OF GRACE. Grace needed then; Grace certainly needed now. This was the primary outcome of Luke's investigation – our need for Grace fulfilled. One of my favorite songs of all time is a song by REM[59] called "Losing My Religion." It is a prophetic song for our time. At the very least, it is a song about self-discovery, or self-identity if you will. Written on the brink of a day when self-identity was to become a dominant theme for a generation, this song takes us on an internal journey that occurs when *"who I am"* and *"who I am told to be"* are conflicted. At one point Michael Stipe, lyric writer, and lead singer, draws attention to his own journey. He sings as a man in a corner, spotlight revealing the fact that he cannot keep up with what is required of him.

---

[59] R.E.M., named for a dream-state condition (rapid eye movement), formed in 1980 in Athens, Georgia, a university town about 65 miles (105 km) northeast of Atlanta that was already internationally noted for its local pop scene by the time R.E.M. released Chronic Town, its 1982 debut extended-play recording. (Information taken from "R.E.M. American rock group", Britannica (July 26, 2023). Written by James Hunter, Freelance Writer Fact-checked by The Editors of Encyclopaedia Britannica)

I have personally experienced this sensation in dramatic ways. I was once running as fast as I could from my own religion because I could not keep up with the demands placed on me by those who declared themselves to be interpreters of the faith. Without suggesting this is exactly Michael Stipe's intent as he writes, this is the way his words hit many of us, who have at some point experienced religion as a burden to be carried. In a day of intense searching for self-identity, where we have the freedom to *self-identify* and *self-declare* the truth as it relates to me or you, why not embrace a song which celebrates our right to do so?

Stipe is not finished with us. He wanted us to understand that life is "bigger than me and you" and the problems we face. Though we go to great lengths to feel accepted, needed, and loved, we fail. We will let others down and they will let us down. However, there are places where this is not allowed. For example, I grew up within a Pentecostal church environment. As a teenager, I found myself going to the altar every Wednesday night and Sunday morning. I knew I had failed during the week, and if Jesus returned during a down time in terms of my behavior I was in lots of trouble, so I thought. I would pray and pray that Jesus would not come back on a Friday or Saturday night, for I needed to get to that Sunday Morning Altar. I was a teenager in the spotlight, not able to hide, and every time I took my guilty conscience to the altar I did so to escape hell. This was what I believed, so I climbed toward the altar for mercy. I knew deep inside this just marked me as sinner and backslider, in the spotlight for all to see, which is precisely why I tried to hide at the very corner of the altar. I was "saying too much" for an audience that was pretending to have life figured out, at least the religious side of things. It was like people despised the truth of the human condition and lived a false reality for the sake of religious reputation.

"Losing My Religion" contained a powerful message for a generation of church goers who were living a lie (baby boomers).

It would be years before I would understand that God's grace was able to "take me as I am" every single day of my existence, that the spotlight was ok when speaking of God's gaze. I spent decades trying to communicate this message inside the American Baptist Tradition. However, I learned there are groups of people who simply refuse to hear. They believe I have lost my religion when I say things like: "God loves us for who we are more than what we do" (As if we really do all that much to begin with) or "Sadly, we do a much better job of making people feel guilty than we do of delivering them from the guilt we create. We need to confess this and change our ways."[60]

Though many within our churches claim to believe these concepts as Truth, their lives represent something else entirely. Many believe there is a line people are not allowed to cross, for when they do, damnation is certain. In my experience, many inside the Church have these imaginary lines, and place artificial limits on God's mercy without realizing what they do. At the end of my teenage years the weight of it all grew so heavy on me that I decided to leave it behind, to resign from Christianity, to forfeit my "get out of hell free" card, to stop striving to be what I always knew I could not be. I decided to quit. I lost my religion.

However, there is always a "but" when it comes to God. As one comedian said, "God has a big butt." One morning, after I had slept in from a long night out, God decided it was time for me to *un-retire from a life of Faith*. There came to me a profound word that began with, "But Rick." I woke to the sound of poetry in my mind, as I ran to find a pen and paper to record my thoughts. I began to write, and I have been writing ever since. I have no way of knowing if this was a direct message from God or the musings of my unconscious mind, but God broke through to me during this season of my life. And this is what I wrote. I call it:

---

[60] Both of these concepts I learned from listening to Tony Campolo. See Tony Campolo Quotes, AZ Quotes, azquotes.com

"My God is not Surprised"

I fail you oh so terribly, yet You cast me not away.
I deserve to be afflicted, yet You bless me every day.
I deserve the chains of bondmen, yet Your free Spirit shines.
I deserve Your cross dear Jesus, yet You took my place one time.

You knew before the world began, before the birds did sing,
Exactly what I'd do and say, exactly what I'd bring,
And lay it there, at Your feet, You paid the price - I'm clean.

My God is not disappointed, My God is not surprised.
Though I fail You every day, You loved me enough to die.[61]

I began to understand I was set up for failure through my understanding of religiosity, what I now deem to be short sighted human interpretations of Metaphysical Truth. I was set up to lose my religion quite naturally, as are so many of our youth today. This song, "Losing My Religion," is brilliant in its ability to touch the depths of the late 20th century experience, but it is one of few songs I know without a true chorus. Instead, it is a continuous story of personal struggle and pain, without a chorus or a bridge built into the fabric of the song. Michael does not offer an answer. Instead, he offers a loop toward a dead end. Whether it relates to a breakup with a woman, as many claim, or is about the journeys of a "military brat" which led to a son coming up short in a variety of experiences, Stipe speaks to a generation with this lyric. He speaks to me. I was one of those who was caught trying hard yet consistently coming up short, only to be rescued by a Grace[62]

---

[61] For more poetry by Rick A. Farmer, you can find some set to music on his YouTube channel. If the music disturbs your reading, just turn down the volume: https://www.youtube.com/channel/UCtfjXAqBNWNYc-Dz67rKvOg
[62] For a brilliant discussion of the concept of "Grace" I stumbled upon two books: M. Scott Peck, *The Road Less Traveled (1978)*. Simon and Shuster, page 260 and 261) wherein "Grace" is powerfully defined as " *"A powerful force originating outside of*

beyond measure at a time when my hope for acceptance was all but lost.

Phillip Yancey wrote one of the more powerful books on Grace in recent years – "What's So Amazing About Grace? (Revised and Updated)." In the first pages of the updated version he wrote, when speaking of Jesus: "The revolutionary strain of grace changed history, setting loose a stream of liberation that freed slaves, empowered women, lifted the downtrodden, educated the illiterate, and brought healing to the sick......I have found a trail of hospitals, orphanages, schools, and the fighting of poverty, liberation of victims of sex trafficking, response to disasters, all in the name of Jesus. Such is the power of grace."[63] Yancey highlights an "amazing grace," Stipe sings about a world in need of grace, while Luke specifically points to *The Source of Grace*. How can we not consider the evidence Luke presents?

Translating Stipe's words into the stories of our day is easy to do. We are a nation struggling with *self-identity*. We see this as we listen to the personal proclamations of individuals. "I identify as…," "My pronouns are" … and we are not allowed to question the line that follows these words… "Man, woman, non-binary, cis, trans, bobcat" …. for we are absolutely allowed to *self-identify* and declare who we are. But this postmodern post-truth ideological right comes at a cost, as a denial of classical Truth leaves us unsure and speculative when it comes to faith and reality. For too long the Gospel has been misappropriated in the West by those who ought to know better. America voluntarily declares herself to be "Losing My Religion" for the sake of her people.

For some, this is the only absolute truth left for us - *Self Declaration of Being.* We have transformed the words of *DesCarte*

---

human consciousness which nurtures the spiritual growth of human beings?" and What's So Amazing About Grace, Phillip Yancey, 1997, 2023. Zondervan Press, Grand Rapids, Michigan.

[63] Phillip D. Yancey, *"What's So Amazing About Grace? Updated and Revised"*, 1997, 2023. Zondervan, Grand Rapids, Michigan. Pg. XV.

from "I think, therefore I am" into "I think I am, therefore I am." We have declared ourselves deity when it comes to defining what it means to be a human being. Society, we are told, is obligated to accept and embrace our personal declaration of sexual identity and gender. Evidence or not, reasonable or not, compassionate people are expected to embrace a person's self-discovery. But this is not simply an affirmation of being, as proclaimed. This turns out to be an affirmation of ideology, in which science and religion are both given a back seat in the discussion. **Instead of celebrating Grace, we celebrate a denial of Truth so that we no longer need Grace.** We all exist in the "spotlight," but this is not for transformational purposes. It is so we can stay the same without pushback, without true growth, without challenge or critique of personal ideology.

The ironic thing, we have yet to extend the same courtesy to Jesus. We have little difficulty denying Jesus His self-proclaimed identity, for many find his declaration of self to be offensive. It is interesting that some self-identifications are allowed, offensive to others or not, while public religious declarations are considered taboo. I wonder, could this be because of the pain we religious people have caused in the lives of so many people in marginalized groups? "Losing My Religion" is a common experience, as we find ourselves unable to sustain the out of touch traditions of our church or society, and the constant scrutiny of people who place us "in the spotlight" for their own condescending purposes. Few of us can survive this spotlight, and we are left alone in the corner tending to our wounds.

Jesus is different. He was not driven to his identity by years of self-discovery or social contagion. On the contrary, He embraced an identity that was set for Him before time began. He grew into a pre-prescribed identity. Someone else decided for Him and He voluntarily embraced His destiny. And when He declared His identity to others, He was met with rejection, both then and now. I am inviting all of us to "consider this" as we consciously deal with the reality of Luke's claim about Who Jesus' followers understood Him to be. Allow room for His claim, just as you would anyone else claiming an identity difficult to embrace.

"Consider this, Consider this, the hint of the century.... Consider this, the slip.... That brought me to my knees," (Michael Stipe, Losing My Religion)

**Jesus' Self Discovery: Jesus lived a life, from day
one, of "consider this" from His knees......**

Have you ever wondered how Jesus was able to understand who he was by the time we find Him teaching in the Temple as a twelve-year-old? (Luke 2:41-50) When I was twelve, I was trying to figure out how to say my first words to a girl, wondering whether my friends were talking about me behind my back, and questioning if Santa was a real person or not. I had little sense of self, almost no understanding of self-esteem, and not a clue what I was supposed to be doing with my life. I was at the end of my twenties before I had a good idea of why I was placed upon this planet. Jesus, at age twelve, already knew of His unique identity, His life calling, and His pre-determined yet freely chosen destiny.

I have an inkling that two things were key to this understanding. First, His Parents, who relayed to Him the stories of Angel visitations, Shepherds and Astrologers, *Ana and Elizabeth*, among others. Second, The Scriptures themselves, containing hundreds of prophetic words that connected directly with His birth and His life. I believe Jesus discovered His own identity, at least in part, the same way I did – in the Scriptures. This is where I discovered I am made in the image of God for a high purpose. This is most likely where Jesus discovered He is the exact representation of God in human form made for the highest purpose of all.

What if Jesus were to say in our hearing? - "Messiah was to be born in Bethlehem. Well, low and behold, Mom and Dad traveled there for the census right as I was being born. We returned to our roots. Messiah was to be the son of David. Mom and Dad both came from David's line. Coincidence? Messiah was to be acquainted with suffering. From the time I was a little boy, people have pointed, whispered, and teased me as a child born out of wed lock in a culture in which this was royally frowned upon. And do not let me get started about my trial and execution. A story for another day. Mom taught me that Messiah was to flee to Egypt. We still have the items given to us by friends from when we lived there. The Messiah was to be a Teacher, a Prophet, a Servant, a Leader of the people. I am all of these, all rolled into One Person. Messiah was to be rejected by those close to him. I forgive you Judas and Peter. Messiah was to suffer and die, though innocent of all charges. Please understand, the pain of unjust suffering, of abandonment, of family rejection, of betrayal, of legal problems, of poverty, I get them all. I feel you. I was there just like you. The interesting thing is that repeatedly I was asked to embrace a purpose already established for me and declare it as my identity - the Son of David, The Son of Man, The Son of God. It seems that if any generation could understand the power of self-identification, it would be 21st century America. Yet my self-identity within this culture lies often rejected and forgotten. I am not allowed to be who I declare myself to be. Will you give me a chance to make my case to you?" (Dr. Farmer imagining a conversation with Jesus today.)

"Dialogue about doctrine seems to have become a mostly aimless conversation for conversation's sake. The goal isn't to arrive at any common understanding or settled condition about what's true and what's false. Instead, the whole point seems to be to get as many different opinions into the mix as possible, and then perpetuate the lavish, lighthearted friendliness of the discussion indefinitely."[64] (John MacArthur)

[64] John MacArthur, "The Jesus You Can't Ignore: What you must learn from the bold confrontations of Christ," 2008. GALE/Cengage Learning and Published in 2010 by arrangement with Thomas Nelson, Inc., Detroit/NY/San Francisco/New Haven, Conn/Waterville, Maine/London. Page 37

Day 5

"I have carefully investigated everything from the beginning....I have decided to write an orderly account for you..." Luke 1:3

Setting the stage: Luke's Gospel is a flowing "I message"

Luke is the only Gospel where the author steps forward to identify himself, using the pronoun "I" to identify himself for the recipient of what is to follow. He is about to "draw up" his own account of the things that had been going on in and around Jerusalem, on the way to the very streets of Rome. The "I" within Luke's Gospel tells us three things, at the very least.

1: He was personally acquainted with the recipient. He wanted this "most noble" man, whom he obviously loved and respected, to know these are his words coming to him. This "most noble" title given to *Theophilus* identified him as a Roman Officer of some sort.[65]

2: Luke had no problem staking his life and reputation on what he was about to write. He believed this message to be far too important to keep concealed, so he wrote a Gospel intended for

---

[65] For a great discussion about the identity of *Theophilus* see: WHO WAS THEOPHILUS?
11/28/2017 CHRISTIAN AMBASSADOR (SHAWN BRASSEAUX), forwhatsaith thescriptures.org

Greeks and Romans, and those who might be able to do him harm if they read it.

3: We see why Luke wrote with such precision and highlighted historical details. He wanted people to check his work. He wanted people to validate the facts he was presenting. He was not satisfied with anyone else's telling of the story. For example, in Luke 3:1 Luke dated for us the precise moment the Word of the Lord came to John the Baptizer. It was "the fifteenth year of Tiberius Caesar, when Pontius Pilate was governor or Judea, etc." He set the stage for any hearer or reader of his words to verify on their own the stories he highlighted. He wanted to be precise with his accounting of events for the sake of those who might hear his testimony. This was a confident writer indeed.

A carefully investigated orderly account... Luke 1:3

Knowing dates is often of utmost importance. Ask any husband who has forgotten his wife's birthday or anniversary. Or talk to a poor elderly person about the beginning date for their Social Security Check. Inquire of a College Professor the starting date for classes in the fall. Make plans for tailgating before the Ohio State/Michigan game on the wrong date. Fail to show up for a job interview you thought was tomorrow. Times and Dates matter. Life is, in many ways, all about timing. Being in the right place at the right time is of huge significance. I have gotten time and space relationships wrong before. As far as I can calculate, there are three ways we can do this.

We can be in the right place, at the wrong time. I was once asked to speak at a funeral, but mistakenly showed up a day early. At least I got to experience the celebration of life for a kind, good-hearted grandmother whose children greeted me as if I were her friend. "How did you know her?" they asked. I wonder, would you lie? I was in the right place at the wrong time.

We can be in the wrong place at the right time. Driving my

sister's car one Sunday evening a deer jumped out of the woods right onto our windshield. Glass everywhere. (Thank you Dr. Jabour for cleaning out my eyes that night.) After we shared with our mom what happened during my sister's visit my mother summed it up beautifully: "That's what happens when you don't go to church." I was in the wrong place at the right time.

We can also be in the wrong place at the wrong time. Have you ever stood behind the slowest human being on earth in a grocery store line when you were already running late for an important meeting? I have. I jumped in the shortest line, but the lady in front of me was ready for a conversation, which kept her from signing her check, which caused her to write the wrong total on the check when she finally did write it, which caused her to drop her check book from the anxiety of doing it wrong, which led to her delay in writing a new check, which led to continued laughter from her and the clerk, which now meant I was definitely late for my meeting. Finally, I was up, paid, and off to my car. Great, only one car was waiting to get out into traffic in front of me. "This won't be too bad......Wait, why won't she pull out. There is a gap. Go! Come on! You must go! You will not find a better opportunity than that." At last, she pulled into an open lane with no cars in sight, slow enough for me to see her face. You guessed it. It was the same little lady who I was behind in the grocery store line. I was in the wrong place at the wrong time.

There are times when we get it right. We are in the right place at the right time, for "just such a time as this" (Esther 4:14).[66] Luke was with Paul. Right place, right time. Luke had time on his hands as Paul served under house arrest. Right place, right time. Luke was surrounded by witnesses to the events that unfolded in

---

[66] For a fantastic Old Testament Story highlighting the idea of being in the "right place at the right time" I recommend reading the short Old Testament Book called "Esther." This fascinating Book will give you fantastic insight into the timing issue and how God so often displays perfect timing in the events of our lives, no matter the scope of the atmosphere in which they happen.

Judea. Right place, right time. Luke was educated to record the events, times, dates, words, and true meaning of these. Right place, right time. And Jesus arrived and thrived just as Luke was being prepared to write about these events. Right place, "write" time. And now we live in this free land, where we are given the privilege and opportunity to study Luke's Gospel that we might be grafted into the greatest event in Human History. Right place, right time, for each of us.

More importantly, the place and time of Luke's writing gives striking evidence to three things that make his Gospel a Source of Trustworthy content. First, he traveled extensively with the most prominent Apostle in the New Testament record - Paul. This is of primary importance when dating the testimony Luke gave. Paul's journeys covered the period of the mid-thirties until the 70's A.D... This means Luke is communicating material that was gathered within 30 years of the actual events, which is unheard of reliable historical documents. Opponents of Christianity often attach this fact first, believing that if they can put time and distance between writer and event, they can undermine the trustworthiness of the testimony given. Their problem is quite simple, for both the internal evidence of the document and the testimony of early church historians both point to the pre 65 A.D. dating of Luke's Gospel. For a myriad of reasons, we can discern he was writing before the fall of Jerusalem in 70 A. D. "When (all the evidence) is combined with the general accuracy of Luke's account......the case for dating (Acts/Luke) in the 60's and for seeing it as written by a close follower of Paul appears very solid."[67]

Second, Luke's account is written as a theological testimony that takes place within public world history. In other words, he intentionally built a case that is intimately tied to the details of historical events, and he obviously knew this as he wrote. He was intentionally building a case from history, and he believed himself

---

[67] Gregory A. Boyd, "Cynic Sage of Son of God", page 255

to be the most credible witness interviewing credible eyewitnesses about especially momentous events that were taking place under the noses of the people of his time. He purposely invited his readers to challenge the facts by placing so much public material inside his Gospel.

Third, Luke claimed himself to be writing a reliable history, "an orderly account," which was the reason he gave for masterfully researching these events. It amazes me that people so often easily dismiss statements like this when speaking of the Biblical Record. Luke risked his life to write, knew that prison would be a likely outcome, sacrificed his claim to status and income, purposely addressed Roman authorities, and showed little concern for consequences for himself by writing what he wrote. After affirming the overwhelming evidence of when Luke wrote his Gospel, it would have been quite alarming for him to write a Gospel that threatened his own safety, if in fact this Gospel was not worth his writing and a Source of Life Transforming material. Luke was in the right place at the right time for those he was trying to reach, not for himself.

(LAUGH WITH ME...)

A man is trying to understand the nature of God, and asked God: "How long is a million years to you?" God answered: "A million years is like a minute." Then the man asked: "God, how much is a million dollars to you?" And God replied: "A million dollars is like a penny to me." Finally, the man gets to the point and asks God: "Can I please have a penny?" And God said: "Yes, in a minute."

A guy is on a trip on a small airline. The steward says, "Would you like dinner?" He says, "What are

my choices?" She says, "Yes or no." (When it comes
to God, there are two choices......yes or no).

Life is a search for Truth. But even facts and the best evidence
are only as useful as one permits them to be. Consider the
example of the fellow who was convinced he was dead. He
visited his doctor with this complaint several times and
the doctor was unable to change his mind. Finally, the
exasperated doctor demanded whether his patient would believe
otherwise in the face of physical evidence that he was alive.
"Of course," said the man calmly. "I'm a reasonable fellow."
"Would you agree that dead men don't bleed?" said the Doc.
"Of course," the dead man replied.
"Fine. Give me your hand," ordered the Doc. Taking a
needle, he softly pricked a fingertip, then squeezed it
until a drop of blood beaded up. He thrust it in front
of the man's eyes. "Look! Is this not blood?"
"I'll be darned," said the patient after astonished
reflection. "Dead men do bleed!"(How stubbornly
do we hold on to our versions of Truth?)

Day 6

Who is this Theophilus? (Luke 1:4)

Setting the Stage: A *Greek* Letter about a *Jewish* Messiah for a *Roman* Officer = Diversity.

THE 1ST CENTURY GOSPELS, INCLUDING THE GOSPEL OF LUKE, were not read by the 1st century population, since 85 to 90 % of the people were illiterate. Writers and then Witnesses, those called Evangelists, would memorize manuscripts or parts of manuscripts, then perform the Gospels as an evening of entertainment usually lasting two to four hours. The Gospels were brought to life by gifted story tellers, but the manuscripts guided the shared content carried throughout the Roman Empire. It served as a night at the theatre. New Testament letters were shorter, and were read at church gatherings, first to the churches they were addressed to, and then to the surrounding churches in that region of the world. It is quite apparent that the letters existed first, then came the Gospels, as the demand for the stories of Jesus increased throughout Rome. Five historical truths prepared the Roman Empire as the perfect place and time for this strategy to work, and these are five truths that have parallels in our time: The Roman Roads the Evangelists traveled (Social Media and the Internet), the universality of the Greek language (The English Language and translators galore), the *Pax Romana* (peace of Rome) which protected the Evangelists on their journeys (The United Nations and NATO), the oral traditions adopted by Jewish and Greek Culture (the Comedian, the Cartoon, and TikTok), and the spiritual hunger of the people held under the heavy thumb of Roman rule. (Postmodernism is a search for meaning and purpose which transcends science and technology.)[68]

"At the proper time, the God of history caused *Caesar Augustus* to issue a decree for the entire world to be taxed. Thus, as foretold by the prophet in Micah 5:2, Jesus would be born in Bethlehem. **Indeed, the reign of Augustus was hallmarked not only by a global readiness for the Gospel, but also for its rapid diffusion throughout the whole Roman world**" (Marked bold by the author of this article).[69] In addition to the *Augustus* factor," The spread of Hellenism had greatly impacted Mediterranean culture giving rise to history, philosophy, art, literature, and drama. Yet a *lingua franca* (common language and culture) and abstract thought for religious debates remained the greatest contributions of the Greeks to herald the coming Christ." (See footnote on previous page). For the first time in human history a conquered people spoke a common language throughout the land.

Alexander the Great emphasized conquest of nations and of minds.[70] For this reason, the Greek language had spread throughout the lands he conquered, which eventually became the Roman Empire. "Most significantly, the translation of the Hebrew scriptures into the Greek Septuagint in the 2nd century BC made synagogue worship by the Jewish diaspora possible and an attractive alternative to Greco-Roman paganism. By the 1st century AD, there were 'God-fearers' in every town in

---

[68] For further insight into 1st century Gospel transmission please see Thomas E. Boomershine, *"First-Century Gospel Storytellers and Audiences: The Gospels as Performance Literature" (July 2022)*. Cascade Books.

[69] Missions History: Precise Timing of Advent, Douglas Batson, December 8, 2022. Global Frontier Missions – *Until All Have Heard....globalfrontiermissions.org*

[70] Alexander the Great & Hellenism, History & Conquests, Joseph Cataliotti, 2024. Study.com, https://study.com/academy/lesson/alexander-the-great-and-the-birth-of-hellenism.html

the Mediterranean basin, eager to study and debate Epicurean and Stoic philosophies as well as one sovereign Creator-Savior God. There was a common language spoken by the people." (See footnotes above) Though Paul and Luke most certainly were called to Gentiles as missionaries, it was without doubt the most practical strategy they could have taken, given the landscape of the people they wanted to reach. Speaking a common language along protected roads there traveled two Roman citizens who spoke fluent Greek with both the knowledge to take the Gospel to the World, the education needed to debate in the public squares, and the passion of their own visitation (See Acts 9) and interviews of eye witnesses (See Luke's Gospel) to energize the most important mission which had ever been given two men. Thus, Paul wrote letters to Greek speaking churches, and Luke wrote a Gospel to his beloved Roman officer *Theophilus,* the two people groups Paul and Luke spent their lives trying to reach, all set up for them by God's Perfect Timing.

*Galatians 4:4-7: **4** But when the set time had fully come, God sent his Son, born of a woman, born under the law, **5** to redeem those under the law, that we might receive adoption to sonship. **6** Because you are his sons, God sent the Spirit of his Son into our hearts, the Spirit who calls out, "Abba, Father." **7** So you are no longer a slave, but God's child; and since you are his child, God has made you also an heir.*

A Roman Road

Let's Meet *Theophilus...*

There are at least three ways to approach a question of the identity of *Theophilus*, or *Theo*, as I will affectionately call him at times. First, some think him to have been a friend of Luke, and that Luke took upon himself to write Luke/Acts as a type of persuasive apologetic for his friend, assuming *Theo* had learned a limited amount of content. Possibly, Luke attempted to persuade a friend who was yet to embrace the full truth of the Gospel of Jesus Christ because he believed his friend to be in a tremendous position of influence in the Roman World of this time. A second possibility – *Theo's* name was being used as metaphor for a particular group of people; therefore, Luke used this name as a sort of code for the people who were his intended audience. These would have been Gentile converts or potential converts. A third scenario - Luke needed a publisher to fund his writing project and *Theo* was the guy, so Luke addressed this work to him out of professional courtesy. All three have some merit. I cannot claim to know which one, if any of these three, was Luke's reason. However, I want to focus on the name itself, and what Luke might be teaching us today through the name *Theophilus*.

(Imagining the transformation of *Theophilus*).

Theophilus is a creative combination of two Greek words: *Theos* (*Θεός*) meaning "God," and *phileo* (*φιλέω*) meaning "brotherly love." *Theo's* name means "God lover." Taken another way, flipping the emphasis onto Love rather than God, it could mean "Loved by God." Either way, we have two beautiful Greek words to think about, built into a single name. Luke's Gospel is abundantly full of both themes. In the writings of Luke, we meet Mary, Elizabeth, some shepherds, Anna, Simeon, Martha, Mary, some tax collectors, prostitutes, and some unnamed but immensely powerful "lovers of God." The woman weeping at Jesus' feet in Luke 7 and the father of two sons in Luke 15 are two splendid examples. Luke's Gospel is filled with real life illustrations of what it looked like to be a "lover of God" in relation to Jesus. This Gospel also gave us the most vivid illustration of a "God who loves." No person is so far lost, no son is too far gone, no tax collector is so hated, no leper is so unclean, no "least, last or lost" is so "least, last or lost," that Jesus did not show that one the Limitless Love of God.

Luke included some parables that no other Gospel writer included, like "The Prodigal" in Luke 15, "The Two Debtors" in Luke 7, "The Good Samaritan" in Luke 10, "The Rich Man and Lazarus" in Luke 16, or the "Publican and Pharisee" in Luke 18. All of these were illustrations of the length God is willing to go to show love for the least, the last, and the lost. In my mind *Theophilus*, "Lover of God" or "Loved of God," was the perfect recipient for this Gospel. For we are all *Theo*. Each one of us has the potential of learning to love God, for we are most certainly loved by God. By the time *Theo* finished considering the Gospel of Luke, there is little doubt that two things would have occurred to him. He knew he was loved, no matter where he had been or what he had done. And he had learned that each person can learn to love, can learn to participate in loving acts as we imitate the Subject of Luke's Gospel - Jesus of Nazareth.

Luke seemed to understand that the certainty of the life of Jesus is wrapped up in the evidence wrought by clear illustrations of God's love for humanity through a record of His life, His deeds, and His words. His Gospel took *Theo* on this quest, takes us on this quest, as we discover the Love of God through His birth, His Life, His teachings, His death, and then His continued activity through the Church in Volume Two of his work (Acts). So, read on *Theo*, who happens to be me and you in the end, as we continue to rejoice in the true reason we celebrate Advent - The Love of God for and through each of us discovered in the Life of Jesus.

Finally, I want to stress that the naming of *Theophilus* is more important than we may realize. Not only does it direct the content Luke would write, not only does it highlight the fact this was a Gospel for the Gentiles, not only does his name combine two very powerful Greek words that point toward the Love of God, but the naming of *Theophilus* gives us major insight as to how to read Gospels in particular and Scripture in general.

In the world today we have conflated Gospel with the word

Theology. Instead of allowing the Text to speak, embracing the words of Scripture as a Light for our path as it stands, we have convinced ourselves that the Gospel must be reinterpreted for each new Generation, at least considering each new Worldview. "It is the content of belief that concerns Scripture, not eradicating unbelief by means of a believable theology."[71] This may seem straight forward on its surface, but it is my contention that fewer and fewer of those involved in what we call theology have followed this principle.

Luke believed himself motivated by God's Spirit (we call this inspired) to write an orderly account of the events of his day, and then addressed this work to *Theophilus*, a Roman Official of Status. The Gospel he wrote stands on its own as a powerful document about a world transforming Gospel centered around the person of Jesus of Nazareth. Luke was not so much concerned about *if* we shall believe. He is much more concerned about *what* we believe. So, he entrusts this message to a person he trusts to help ensure this message is carried forth to those who are like him - The Gentile World. It Luke were with us today he would no doubt say to us: "Don't spend so much time concerning yourself with making the Gospel relevant to the modern world. This task is both endless in nature and fleeting at best." The Jesus Event, and specifically my topic, the Advent Event, speaks for itself. It is a "Timeless Script," it never grows old, and it will always have the power to transform.

In other words, we are not called to surrender to Christianity as people of faith. We are called to surrender to a Person, namely Jesus. As a Christian I can conveniently incorporate the tenets of the faith into a relevant and modern lifestyle, while at the same time remaining the ultimate authority in my own life. Most Christians live here. However, Luke is not introducing a lifestyle among others, to be made relevant in new ways by every succeeding

---

[71] Stanley Hauerwas and Wiliam H. Willimon, "Resident Aliens: Life in the Christian Colony", 1989. Abingdon Press, Nashville, TN, page 22

Generation. Luke is introducing a World-changing Event, The Birth of a King. Within his testimony of the birth, "Life, death, resurrection and ascension of Christ, all Human history must be reviewed.........In Jesus we meet not a presentation of basic ideas about God, world, and Humanity, but an invitation to join up, to become a part of a movement, a people."[72]

Allow me to explain what this means for us as we read. *Theophilus* was the intended audience. He was no doubt intentionally chosen by Luke for at least 2 reasons. Luke knew him, and Luke knew his name would introduce his Gospel. The meaning of his name, "Loved of God," would be well known by all Gentile Greek speaking listeners. But Luke did not intend this Gospel for *Theo* alone, for his audience is the people *Theo* represented, those "loved by God." *Theophilus* alone makes this a Timeless and Universal Gospel, in Luke's mind. His name means we are all included in his audience.

Luke had no knowledge of modern theological ploys, whereby we allow the modern world to determine the questions we ask, which automatically limits the answers we find. This is one reason the Advent Story is so diminished in our time. We ask the wrong questions! Questions limited by our Worldview options. Luke wrote what he wrote for any time to be understood by any audience falling within the framework of "Gentile" (See later footnote about "Gentile"). Modern theology tends to read back its premises into the Biblical record, which of necessity will distort the message. Luke is to be read as a Gospel that dictates theology, allowing his content to direct our thinking rather than allowing our thinking to limit his message. This would be the equation of such a task: God at work in Israel through history in Old Testament Scripture followed by the Jewish expectation and longing for Messiah who would be "God with us" followed by a prophetic profile of this Messiah followed by longing and expectation followed by birth of

---

[72] Hauerwas and Willimon, Resident Aliens, page 24 and 21

this Messiah followed by "God with us" in real time in the Person of this Messiah followed by fulfillment of the prophetic profile by this Messiah in such a way that human history begins anew followed by people surrendering to this Messiah King followed by stories of the actions of this Messiah being organized into a written record by the likes of Luke followed by the gift of a Timeless, Universal Gospel to the world which we are now exposed to.

"The challenge of Christianity has become an intellectual one involving a clash of two different systems of belief: how to make old Christianity credible to the new world."[73] I am suggesting that because Luke specifically addressed his Gospel to *Theophilus*, he is asking us to allow his words to stand on their own as a message from a real Jesus follower to all people who share a non-Jewish heritage. Rather than striving to make Luke's Gospel a document that "makes sense" considering our modern sensibilities, let us treat his Gospel as a document that speaks what needs to be heard by all of us, for it contains Timeless Truth which will never cease to speak to its intended audience. We stand at a precipice, yes, but so have other generations before us. And Luke has a message for us all, which is always and forever "contemporary."

---

[73] Hauerwas and Willimon, "Resident Aliens", page 23

God's Love Never Runs Short....

"There have been multiple attempts to create a society where freedom reigns. The Roman and the American Empires are two primary examples, both riding the coattails of Greek Culture and Philosophy, Incredible Wealth, and Military Might. One Person presented himself to both empires, offering a reign of freedom for all. In reality, there is only one person in all of history that demonstrated authority over the very enemies that destroy freedom – death and tyranny. Luke tells us the story of this very person." (Rick Farmer)

"If we could be reborn wherever we chose, how crowded Rome would be, populated by souls who had spent their previous lives longing to inhabit a villa on the Janiculum Hill." (Francine Prose, American Writer)

"It is the will of the Father to provide a space and a time wherein men and women can both give their allegiance to the Kingdom in the only way it can be given – namely, in freedom." (Lesslie Newbigin, Foolishness to the Greeks, page 138)

Day 7

"Elizabeth could not conceive, and both of
them were well along in years..." Luke 1:7

Setting the Stage: Is One ever enough?

IN 2020 AMERICAN WOMEN AGED 15-49 AVERAGED 1.64 BIRTHS
per woman in our country (USA). This rate was lower in both
Canada and China. We have discovered over the past few decades
that growing economies equal fewer children. One report suggests
even lower rates, considering the survival rate after one year,
stressing that "by 2019, the average female aged 15-49 had given
birth to 1.3 children, and the average male had fathered 0.9 kids."[74]
The number varies depending on the age of women we include in
the study, but the consensus is clear - Women are having fewer
than 2 children on average. This is in comparison to the same data
through the 1950's and 60's, where women peeked at a birth rate
of around 3.8 children in a lifetime.

Why is childbirth in decline? We can speculate: "According
to a report, the reasons for these trends are many: Better access
to contraception, more women seeking higher education, more
women entering and staying in the workforce, changing family
values, relationship instability, and concerns over personal finances

---

[74] All the statistics in these two paragraphs are gathered from and highlighted
in: U. S. News and World Report, *"U.S. Birth Rates Continue to Fall"*. *By Ernie
Mundell, HealthDay Reporter, Jan 10, 2023.* USNews.com

and the high cost of childrearing."[75] Almost half of these births are pre-marriage or no marriage births (around 48%), as the family in our society continues to evolve and transform. We are yet to understand the impact of these changes. A discussion for another day. What we do know is that fewer women are choosing to have children in our country, and those who do have children are having them later and having fewer children in terms of number. Whereas children used to be a commodity in pre-industrial times, children are now considered a financial burden and a career threat.

Political policies leading to population practices are no doubt influenced by the practical palpability of 21st century life. Simply stated, children are more likely to be seen as an inconvenience rather than commodity. We will say more about this later as we focus on only children, but for now let it suffice to say that our attitudes toward children in the 21st century say a great deal about the transformation taking place in the hearts of people at a deeply cultural level of existence.

---

[75] All the statistics in these two paragraphs are gathered from and highlighted in: U. S. News and World Report, *"U.S. Birth Rates Continue to Fall"*. By Ernie Mundell, HealthDay Reporter, Jan 10, 2023. USNews.com

"Elizabeth could not conceive" …

In 1st Century Palestine, there was a strong belief that to be without child was to be without God's blessing, some making the case that to be childless was to be under the punishment or "curse" of God. We see this theme in several Old Testament stories, such as, the stories of Sarai, Leah, Rachel, or Hanna (See Genesis 21 and 29, 1st Samuel 1 and 2). These women struggled for identity and purpose and longed for The Blessing of God. If you were a woman of childbearing age in that day, it was exclusively found through childbirth. Modern scientifically minded people now understand there are many reasons we are not able to have children – genetic deficiencies, environment, low sperm count, even stress. Seldom will we connect the inability to have children with the hammer of God upon a potential mother. In addition, we do not instantly connect childbirth with evidence of God's blessing or favor. We believe ourselves more sophisticated in this postmodern age.

My son is a miracle child. My wife had issues that made it medically unlikely to conceive. So, when Josh came into this world, we knew he may be our only one, and we felt quite blessed to have him. As parents we did our best to spoil him in the name of this "blessing," and I sometimes wonder if we did swing too much in that direction. However, three decades into this parenting thing we realize our mistakes are behind us and it is what it is.

I can only imagine what it must have been like to be *Elizabeth*. Not only was she pregnant at the age of a grandmother, but her husband was made aware that this child was to be the forerunner of the Messiah, his purpose having been announced before he was conceived. A miracle pregnancy which pointed to a unique child. Not only was Mary to bear a son at such an advanced age (likely in her 60's), but she was told of his future before he was born. She and *Zac* knew they were not raising him to run the family business, to marry and bring up grandchildren, or even to be the kind of son that would sit down for a normal meal during the holidays. Instead, they were given a son who would wander in the wilderness eating locusts and honey, preparing for a time when he would disappear from the scene to make way for the whole reason for his existence? Yes, John the Baptizer was a miracle conception, born despite his dad's lack of faith, and despite Mom's age. It was here Luke's Advent Story began.

The concept of having children has changed drastically over the past two thousand years. There was a time in western society when children were our greatest asset. They gave us status, a legacy, workers for our fields, new minds for business ventures, lots of grandchildren, and of course a sense of prestige within one's community. In other words, children were meant to serve parents' business ventures and reputation and were of immense value. However, in terms of legal rights, children were lowest on the totem pole of 1st century life. Unless they belonged to a royal family or stood out among their peers in some incredible way, children were simply tools in the hands of adults. Their value to the family was determined by service to the family, not the sheer fact they were children. However, in this account we are introduced to a child that violated the norm, broke the 1st century mold, and transformed his parents. John was special. Not only was he an only child (I fathered one and married one. The stories I can tell….), but he was a miraculous child, an unexpected gift, and a child with a unique calling all rolled into one.

In our world today, the Advent season is set up to honor children rather than "The Child." We buy them gifts without expecting them to return the favor. We honor them in churches, schools, and family gatherings. And we creatively gifted our children a Saint who exists just for their sake - Saint Nicholas. Christmas morning is completely dominated by the thought of Santa's visit the night before. We ask nothing of our children on this special day, for they remind us of the best things in life - joy, giving of ourselves, sacrifice, a child's smile, the love of family (and "getting stuff"). Somewhere along the way we have forgotten that the Advent Season began with the story of John, a gift for two aging parents who set the stage for God's Eternal Gift to the world.

People from my childhood remember a world where one or two gifts were the norm, where Christmas morning was more about the excitement of the day rather than the money we spent. I failed at teaching my son these truths, for during the time of his childhood Capitalism had a hold on me, and the Advent Season was more about profit margins than a story beginning with the miraculous birth of John. Could it be we have lost our way? Could it be we have adjusted our vision downward? Is it too late to "buy back the day"?

Each Advent season we are invited to adjust our vision upward, beginning with a miracle of God we learned to take for granted - our children. I am not here speaking of the happiness they bring to us, the stuff we buy for them, the survival of our family name, or the difficulty of parenting in a complex world. All of these have their place. But let our hearts be drawn to the miracle of new birth and the possibilities each child brings. Each is a miracle. Each birth is a symbol. Each baby a gift from God. Each one is brought into this world with purpose and value and a Plan to embrace. John stands as a symbol and calling for each of us - "Prepare the Way for His Coming!" Declare to the world that God is ready to do a new thing in a new way for a renewed people. Luke's renewal story began with the miraculous birth of John the Baptizer, *God's Gracious Gift.*

"I stopped believing in Santa Claus when I was six.
Mother took me to see him in a department store and
he asked for my autograph." (Shirley Temple)

Interlude

There is a time for silence......

"Women like silent men. They think we
are listening." (Calvin Coolidge)

"If we chose not to say anything unless we knew
what we were talking about, a ghastly hush would
descend upon the earth" (Alan Herbert)

"It's better to keep one's mouth shut and to be thought a fool
than to open it and resolve the issue" (Abraham Lincoln)

LESSONS IN LIFE ARE SOMETIMES EXCEEDINGLY DIFFICULT TO carry. If left up to me and you, our learning would be cut short most times. Nine months of silence seems a bit overdone. Let us be real, which one of us would readily embrace that our "senior citizen wife" is to be with child? Who among us would not have some doubt, require some evidence, or balk just a bit at such news? The result of such unbelief in the face of God's miracle gift? - Silence. From the time we wake until our heads hit the pillow our lives are full of noise: TV on; Social Media shorts; Music blaring as we lie or as we walk; Bluetooth in our automobiles, Restaurants full of laughter, Baby monitors, Protests everywhere protests; Sold out events; Construction crews; Notifications on your phone, On and on we can go. Our world is a noisy place, especially in the USA.

"Quiet times" have now become synonymous with "devotions" in the contemporary church, symbolizing for us that time alone with God may be the Church's last hope for some restorative silence.

The quietest place in my life is inside my car. Tranquility. Peace. Silence. A time when God is allowed to speak above the noise of the day. This is a place and time when silence becomes a haven for me, as I can think through my day in a way that is always beneficial. How about you? *Zac* the priest is set aside for a much-needed time of silence, and painful as it would have been, he came out the other side a changed man and a prepared father for a unique son that would speak a Word into the silence of Israel. For 400 Years Israel was left without a prophetic voice. This silence within a nation is symbolized by silence within a priest (Zac), which led to a Vibrant Voice in the Wilderness. Silence used to announce the Loudest Event in Human History - The coming of Messiah.

From the Author's Journal: *There are times when silence can be excruciatingly painful. Yell at me and I know at least I evoke passion from you. Show me your anger and we can deal with the reality of something wrong between us. Tell me what you understand, and I can see if you really do understand. But ignore me, avoid me, speak not a word to me, and I feel as though I do not exist for you. There was one time in my growing up years that my dad would not speak to me, and I would not speak to him. For over a year! He needed to say, "I am sorry," or he needed to scream his displeasure with me. He did neither. He simply did not speak. We did not speak. I answered his silence with silence of my own. That was the most painful time of my life growing up, and it took us years to recover. From the Author's Journal:*

The Awesome Voice of Nothing Said

The Awesome Voice of nothing said
Empty sounds of no reply
As silence loudly rips my heart
With the cutting edge of an angry eye

Always answers hide from light,
When shadows creep within
As voices I have never known
Slowly, silently, guide my sin.

Words from pain-filled valleys
They hide beyond my view.
Speaking only to themselves
In tongues unknown to me and you

They feed on fear within us
These voices yet unknown
Deafening silence grows without
Empty enemies call hearts their home

Known only in a day removed
We live this silent death
As the Awesome Voice of Nothing Said
Lies unspoken under lonely breath

Oh, that I might know you
With words so real, yet free
But silence seems to drown our voice
Til time does claim our right to speak
(Written by Rick A. Farmer)

Silence can be so Deafening!!! In Christ, our words are redeemed, and silence is overcome with the sounds of grace and mercy. Lessons learned. Words renewed. And lives changed. Truly a gift, this power of speech we have been given. Ironic that the dad of the one who was born to pave the way for Christ learned the importance of faith's voice by having his own voice removed. A Muted father gives way to a "Voice in the Wilderness" - A Lighthouse for a world in need.

"Were I Roman Catholic, perhaps I should on this occasion vow to build a chapel to some saint, but as I am not, if I were to vow at all, it should be to build a lighthouse."[76] (Benjamin Franklin)

---

[76] Letter to his wife, 17 July 1757, Benjamin Franklin, Memoirs of the Life and Writings of Benjamin Franklin Volume 2

Day 8

Zacharias the silent priest.... Luke 1:5

Setting the Stage: The first Silent Night

THE NUMBER ONE CHRISTMAS HYMN OF ALL TIME IS *SILENT Night*. Legend has it that "it was 204 years ago when *Silent Night* was first heard by Austrian villagers attending Christmas Eve mass in St. Nicholas Church in Oberndorf. Joseph Mohr, the young priest who wrote the lyrics (1816), played the guitar, and sang along with Franz Xaver Gruber, the choir director who had written the melody." [77]

Mohr wrote the Lyrics not long after the Napoleonic wars had wreaked havoc on the citizens of Austria. The sounds of War stood in stark contrast to a *Silent Night*. A town at peace, finally. The sounds of war gone. For the people of Austria "peace" was a Silent Night experience powerfully heard by those who have been through the 'terrestrial thunderstorm' of War. Today, *Silent Night* has been translated into over 300 languages, and is sung on Christmas Eve by more people than any other song on the face of the earth.

As the most diversely recorded Christmas Hymn in history, all who celebrate Christmas in our churches sing this song on Christmas Eve. The frequency and diversity of languages used in

---

[77] *This Is the Most Popular Christmas Song Ever* by Chris Wilson. Published December 2, 2014. Time, time.org

the recordings of Silent Night was affirmed by a study done by Time Magazine: "Silent Night," which Mohr wrote the lyrics for (in German) in 1816 and Gruber put to music two years later, is the most recorded Christmas song in the modern era of the holiday's substantial oeuvre," recorded in over 300 languages.[78] With 733 copyrighted recordings since 1978, it is nearly twice as dominant as "Joy to the World," a distant second with 391 records to its name. Though the night was no doubt silent, as far as the world is concerned, it has been creating lots of noise ever since. This noise is precisely what Luke has written about, and the event is now marked with a song that has grown into a universal tune celebrated every year by millions of people all over the world.

The Silent Priest ……

There are times in my life I have experienced extreme silence. On a Solo Adventure deep in the Appalachians, one of the numerous times that my wife sent me to the doghouse, the week I had laryngitis, in a movie theatre, church when I was growing up, or the time I went for a late-night walk in my old run down heavily depressed neighborhood, among others. Silence is a commodity in our world. Even when we are home alone or in our cars we are used to sound – the radio, the television, our earbuds, and our phones. Whatever it takes to drown out the intense volume of unwanted silence.

Zacharias was a priest. It was his job to speak. He spoke to God on behalf of the people, to the people on behalf of God, and to his wife in response to a miracle. For nine months he would do none of these. Not one word was to come from his mouth, and he was to become an expert at charades. I would love to have been a fly on the wall as he tried to communicate with his sixty something

---

[78] *This Is the Most Popular Christmas Song Ever* by Chris Wilson. Published December 2, 2014. Time, time.org

wife about "the bun in the oven"; Or how God silenced him for his lack of faith; Or how the Angel had greater news as to the role their son John would play.

The silence of *Zacharias* was a metaphor for his time. For four-hundred years the voice of God had disappeared from the land. This resembled what we find in Revelation 8:1, as all heaven is silent for a half hour before something amazing and extremely major is about to take place on earth. Silence for John's father served as a type of trumpet call, to which even the sound of a trumpet would be inadequate for announcing what was to come. There was silence in this priest for nine months, the Trumpet call of God. In Scripture, silence is a sure sign that it is time to prepare ourselves for what is to follow. Silence is a call for internal reflection, other worldly preparations, as we try to place language next to an event that no language can describe. *Zac* was not yet prepared to speak to the miracle of John's birth, much less the miracle of Mary's Son, so God set him aside for a time of reflection as he contemplated the most important event in human history, which would become a part of his own life story.

The reason for this is quite interesting. *Zac* was silenced because he asked for some proof. Can you imagine his question being "the wrong question"? In this case we learn asking for proof is not an act of faith, although proof is never a terrible thing in and of itself. Some things can only be embraced by faith. Although science began its journey as an attempt to understand the order and wonder of God's Creation, it has now been set by many in opposition to faith as the dominant way our closed universe is to be understood. Faith has lost its place in the discussion, although science itself requires a good bit of "faith" at every turn (i.e.; It is assumed we will one day understand the gaps in the fossil record. Faith.). The Enlightenment Age opened the door for the necessity of science and reason to explain all things in such a way that faith became a *personal* rather than a *public* journey. In our culture, we seek proof. We seek reasonableness. However, "the west is coming to realize the fearful human cost of its science and technology and cannot assume that it will continue to enjoy forever the almost universal authority that is now accorded to them."[79]

We have entered a time of public silence known as "cancel culture," as science, technology and reason are no longer allowed to freely speak for the masses. Individuals are struggling to find a different truth, a new vision, a deeper understanding of reality. This is ripe soil for postmodern and post-truth thinking, where personal meaning and autonomous value positions are being explored in private and progressive ways. The pendulum is swinging back toward "faith," but without tradition and orthodoxy, we have no real foundation for Faith grounded in Truth. Silence can provide a solid foundation for evaluation, but only if we embrace the possibility that something beyond personal preference provides the answers we are searching for. *Zac* wanted personal proof for a public transcendent truth in need of a genuine faith commitment. Silence gave him the opportunity to find this faith.

When I was young, I would attempt to employ the silent treatment when I was "hurt in my heart." I had some strange notion that if I did not talk to someone, that person would get the core of the message I wanted him to receive through osmosis, that she would somehow understand exactly why I felt they had hurt me. My talents were lacking in this area, though my intent was clear. I would employ such a tactic to bring hurt or discomfort into the other person's life. Little did I realize that my silence was most often a gift, since I was the type that would attempt to argue that a black horse was a white horse if the mood for such a discussion hit me. My silence was often a gift to others, and torture for me. However, on most occasions silence created a void

---

[79] Leslie Newbegin, *The Open Secret: An Introduction to the Theology of Mission (Revised addition),1995.* Eerdmans Publishing Co., Grand Rapids, Michigan. Chapter 1.

in communication that was not easily bridged. There are people who will never tell us what is really bothering them, leaving us to guess, often wrongly!

Silence often means that a key piece of information is missing, which frequently leads to faulty conclusions and mistaken choices. In the past my wife often looked at me with non-verbal disgust simply because I was unable to finish her sentence or read her mind. We men are often not gifted in this way and will not understand what you want us to know unless you clearly tell us. I imagine there were some frustrating moments during the nine months when *Zacharias* could not speak, as silence became God's method of discipline for a man who ought to have known enough to trust in and proclaim a miracle of God for the people. His silence was involuntary. Ours is often a choice.

There is a drastic difference between voluntary silence for good reasons and forced silence by those who have the power to impose it. Advent makes one thing quite clear – Christianity cannot be practiced without both silence and proclamation. The Advent Gospel only becomes Reality when it is practiced both publicly and persuasively. And it cannot be a meaningful public proclamation unless it is also practiced privately and personally. In this day of cancel culture, we are witnessing a postmodern push to highlight personal preference and celebrate personal opinion, unless, it seems, the preferences are for those things considered Christian. This past Christmas we saw public displays of satanic altars protected, while Nativity Scenes were outlawed in public spaces.[80]

---

[80] "Kim Reynolds calls Iowa Capital satanic display 'objectionable'", written by Stephe Gruber-Miller, December 12, 2023. Des Moines Register, https://www.desmoinesregister.com/story/news/politics/2023/12/12/governor-kim-reynolds-criticizes-satanic-altar-at-iowa-capitol-asks-for-prayer/71891969007/
And "What the Supreme Court says about Outdoor Nativity Scenes", By Outdoor Nativity Store, July 30, 2016. https://outdoornativitystore.com/blog/outdoor-nativity-scenes-and-supreme-court/

This issue sparks a national debate which highlights the importance of worldview in the public arenas of our society. Lesslie Newbigin predicted such an ongoing debate. "Both Capitalism and Socialism draw strength from a vision of human life, and this vision sustains them in the face of their failures. For capitalism it is the face of freedom – the freedom of the individual person to develop his own powers, to achieve the greatest success (she) is capable of and to enjoy the fruit of this achievement. For socialism it is the vision of equality; at its best this has been a vision of brotherhood, of community, but in practice it has often been reduced to the visions of mere equality of rights for each person seen as an autonomous individual. In the one case, freedom is pursued at the cost of equality; in the other, equality is pursued at the cost of freedom."[81] Both are missing reality with their extremism, for both have either redefined or failed to establish Truth when it comes to human purpose. Human purpose is highlighted within Advent.

You see, Zacharias was silenced for lack of faith, just as we attempt to silence individuals for lack of our version of faith. We do this from "the right" and from "the left." What Advent makes clear is that the fundamental Truth by which humanity is defined is relatedness. Humanity - "male and female – is made for God in such a way that being in the image of God involves being bound together in the most profound of all mutual relations" (See footnote below). Advent is God restoring relatedness, both between God and human being and human being and human being. Silence is the natural consequence of the loss of Faith, and *Zac* experiences this for all of us. A Nativity Scene is the proclamation which was historically on our lips and in our hearts. The Proclamation? That God came to us as a babe in a cave to restore the very thing humanity needs most and is born to discover – Immanent relationship with the Divine and the Image of the Divine. "The Lord God said, It isn't good for the man to live alone. I will make a suitable partner

---

[81] Lesslie Newbigin, "Foolishness to the Greeks", page 118.

for him"(Genesis 2:18, Contemporary English Verion). God gave the human couple everything they needed for sustenance, joy, vocation, and family, but the highlight of everything God created was relationship. "Neither *freedom* nor *equality* are the words that can take us to the heart of the matter. The breakdown of relationship will destroy freedom and will destroy equality, but neither of these will be achieved by being sought for itself."[82]

I suggest Advent is not simply a "Silent Night," for it is above all a time of "Joy to the World." Those of us who have endured the "Silent Night" understand the life-giving reality of human relationships. Advent highlights God's desire to restore relationship, and this cannot be made known by a strategy of silence alone, even in this cancel culture we occupy. Do not forget the power of the words we speak and the stories we tell. Take time to prepare, but then speak. Speak to that one who has hurt you, offering forgiveness instead of condemnation. Write to that one you have not heard from in years, celebrating the wisdom and compassion such a person once brought to your life. Tell your spouse how much you love her. Show your children how important they are to you. Invest in time with your grandchildren, knowing that any given day could be your last with them. Give to the needy. Speak to the fallen. Speak and Live Advent a new way each day. Many in our society are working diligently to silence the voice of Jesus around us. This is the power of Advent for our time. If we will not speak, if we do not speak and live a Word of Hope and Compassion to the people before us, it will not be long until involuntary silence will be the result of our lack of courage for all of us. May we not remain another "silent priest" in the land, but instead become *priests with a proclamation – God with Us, Immanuel!*

---

[82] Lesslie Newbigin, "Foolishness to the Greeks," page 119.

"If you don't have anything good to say,
then don't say anything at all."

(Every mother who ever lived, in multiple languages)

"There are many ways to speak forth The
Message, with or without words."
(Rick Farmer)

A Word for the Wise: *"In our country we are encouraged to speak
our truth. We do with little constraint, as long as this truth is "my
truth." However, we are seldom encouraged to remain silent long
enough to open ourselves to challenge when an even greater Truth
begs our attention. Those who can remain silent long enough to hear
the voice of God are those who will always have better things to say
in the end. And once we have been given that thing that needs to be
said, it is impossible to remain silent for long."*
(From the Journal of Rick Farmer)

(LAUGH WITH ME...)

Short one: An oxymoron walked into a
bar.......... The silence was deafening.

Longer one: Mildred was the church gossip and self-appointed
monitor of the church's morals. She kept sticking her nose
into other people's business, even if several members did
not approve of her extra-curricular activities. However,
they feared her enough to maintain their silence. Once, she
accused a new member, Frank, of being an alcoholic after she
saw his old pickup parked in front of the town's only bar one
afternoon. She emphatically told Frank (and several others)
that everyone seeing it there would know what he was doing!

Frank was a man of few words. He stared at her for a moment and just turned and walked away. He did not explain, defend, or deny. He said nothing and just went away. Later that evening, Frank quietly parked his old pickup in front of Mildred's house, got out, and walked home... And left his old pickup there all night long.......

Day 9

Zachariah and Elizabeth both came
from the line of Aaron... Luke 1:5

Setting the Stage: Born to be a Priest

DID YOU KNOW THAT EVERY DESCENDANT OF AARON WAS
automatically a priest? This meant two things, at least. First,
Vocation was a family affair. The sons did what their fathers had
done, and the women from Aaron's line were often wives of priests.
Secondly, there ended up being far too many priests. Originally
meant to serve twelve tribes, they were now serving two tribes -
Judah and Benjamin (And Levi, which did not have land to possess.
This was Aaron's line).[83] The other ten tribes were considered lost
tribes during the time of Jesus and had been non-identifiable since
the Babylonian invasion.

Only during incredibly special occasions were all the priests
serving together. For example, during Pentecost they were needed,

---

[83] Aaron (flourished 14th century BCE) the traditional founder and head of the
Israelite Priesthood, who, with his brother Moses, led the Israelites out of Egypt.
Aaron is a central figure in the traditions about the Exodus, though his role varies
in importance. At the beginning he seems to be coequal with Moses, but after
the march out of Egypt he is only a shadow at Moses' side. Moses is obviously the
leading figure in the tradition, but it is also clear that he is pictured as delegating
his authority in all priestly and cultic matters to Aaron and "his sons." (See
"Aaron, biblical figure", Arvid S. Kapelrud, History and Society, December 20,
2023. Britannica, britannica.com)

during the Feast of Tabernacles, and most certainly during Passover. On this occasion, *Zac* was to light incense at the Altar inside the Holiest Place before the daily animal sacrifice was to be offered. He would oversee this matter during his week of service. There would be a rope tied around his waist just in case God was not pleased with the offering, and in he would go. In total, *Zac* would serve for one week twice a year. The incense was needed to prepare for the morning and evening sacrifices, given daily. This incense was an aesthetic part of the daily offerings, as the sweet aroma would make them a more pleasing sacrifice as the fragrance from the altar rose toward God. Simple math would suggest that not all priests had the privilege *Zac* enjoyed during this week in their entire lifetime.

Altogether, it has been estimated there were as many as twenty thousand priests, and having a wife who also came from the line of Aaron would have been a high-status union in the community. Maybe this is the reason *Zac* enjoyed this privilege. Qualifying would be a bit like being in a lottery to have opportunity to spend a week looking for a shooting star. Maybe it happens; likely it never does. This was a blessed honor for *Zacheriah*.

"Both of them were righteous in the sight of God" .... Luke 1:6

Can you imagine being referred to as "righteous in the sight of God"? Luke made a special effort to include this, since Jewish women who were not blessed with child were viewed as under the judgement and condemnation of God. We have similar practices today. I have often heard preachers or church leaders pronounce God's condemnation upon specific sins. There are the normal church people condemnations, such as divorce or sexual orientation or not taking Communion. But there are more, and the list can seem endless. In my lifetime, I have heard people condemned to hell for a myriad of sins – gambling, drinking alcohol, skipping church, failing to confess, playing cards, long hair for the man and short hair for the woman, working on Sunday, reading something other than the King James Bible, watching an R rated movie, cohabitation; on and on this list could go.

To be honest, if God uses such a list to determine righteousness, no one is going to survive God's judgment, which is precisely why it makes little sense to develop such a list. Luke did not. He simply stated, they were "approved in the sight of the Lord, walking blamelessly" (Luke 1:6 from the Amplified Bible Version). Luke focused on the walk, not the rules. *Zac* and *Elizabeth* lived a life of faith. They set a standard to live by, and they strove each day to live by this standard. Such a life is not about "not doing this" or "avoiding that." We cannot live in this world without interacting with this world. Nor would we want to, for "the earth is Lord's and everything in it, the world and all who live in it." (Psalm 24:1) Rather, let us live a life focused on a specific way of "doing," a specific way of "being," a lifestyle, where one's choices are steady, consistent, and flowing from faith. This, I believe, was *Zac* and *Elizabeth* in the context of Luke's Gospel.

Commandments by nature are about opportunities to do, to be, to act. We all live by them. You may not be aware of the commandments you live by, but we all have them. I have them. For my wife: "Treat me with respect." For my son: "Honor your father." For my students: "Pay attention in class if you want to pass." For my Zoe: "Walk with me so I don't have to chase you." For me: "Stop being such an idiot." Most often, they involve taking care of ourselves, meeting our own needs, or protecting our own reputation.

Church people are not immune from these motives and may be even more prone to having them. We all need a scale from which to evaluate ourselves and others. Even God is accountable to our standard of judgement. How many times have I heard people proudly proclaim exactly how they would run the universe if they were a Divine Being in charge? More than I can count. Can you imagine the audacity we must possess to suggest to God how God might better do God's job. But we do. We are lost without our "good person scales."

Jesus once summarized the entirety of the Law as this: "Love the Lord your God with all your heart and with all your soul and with all your mind. This is the first and greatest commandment. And the second is like it: 'Love your neighbor as yourself.' All the Law and the Prophets hang on these two commandments" (Mat 22:37). It is important to note that Jesus was speaking these words to those who believed themselves most righteous, the religious leaders of His day, the "I'm a good person how about you crew."

One illustration from my past might help us understand the difference between "The List" as opposed to "The Lifestyle." As a pastor, I was once a part of an Opiate Recovery Group Outreach. I lived in a State of tremendous need in this area, so it seemed a thing God would have us do as a church community. We were at a downtown church in the middle of downtown in a small city ravaged by rampant unemployment, the highest divorce rate in the country, and lying smack in the middle of a drug trafficking route on the way to Columbus. Yet, we were a church full of suburban attendees ministering to suburban people. It made sense for us to begin this outreach, given our location. Often, however, the church is oblivious to the people right outside our door, so, we invited them in, in the form of a recovery group focusing on sobriety, reuniting families, teaching Scripture, and Life Learning Lessons. Our purpose was *Offering the Gospel in Real Life and in Real Time.*

Soon this group grew out of the office space we were using, and we began to use larger church facilities. With more need comes more responsibility, so we found ourselves "baby sitting" around thirty children every Tuesday night as their parents attended a recovery meeting made up of drug testing, Bible studies, and small group mentoring meetings. Our normal children's night was on Wednesday, where many volunteers served in the teaching and training of children in the Christian Faith. It was a well-run program. However, we did not have the resources or the volunteers to duplicate this on Tuesday night for the children from Recovery Group parents, so we gave them pizza and played games with them.

One night, someone had a brilliant idea! Why not mix the Tuesday night kids with the Wednesday night kids and teach all of them together? In other words, why not be the church for both groups of children? There was a problem. We knew we would not get these recovering parents and their children back with us for two nights, so we decided to change all children's programs to Tuesday night. With this choice came the second problem. Many Wednesday night parents did not want their children on campus during the Tuesday Night Recovery Group time. Some of them surprisingly stated this aloud.

Yes, we were a church full of "church people." They did not believe their children would be safe, would get the training they deserved. One quote from one of these parents stood out to me - "those parents are not giving financially toward this program and therefore should not be rewarded with this change of programming." Two things became obvious with these words. Recovering Addicts were for many "those parents," not "our parents." And there was an obvious link, for many, between financial contribution and status in our church. The one speaking this line may not have known this is what he believed, but his words gave it away. Several of our most prominent families left the congregation because of this issue. Meanwhile, all these children were exposed to the Gospel, most for the very first time. In addition, more than a hundred of the parents were baptized into the Christian Faith. Advent won the day!

You can already see the difference, right? Some churchgoers use "The List." There are things we are simply not supposed to do, people we are not supposed to be around, places we are not supposed to be seen, sins we cannot tolerate. We do this in the name of things like, "coming out from among them" or "remaining above reproach," making theological cases for dismissing people who are not like we are. On the other hand, many people of faith are simply trying to show love for people in need, whatever it takes to do so. They are prepared to burn incense at the Altar of Faith, as they offer their lives in loving service to God and others. There are those who work for God's approval and know precisely how to get it, for themselves and for others. And there are those who are simply living in The Faith, doing the good, sharing the love, doing so many "do's" they have little time to contemplate the "don'ts." I have a suspicion this will need to become the Church moving forward, if we are to regain the trust of those on the outside looking in.

Elizabeth and *Zachariah* were labeled by Luke as "righteous." In their time this would have meant a heart-felt commitment to the tenets of their Faith, a continuing trust in God despite the fact they were not blessed of God with a child. It did not mean they did not make mistakes, as we clearly see in the case of *Zac*. It meant the mistakes did not rule their understanding of faith; it meant that faith is an ongoing struggle through life that often encounters speed bumps of our own making, it meant an openness to new things from God that had never occurred in their lifetimes, it meant embracing a new day for the people of God even if this meant a miracle was needed to see that day. These possibilities are most certainly true in the day in which we live. Let us open our eyes and behold the miracle occurring all around us. Let us take our eyes off "The List" and look for "The Life." We might end up amazed as to what we find.

(LAUGH WITH ME...)

"Adults are always asking little kids what they want to do when they grow up cause we are looking for ideas." (Paula Poundstone)

"Any kid will run an errand for you if you ask
them to do it around bedtime." (Red Skelton)

Day 10

Elizabeth the joyful mother... Luke 1:13,14

Setting the Stage: Children change our world

QUESTION: *DOES HAVING CHILDREN MAKE US HAPPIER THAN IF WE would be without them?* According to recent studies, parents from Norway and Hungary are happier than childless couples—but parents from Australia and Great Britain are less happy than their childless peers. The country with the most significant decrease in happiness after having children is the United States. Although many studies suggest that having children usually leads to less happiness, this varies according to numbers of children, sex, location, and age. For instance, single moms in almost any nation are less happy after they have children. One study found that men aged 26-62 get a happiness boost after having children, while young parents and single parents slide toward greater unhappiness if they have "children" (more than one child). "Children make some happy and others miserable; the rest fall somewhere in between—it depends, among other factors, on how old you are, whether you are a mother or a father, and where you live. But a deep puzzle remains: Many people would have had happier lives and marriages had they chosen not to have kids—yet they still describe parenthood as the 'best thing they've ever done.'"[84]

---

[84] Taken from an *article adapted from Paul Bloom's new book,* The Sweet Spot: The Pleasures of Suffering and the Search for Meaning. *The Atlantic, "What*

The Bottom Line: Context and Expectation helps create emotional response. I am reminded of my grandfather's words, which he spoke quite often - "happiness is overrated." When it comes to having children, this is a good philosophy. "Some things are just more important than happiness" (My Grandpa).

Zac and *Elizabeth* had an only child. My son is an only child, whose mother is an only child. Only children are a growing majority, and we are within a couple of decades of this being our norm for children. I will have more to say about this trend, but for now ask yourself, "Why are modern Americans trending toward single child families? What does this reveal about us?"

"The Joyful Mother" ....

Elizabeth is one of my heroes. I see her as elderly, empathetic, a silent sufferer who had been denied the joy of a child that she might celebrate family in a society that truly values children and family. She reminds me of a lady in one church who was always there to serve when serving involved children, even though she never had the opportunity to raise a child of her own. She became the mother of all. She served as the grandma for the least, a mother for the isolated, a comforting arm for those who had suffered loss. Her life was a daily experience of suffering, which she had learned to turn into joy. Every December we would share an evening of celebration and communion together in her home with about fifty college students. She would always recite a poem called Keeping Christmas and knew every Christmas Hymn by heart. It became one of our most important traditions during the years I lived in that town. She had more children than she could count, though never having given birth. (The Poem you will read later in this

---

Becoming a Parent Really Does to Your Happiness", by Paul Bloom (Nov. 2, 2021). TheAtlantic.com.

manuscript is in celebration of this mom, but for now, take a moment to read *"Keeping Christmas,"* her favorite.)[85]

To be without child in *Elizabeth's* day was not only thought to be a sign of displeasure from God but was often viewed as a true reflection of the quality of faith in the heart of the barren mother. Giving birth was salvation for the Jewish mother. The Old Testament is full of the pain filled days of mothers who had no children – *Hanna, Rachel, Tamar, Sarai.*[86] All these mothers pleaded for the gift of a child. All these mothers suffered through the condemnation of others during their infertile days. And all these mothers were trained through their suffering, for their children were to be granted in miraculous ways. Often it is the individual who is forced to go without who truly knows how to appreciate a gift when it finally happens.

Advent is for most of us a time of celebration with family. It is a time when the child in us connects with the child in others, as we are lifted to a place and a time of meaningful nostalgia. I find it so interesting that the first Advent was just such a time for two women of faith. *Elizabeth and Mary would share a connection that would forever be proclaimed in the Advent Story.* Two boys. Cousins. One born to a woman in her 60's, who had spent her entire adult life longing for the day when she might experience the miracle of a son in her womb. The other born to a teenage peasant girl, who had her entire life ahead of her, who had not yet had time to formulate her dreams, as her plans were derailed in favor of a virgin born son that would now define her every thought and choice for the rest of her life. We are left to wonder why Luke included the interaction of these two women for us to read. Could it be that Luke understood the importance of family

---

[85] Henry Van Dyke, *Keeping Christmas. Six Days of the Week, NY: Charles Scribner's Sons, 1924 and 1952.* https://www.appleseeds.org/xmaskeep.htm
[86] You can read the account of these women in 1 Samuel 1, Genesis 29, Genesis 38, Genesis 16 respectively.

and community when we feel alone and abandoned? Could it be that Luke understood the tendency of human beings to migrate toward those who might understand our plight, when our plight is indeed difficult to understand or explain?

Notice what *Elizabeth* did not do. She did not question *Mary's* news, or speak of infidelity, or question *Mary's* sanity, or try to get behind her story. She simply embraced the miracle and celebrated their bond.

I find myself drawn to their conversation, as two miracles encounter one another, rejoice in the Power of Almighty God, and hold each other tightly as if they began to understand their lives and this world would never be the same. *Elizabeth* seemed unsurprised, just honored by her visit. I imagine that being pregnant at such an age would have made the miraculous commonplace for her. She needed no Angel to convince her, for she felt the stirring of a son in her womb. As her eyes locked onto *Mary's* gaze, this hero of faith became the first to testify to the birth of the *Messiah*. *Elizabeth*, my hero, grandmother to all, mother of John and the first Advent Evangelist - "*Messiah* is coming!" *Mary* needed her embrace. As do we, as we bring a daily testimony to The Miracle of Advent in a time full of indifference and hostility toward the story we must share with the unwed mothers and lonely grandmothers in our midst

The Mother

Pain gives birth to love
For one who loves a child
For in her heart the endless tear
At once reborn life-giving smile

Hearts resurrected through her pain
As children reap new life
Flowing from the hands of one
Gifting hope amid the strife

Tis Jesus who has taught her
His suffering set her free
Becoming a mother of soul embrace
Though her body would not let it be.

Life may hold us back at times
Can seem an endless day
But when a child smiles back at you
Yesterday's pain is wiped away

So, love the child living in your eyes
And know, it's life you bring
Pain is turned to brightest day
As we teach another child to sing.
(Rick A. Farmer)

"Christmas is a baby shower that went totally
overboard." (Andy Borowitz.)

Day 11

Elizabeth the joyful mother, part 2... "then her neighbors and relatives heard that the Lord had shown her His great mercy, and they shared her joy." .... Luke 1:58

Setting the Stage: For Mothers and Fathers of Only Children

MENTAL HEALTH PROFESSIONALS HAVE CONFLICTING IDEAS about how an only child operates within family dynamics. "They often have problems when it comes to delayed gratification, overly seeking attention, difficulty separating from parental influence, immaturity, independence, giving and receiving, [and] sharing," (John Mayer, Ph D, April 12, 2019, written in an email to a colleague). "Being an only child is a disease in itself" (G. Stanley Hall, first president of the APA (American Psychological Association), 1907). However, these are but one side of the story.

"Only children are considered to be more self-reliant and independent," says Dana Dorfman, Ph.D., psychotherapist and co-host of the podcast "2 Moms on the Couch." "Though they may have had parents readily available to them or not distracted by the needs of other children, only children are typically self-sufficient, learning to function on their own without the assistance of others."[87]

---

[87] For a thorough and very readable discussion of the psychological well-being of Only Children you might consult: "The Truth about Only Children: More evidence that birth order is not destiny", Susan Krauss Whitbourne, April 9, 2022. Psychology Today, PsychologyToday.com

Only children are excellent candidates for growing up to be ultra perfectionists."[88]

I have mixed feelings about the challenges and joys of an only child. I married an only child, and my son is an only child. They educated me in terms of how to be heard, how to get what you want, and how to find a way to enter any conversation no matter the content. We consistently interrupt one another. It is a family art-form to choose the best time to dismiss the other for the sake of what "I" want to talk about. Only children carry this gift. As two Only Children were taking over my home, I began to learn they were also taking over the world.

Current statistics reveal a rise in the only child phenomenon. Presently, 26.3% of parents in the U S A have one child. This percentage is on the rise. It is estimated that the number of only child families will double by 2050. If this holds true, only child families will be the most common scenario by 2050. 47% of women who had their first child between 1995-1997 had one child. The 90's are known for many things (great music, Bill Clinton, cell phone takeover, the birth of my son, and much more), but the turning of the American Family toward having only one child was a happening that ran under the radar during this decade.

Around this time, China was creating a massive society of only children, as more than one third (around 40%) of all Chinese people aged 25-29 had no siblings. Considering the huge population of China, this means a significantly substantial portion of the world population are only children. Germany is tops in Europe, as 24% of families are only child families. Almost half of all children in Canada are only children. Bangladesh stands at around 71% one child families. Half of all single parent homes in Japan are one child families. Exceedingly rare is the Italian tendency, as only

[88] Dr. Kevin Leman, *The New Birth Order Book: Why You Are the Way You Are,* 1998. Fleming H. Revell, A Division of Baker Book House Co., Grand Rapids, MI.. Chapter 7.

13.7% of families in Italy are single child families.[89] This trend toward single families is worldwide. The question: *How long before entire cultures are catering to the needs of only children?*

I asked before if you had any ideas why this trend of one child families is growing in our society, and as it turns out, in much of the world. In my view, a major reason is the postmodern emphasis on happiness and contentment. Lifestyle, career, hobbies, and interests seem to have grown in importance for so many of us over the last 50 years, especially with Millennials and Gen Z. However, they inherited this trend from parents who were growing increasingly dissatisfied with life as we know it. Millennial and Gen Z people simply have the courage to make life choices reflecting this truth.

In Europe, each child a woman has means an average drop of 3.6 % in salary expectation. In the USA, the drop is 13% per child, and women see a 17.5% decrease in income at three children.[90] Each child costs a parent, on average, $194,607 in the UK and even more in the USA. This is a primary reason Millennials began to question the strategy of having more than one child, this, and the overwhelming emphasis on climate change. In other words, "the happiness factor" is now in play when it comes to having children. Research reveals that one child bumps happiness, at least for fathers, but with two or more, life happiness and satisfaction take a hit with each subsequent child, especially for mothers.

The rise of only child families is also likely connected to the growing empowerment of the female voice in our society. One study covering an analysis of eighty-six countries clearly shows that "happiness decreases with the number of children parents

---

[89] "*The Most Surprising Only Child Statistics and Trends in 2023*", Author: Gitnux (August 2, 2023). Market Data, Parenting Statistics. blog.gitnux.com

[90] "*The rise of 'one-and-done' parenting*" *(January 11, 2023),* Amanda Ruggeri. B B C. bbc.com/worklife

have,"[91] and mothers benefit most from this growing phenomenon in terms of happiness and career satisfaction.

The crux of the matter is this: If contentment and happiness become our goal for life, birth rates will drop, abortion rates will rise, and children will grow up increasingly isolated and depressed. A deeper question for us might be: "Did the Founders have it right when they emphasized the "pursuit of happiness," rather than guaranteeing happiness to the citizenry? What happens when we make happiness our chief goal, at the expense of purpose, meaning, and our contribution to humanity? As the "one-and-done" phenomenon takes over, will it cause us to quit asking these questions? Will we simply settle into a worldview which counts financial security, a comfortable life, contentment, and happiness as the reasons we exist? Advent calls us toward more, demonstrates what more looks like, and celebrates the cosmic consequences of a life that searches for more. Something for all of us to think about.

**"The Lord had shown her His great mercy,
and they shared her joy." ... Luke 1:58**

The day my son was born is one of the most powerful memories of my life. It was a long-drawn-out affair. Thirty-Six hours of labor that my wife still cannot speak of without pain. Almost four hours of pushing him into this world. He was as stubborn then as he is now. He simply did not want to leave that safe, warm, eight-and-a-half-month home he had grown accustomed to. Am I really surprised that he lived with Mom and Dad at age 23? The infant Josh would not let go of his mother. Through the screams of Mom's labor and the panic in the room on the face of every nurse involved, which grew from two to six nurses, Dad was experiencing a form of anxiety unknown to medical journals. I had prepared myself to

---

[91] All the statistics in these two paragraphs are gathered from and highlighted in: U. S. News and World Report, *"U.S. Birth Rates Continue to Fall". By Ernie Mundell, HealthDay Reporter, Jan 10, 2023.* USNews.com

see that which I had never seen, but the images I had in my mind were nothing like what was taking place. At one point I witnessed Josh's mom sleeping between attempts to push, and I found myself wondering if son and mom would survive the ordeal at all. Helpless in the moment, I laid my hand on my face and began to pray. One of the nurses interpreted this as a sign of desperation and a prelude toward fainting, so she ushered me into a chair while supplying me with a glass of orange juice. I am not sure what the orange juice was supposed to accomplish, but I was not the one trained for such a moment, so I did as I was told.

It seemed my son would never arrive. It seemed like a lifetime was built into that single day as I waited for him. So many emotions filled the room. Anxiety on the part of those trying to deliver him. Contemplation on face of the Doc as he planned what to do next. Pain and exhaustion on my wife's face. And sheer helpless fear seized my entire being. I remember bargaining with God. "Please just let her live. I cannot raise a son on my own. If it must be one of them, please do not take her." I sensed this delivery was not normal, and later found out it was far from normal, as far as births go. Knowing what I now know about my son, abnormal is "normal."

When he finally let out that newborn cry, I was battling fear, anger, and helplessness, all rolled into one man's heart. Josh's mother was too exhausted to rejoice. The doctor and nurses just seemed relieved. At that moment it was all on me. Someone needed to celebrate. As I picked up my son for the first time, as I looked down toward that tiny little face with that tiny little nose and those tiny little hands grasping for a warm home that had just been taken from him, every emotion I had ever felt while anticipating his arrival had disappeared and all I could feel was elation and joy. Any doubt I ever had about the power of our God, the miracle of Life, or the Truth of the awesome Glory of our Creator, was forever dismissed. In my arms lay the beginning and the end of faith, the gift of life through the door of suffering. I had a Metaphysical Experience.

Elizabeth's joy in giving birth to John must have been the most incredible day of her life. She had already given up on such a day ever happening for her. She had embraced her life as a barren woman. She had already accepted her fate. She could not number the months and months of prayer she had offered up as she longed for a child of her own. God had said "no" repeatedly. Her lot in life was to be something other than a mother. Now? Praise be to God for making the impossible possible! Joy for her, Joy for *Zac*, and joy for the entire community of faith. The emptiness of longing was replaced with the celebration of a son! God began a process of redemption which could not be undone or thwarted, and Elizabeth was forever to be part of the Advent Story. A son. A gift. An unlikely mother. Every emotion she had ever felt, every doubt she had ever had, every tear she had ever shed, erased in one moment of euphoria as she held her son in her arms that very first time. *Zac* and *Elizabeth* had a Metaphysical Experience which still speaks to us today, and Luke wrote it down for us to hear.

If I am correct in my assessment, the future of this world is intimately linked to family connection and family thriving. When I was young, I envied the connection I witnessed in so many of the black families I grew up with. I saw family at the core of their lives, where despite having considerable amounts of discrimination and poverty thrown in their direction, I witnessed a love and connection within the black family that explained to me how they survived centuries of slavery and inequality. It was family. However, after the Civil Rights movement of the 60's, that which had sustained them began to undergo a transformation, and not for the better. An age of mass incarceration, the impact of the welfare state, and single parent homes began to wreak havoc in the black community. Whereas family and faith had been the constants which had carried African Americans through horrific times, both entities began a massive decline.[92] There are many explanations offered on this side of the transformation, but we are left with a common denominator which history affirms repeatedly. Strong family leads to strong community. It is not coincidence that the Christian Faith is referred to as a "family," for Family is the entire purpose of God described with one word. "We are family." And without the relationship stability and value instruction we traditionally receive within family, our future as a nation is quite uncertain. We may believe the most important contemporary journey is an autonomous search for self-fulfillment and the individual quest for happiness, but history clearly teaches us otherwise. Advent is God's declaration of that which matters most throughout the entire human journey over time.

Simply stated, some things cannot be defined by Science, Philosophy, Religion, or Personal Experience. The power of family and human relationships is one of those things. Such entities transcend normal human experience and take on a Life and Meaning of their own. The birth of a child points us in the direction of Transcendence if we have eyes to see this. And Joy seems the only rational response for those who were there at the time of His Birth, and for those who travel back to His birth to find themselves today.

---

[92] For an excellent discussion of the attack upon the Black Family see: "The Breakdown of the Black Family,", Chris Bodenner, Oct. 11, 2015. The Atlantic, theatlantic.com. *Editor's Note: This article previously appeared in a different format as part of The Atlantic's Notes section, retired in 2021.*

(Pure Joy transforms the Day!!)

Joy comes to us at unexpected moments. However, there is one season which is the epitome of Joy, beginning with two mothers faithfully embracing an unparalleled miracle. This is the reason Advent lives forever, as we reflect on the enduring story of the eternal God who empowered two special women from the same family to forever change human history. This is the miracle of the season. This is the Joy of the moment. This is the beginning of the Story Luke was entrusted to proclaim.

"Three phrases that sum up Christmas are: Peace on Earth, Goodwill to Men, and Batteries not Included." (Unknown)

(LAUGH WITH ME...)
ONLY CHILDREN ARE THE BEST!

-I am the only child in my family. My mom
said she learns from her mistakes.

-I was raised as an only child, which really annoyed my sister.

-I sat my daughter down and told her she was my least favorite child......she laughed and said, "Of course I am, but I'm your only child!" With no hesitation Dad said, "No, you don't understand, I mean globally."

-If you are trying to decide if having kids is right for you, my son just said, "As an only child I get all your stuff when you die."

-Living with two only children taught me two valuable lessons: Never assume you get a vote on family matters, and Two against One is the way God intended the world to be so just go with it.

-One Christmas, to save money on Christmas for our only child, we hired Taylor Swift to perform a concert for our son. We saved $10,000.

-If I had a nickel for every time I gave in to my only child daughter, I would be able to fund space travel to the Moon and buy Happy Meals for everyone once we arrive there, if my daughter lets me of course.

-Two entities are most blessed when raising an only child. Parents, of course, being one of these myself. And the entire Capitalist Society in which we live.

- "Children are such a great comfort in our old age, and they no doubt help us to get there faster as well." (My Grandfather)

As for me (your author) - Living with two only children has taught me four things I would never have known otherwise: *1. I am always wrong. 2. She is always right. 3. The only time she is wrong is when my son overrules her and then he is right. 4. Rightness follows this order: Son, Wife, God, never me (The truth being, I work ridiculously hard to deny this chain of authority. As a misunderstood middle child, I simply never learn).*

"There are those who desire to turn Jesus into an "only child." My case: He is and he isn't. He certainly had the complexity that comes with having siblings. On a scale of one to ten, I am a "3" sibling. I do not have sibling talent. My sister got all of it in our family, and my brother and I were in the back of the genetic line. However, Jesus ended up being the big brother of the century. Just ask James. But Jesus is also an "Only Child." He is the "Only Begotten son of The Father." And this He did so that all siblings in all families can become a new sibling in a new family where we will never be rejected, ignored, or nullified. We will matter, from this day forward and forever more, as brothers and sisters to Jesus and each other. This is the very family Luke introduces for all to read. This is our "Metaphysical Family" which becomes "Existential Reality" by Faith. (From the Journal of Rick Farmer)

Day 12

His name is John…. Luke 1:63

Setting the Stage: I know a man named John…

"John" is a common biblical name, first appearing in its Hebrew form in the Old Testament. The New Testament, written in Greek, adapted the Hebrew name *Yohanan* as *Ioannes*, later *Johannes* in late Latin, which then became "John" in English. "John" was the number one name for boys in America from 1900 to 1923, dropping to number six by 1973. "John" dropped out of the top twenty for the first time in 2009, and now places number 27 (as of 2021). The meaning of the name in the first century captured the essence of John's Mission - "graced by God." There are two very prominent "Johns" in the Gospels: "John the Baptizer" that we read about here; "John the Apostle" who was commonly referred to as "the disciple whom Jesus loved" (See John 21:20), the apostle who ended up living the longest life of all of Jesus' original twelve.[93] (My Dad used to say that John the Baptizer was the first "Baptist," but I never believed him, seeing the Baptist tradition began after The Reformation.)

This John, son of *Zac* and *Elizabeth*, held a special place in Luke's storytelling. First, Luke used John's arrival in the Judaean countryside to date the Jesus Story. "In the fifteenth year of the

---

[93] Very Well Family: *"What Does the Name John Mean?"* Written by Wendy Eisner. (Updated March 8, 2023.) Fact checked by Daniella Amaro. VeryWellFamily.com

reign of *Tiberius Ceasar*, while *Pontius Pilate* was Governor of Judea, *Herod* was tetrarch of Galilee, his brother *Philip* tetrarch of the region of Iturea and Trachonitis, and *Lysanias* tetrarch of Abilene, during the high priesthood of *Annas* and *Caiaphas*, God's Word came to *John* the son of *Zechariah*" (Luke 3:1,2, The Holman Christian Standard Bible, by Holman Bible Publishers). These dates were confirmed by Josephus the first century Roman-Jewish historian. The fifteenth year of *Tiberius* would place this appearance of *John* sometime around 26-29 A. D.. *Caiaphas* was high priest from 18-36 AD. Luke knew about the fact that all through *Caiaphas'* term as high priest his father-in-law, and previous high priest, remained in a major position of power, so he includes him as co-priest. You can read about this relationship in John 18:12-14. The high priesthood was considered a lifelong appointment, even when a new active high priest was named. Luke was placing John inside a true narrative which he chooses to date for us. Luke revealed to his readers an accurate picture of John's arrival, which we would expect from someone taking great care in getting his facts correct.

Second, Luke was issuing a challenge for those who hear and read his Gospel. Luke was saying something like: "Check me out. You will find that the facts of my narrative cannot be disputed. I know who was in charge, I know who was there, I know who was part of the Story I tell. John was not a figment of my imagination but was an actual living person when people held these offices in Judea. He was known by all, and he was executed by one who had the authority to do so – Herod the tetrarch of Galilee." Other historians recognize these names and dates. Luke was placing John inside a true narrative which he chooses to date for us.

Third, Luke chose to highlight the sharp contrast between the rulers empowered by Rome and the lowly wanderer who paved the way for A New King in Israel. It was ironic that the pretend king, Herod Antipas (ruled 26-36 AD), was the one who executed

John, making way for the King who is King in Israel. "Luke ties his account of Jesus' life to major figures of that era (Luke 1:5; 2:1–2). Here, again, is a list of then-well-known names meant to establish a timeframe for these events. Most important of those is the Roman Emperor, Tiberius, whose reign began after that of Augustus (Luke 2:1). That establishes this moment somewhere around AD 29."[94] Luke wanted his listeners to understand the contrast in terms of the people God chose to change the world vs. those who seemed to be in power, and the power of God to rule over events no matter how powerful human rulers appear to be. John was a prime example of both.

"His Name is John" ....

"John the Baptizer" is one of those guys in the Advent story who kind of sneaks up on us. His place is pivotal, his story beyond interesting, and his personality is unique. It is amazing to think about the circumstances surrounding his birth. An Elderly Lady and a Faithless Priest give birth to a child who will pave the way

---

[94] Got Questions Ministries, Bible Ref - Luke 3:1,2, 2002-2024. "What does Luke 3:1 mean?", bibleref.com

for Messiah. However, of all the details pertaining to the birth and life of "John the Baptist," there is one detail that stands out to me as I read the story: "when Elizabeth heard Mary's greeting, the babe leapt in her womb...." (Luke 1:41). **Sa**

I am sure this is not the first time a baby "leapt" in a womb, or the first time we might observe the outside world affecting an unborn child. Science has shown that talking or reading to the unborn, or playing music for the unborn, all impact an unborn child. I loved reading to my son in the womb, but it just put my wife to sleep. These were not her favorite moments. Nonetheless, we are convinced the unborn are impacted by sound from the outside world. We need not dispute this. It was the timing of the leap which intrigues me when it comes to John.

It is safe to say this unborn child did not know Mary's voice. It would also be safe to say that something exciting was going on inside Elizabeth's womb when she laid eyes upon Mary. She knew in her spirit that Mary was highly favored, blessed of God. So, before she could utter a word, a mysterious connection between mother and unborn was unleashed. The baby, who was to become the forerunner of Messiah, rejoiced over this Messiah long before he could understand the source of his own joy. The one who would bear witness to "God's Gracious Gift" bore witness even before he understood the testimony he would bear. The *miracle* child *miraculously* celebrated the Source of all *miracles* before the *miracle* birth took place. In this instant we are blessed to peek inside the connection a mother had with her unborn child, the intimacy shared between God and two faithful women, and the purpose of God celebrated in the tiny heart of an unborn child who had been specially chosen and uniquely called before he was conceived.

I believe every child of God from every mother has such a unique calling. Every child, carefully orchestrated by a Loving Creator, has a purpose to discover, a purpose that will potentially bring joy unspeakable once it is embraced. Just as the Psalmist reminded us, "You knit me together in my mother's womb, I praise you because I am fearfully and wonderfully made...." (Psalm 139:13,14). We do our best as imperfect creatures to thwart this purpose, to undermine God's plan, and to devalue the sheer miracle of the "knitting together" of a new life. The Sanctity of human life is daily debated on the political stage like no other time in U. S. history. The problem is not the debate; the problem lies with the parameters of the discussion.

The purpose and value of the pre-born life are often not a part of the discussion. We treat them as if they are sub-human, as if society is not damaged if their existence is cut short for a myriad of reasons. Whatever the justification, they are not allowed to achieve their purpose for living, as if somehow, we are better off with the void created by their lack of contribution to life. If each life is of immense value, and each person has a purpose to discover and a contribution to make, then ending said life must become a last resort in my view. And this is for the benefit of all of us. Who are we to decide this potential person is not coming to help transform the world around us?

However, it must be said, to live in such a world, morality cannot be the sole argument we offer for life. We must do more. We must battle poverty, the environment which breeds more than half of all abortions. We just step forward as family and church to invest in single moms contemplating abortion, fund agencies responsible for adoption, work as entire communities to create a safer environment for children to be born and raised. Without these efforts and others, it is very unlikely we will ever begin to stem the tide of desperation that mothers contemplating abortion daily experience. This is not a simple issue, and therefore the answers are more complicated than we believe.

The motivation must always be for the betterment of all, the growth of society beyond simple personal concerns. Purpose. I sometimes wonder if we might not have aborted the next MLK or the person who might find the solution to American poverty or the next Abraham Lincoln for our time. If each life truly has immense worth and value, should we not do the best we can to discover the value it might bring? I understand it is easy to dismiss such a question, given that the existential reality of a newborn changes so much for the parent(s). But I also believe that a 43% abortion rate among African Americans in our country and the rising number of abortions connected to poverty cannot be something we simply choose to ignore or dismiss. There must be better solutions if we truly value human life.

I believe God's plan for each living person is as constant as the sun rising in the east or the constellations gathering in our night sky. Sometimes the clouds cover what is there and we are not allowed to celebrate the gifts the sky offers us, but the potential is always there behind the clouds. What if our political posturing is the very reason some problems do not get solved? An unborn "John the Baptist" somehow felt that which he could not understand, celebrated that which he could not yet know, leapt for joy before he even knew what he was leaping about. God's Spirit moved "in the depths" of an unborn son. Such is the connection between God and the unborn. Such is the plan of our Creator for the created ones. Such is the timeless testimony of this unborn child. Mother to Mother, Baby to Baby, Spirit to Spirit, Advent conceptions are celebrated by two courageous women as each son in the womb laid claim to a purpose that could only come from the Hand of God. This is the story of two miraculous pre-born children conceived with a Purpose that would change human history forever. These two unborn children mattered immeasurably to the world. Purpose predated birth.

What is Purpose? And how do we bring the Joy of this first Advent into the discussion of Purpose? The ongoing discussion of Authority was diminished in the Modern world. In the 1st Century *"the Church could have escaped persecution by the Roman Empire if it had been content to be treated as a 'cultus privates' - one of many forms of personal religion. But it was not."*[95] First Century Christians, beginning with the likes of Mary and *Elizabeth*, believed something which has been minimized in the Post-Modern Worldview. First Century Jesus-followers believed God had the authority to ask of them anything God chose to ask, such as: Pregnancy when beyond our fertile years; Mothering a child meant for suffering and death; Leaving our nets behind to take the Gospel to the World; Selling our property to give to the poor; Sacrificing income to spend time with our family; Investing in those who seem un-redeemable; Fighting the "popular belief" to proclaim the "right belief"; Loving those who are vastly different than ourselves, and on and on we could list. If Purpose is a thing at all, then a "Higher Purpose" is the best of this thing.

Purpose as an idea has been explored and discussed for

---

[95] For further study on the modern question of Authority read the discussion offered by Leslie Newbigin, who is quoted here. Leslie Newbigin, *"The Open Secret" (1978, 1995)*. Published by Wm. B. Eerdmans Publishing Co., Grand Rapids, Michigan. www, eerdmans.com

centuries. We might examine the ideas of Aristotle, whose impact on the thinking of the West dominated much of our history. Aristotle believed that "humans are motivated by end goals and need to have a purpose, something to pursue." Aristotle considers the purpose or ends: the final reason for that function's existence. Aristotle used the Greek term *telos* to describe the inherent purpose of each thing, the ultimate reason for each thing to be the way it is. Aristotle defines the *telos* for humans as *Eudaimonia*,[96] which was simply his term for "human flourishing." In his view, we cannot flourish without meaningful purpose.

We have begun to climb out of a closed universe in recent years. Just a century ago Science pretended not to know the difference between a responsible action and a predetermined genetic event. In such an atmosphere Behaviorism thrived and Genocide was reborn. Science had no place for the responsible action, and the only real thing they would admit to were what they deemed to be "facts" (as opposed to values). "To explain behavior in terms of the responsible action of a person who is capable of understanding and accepting a purpose is 'un-scientific'," so they claimed.[97] Why? It was not because of the evidence, but because of the worldview. To create a system, we can explain without the necessity of a Creator and a God, we must destroy the concept of a purposeful and meaningful explanation for human history. The honest scientist will pause to ask the obvious question - Is this not also a faith commitment? Once a system of thought embraces the concept that Purpose does not exist, it is difficult to find meaning and purpose beyond Darwin's survival mechanism - natural selection. However, the denial of Purpose ends up making the

---

[96] *The Five Gifts from Aristotle for Living a Meaningful Life,* Jim Luckman and Elizabeth Luckman, July 3, 2020. Published by LinkedIn Corporation, LinkedIn. com. For a detailed definition of Aristotle's *eudaemonia* please consult: Britannica, History and Society, Written by Brian Duignan and fact checked by The Editors of Encyclopedia Britannica, 2024. www.britannica.com/topic/eudaimonia
[97] Newbigin, "Foolishness to Greeks", page 75

case for Purpose. Survival is a purpose, and we must surrender to the song of Purpose in order to deny it exists. In other words, we need Purpose to deny there is Purpose. Once we all admit to each other that Purpose is a very human system that cannot be denied or escaped, we are allowed the room we need to open ourselves to the concept of Faith. Not to replace science, in the manner science sought to replace religion, but to compliment science as we search for Truth together. And once we admit Faith is Real in a way that transcends what science has to offer, we are set free to explore "A Timeless Script from a 1st Century Doctor" in our present reality.

We might also consider more recent discussions of the power of purpose. "We already have the evidence of the dichotomy that runs through our culture. We all engage in purposeful activity, and we judge ourselves and others in terms of success in achieving the purposes that we set before ourselves. Yet we accept as the final product of this purposeful activity a picture of the world from which purpose has been eliminated. Purpose is a meaningful concept in relation to our own consciousness of ourselves, but it is allowed no place in our understanding of the world of facts."[98] As a Social Scientist I must admit that no place is this self-contradiction more apparent than In the area of Social Science. During research in these areas "the manipulator credits himself with the capacity for purposeful action that he denies to the manipulated" (see footnote above), since only the Social Scientist is claiming 'facts' over values, denying that 'facts' are ultimately based on foundational 'value' judgments made by the Social Scientists pertaining to the reasons we choose to study "this thing" rather than "the other thing."

Purpose is unavoidable. Both manipulator and the manipulated are dominated by Purpose. Aristotle was expressing an idea that scientists have suppressed, to their peril. If we acknowledge

---

[98] I would suggest that any person who is interested in the investigation of the Worldview issue must take time to read and study the author of this quote: Lesslie Newbigin, "Foolishness to the Greeks, 1986, page 78

Purpose, we must also acknowledge Authority. And if we choose to engage ourselves in the asking of questions related to Purpose and Authority, we are of necessity entering an investigation of *Metaphysical Reality* which transcends a strictly *Naturalistic Worldview*, or any worldview where the invisible but True are not investigated. Science is changing amid *postmodern* pushbacks. Scientists already investigate the invisible, claiming that 95% of the universe is what they call "dark matter", which is invisible to us.[99] We can investigate the consequences that invisible reality has upon our universe. Imagine, scientists investigating what they claim is invisible to us. This is what most Theologians are attempting to do - measure and proclaim the impact of an Invisible God as God impacts our universe. But what others call Invisible, Luke declared Visible, beginning with the Story of Advent.

Luke assumed that it would seem logical to his reader that One who claimed Authority would be able to display Authority in a multitude of ways and times. The Universe itself would obey and bear witness. Each Advent we celebrate the birth of Jesus - that sometime between 4 and 1 B. C. his birth was marked in the stars, inviting "Wisemen" from far away to seek this star and celebrate the coming of The Great King. Their purpose was to look at the stars and mark the time. This took place in the eyes of the *Magi*.[100] While the events written about for *Elizabeth* and Mary were transpiring, the Magi were looking to the sky. Once the day arrived, these men followed The Star to their purpose,

---

[99] You can begin an elementary understanding of "dark matter" in the writings of Michael Guilen, "Seeing is Believing."

[100] According to John F. MacArthur, Jr., in his book "God With Us", these Magi were "esteemed for their amazing intuition, wisdom, knowledge, astrology, and occult ability, and rose to places of prominence in the Babylonian, Jedo-Persian, and Greek empires. They acted as advisors to kings…..and helped settle questions of science and law. There heyday lasted from about the 6th century B. C. Through the time of Christ." (page 104) For further analysis see: John F. MacArthur, *God With Us (1989)*. Zondervan Publishing House, Grand Rapids, MI.., pages 99-114

greeting The King. Let us ponder deeper. This star was set in place, whatever it was (some say Comet, some say Star, some say conjunction of Planets), by a Purposeful Creator millions or billions of years before it was discovered by the Magi. WOW. God set God's purpose in the sky eons before the event unfolded in real time, just as God planted two boys in the womb of two special moms. Advent was as much a day anticipated as a day now celebrated. It is the promised past and the fantastic future which serve to amplify the Annual Advent Miracle.

Meaning from our past is always interpreted through a lens in the present. We have a challenging time understanding Advent as a significant event for our time largely because we do not fully comprehend how this day impacted the people who experienced it. Mary and *Elizabeth* are but one example, but a powerful example indeed. Both women had a deep understanding of the event they were a part of. They understood the purpose of their individual lives because they embraced the meaning of the day. They saw themselves as a part of something miraculous, but more than this, a part of something significant. The Authority of God, the Incarnation of God's Son, and their part in the Visitation of God, all gave a meaning and a purpose to their lives that could not have come otherwise.

> "The legitimacy of dismissing everything that does not easily fit our twentieth century (now 21st century) 'closed universe' worldview needs to be seriously questioned. In truth, it seems quite presumptuous to self-consciously enshrine one's own worldview as the final arbiter of what could and could not have happened in history." (Gregory Boyd, page 225)

> "Empiricists have been embarrassed by the increasing recognition that the 'hard facts' of experience are not always so hard. What one observes is strongly shaped by prior expectations, and experience seems to be

heavily influenced by the conceptual framework of the experiencer." (C.Stephen Evans, page 165)

"True tolerance, not indifference to the truth, can be founded. True dialogue is as far as possible from neutrality or indifference. Its basis is the shared conviction that there is truth to be known and that we must both bear witness to the truth given to us and also listen to the witness of others." (Leslie Newbigin, Foolishness to the Greeks, page 139)

Day 13

"The Dawn from on high will visit us to shine on those who live in darkness and the shadow of death, to guide our feet into the way of peace" (Luke 1:78,79 – The Holman Christian Standard Bible, Holman Bible Publishers, 2007)

Setting the Stage: Meaning and Purpose in chaotic times...

JORDAN PETERSON, A WELL-SPOKEN AND SOMEWHAT BRILLIANT Psychologist from Canada, stresses the fact that people are attracted to his lectures because they are hungry for meaningful discussions about the relationship between responsibility and ideology. He believes that we have often settled for a culturally defined conversation regarding human rights to such a degree that we have forgotten some old-fashioned ideas that need to be resurrected for consideration. As a result, he tells us that Western Values and Western Ideals have taken a back seat to a Woke Agenda, that is both alarmist and a complete misrepresentation of reality. Consider his definition of "woke": "A pseudo-intellectual pastiche of postmodern and neo-Marxist tropes, dedicated to the idea that categories themselves do nothing but privilege and oppress."[101]

In plain language, "woke ideology" is a pseudo-representation of

---

[101] Taken from a Twitter post by Dr. Jordan Peterson: **Dr Jordan B Peterson** @jordanbpeterson Best-Selling Author | Clinical Psychologist | #1 Education Podcast | Listen to the podcast here: linktr.ee/DrJordanBPeter

Enlightenment thinking, whereby modern political ideologues create innovative ideas which they claim represent understandings of truth which lie hidden in the hearts and minds of people groups and are brought out in the open as the result of oppression and suffering. They are not new; they are simply revisions of long rejected philosophical ideas. They never explain their precepts in terms of logic, rational thinking, or even historical cultural evidence. They see no need to do so. They simply expect us to accept their proclamations at face value without philosophical, scientific, or rational reasons to do so.

Rising from the royal heap of "woke" nonsense are shallow Marxist concepts and Critical Theory renewed, as those espousing this worldview expect people to naturally understand (which is more emotional than anything) that history is divided into those who oppress and those who are oppressed. The oppressors are responsible for all we deem bad or evil, and the oppressed are victims of their oppression and are not responsible for the plight in which they find themselves trapped. I have never seen any of them discuss Jesus as one of the oppressed, which would have to be true in their paradigm. Those who knew Him and those who wrote of His life never categorized Him this way, for He spoke of love for enemies, personal responsibility and accountability, purpose which often arises from suffering, and transcendent Truth which was more important than political ideology. (Jesus was not "woke").

Luke's Advent narrative took human understanding in the opposite direction. The concept of Authority, Responsibility, and Meaning are deeply rooted in 1st century Judaism, and break forth throughout the Gospel of Luke. Mary and *Elizabeth*, both of whom had reason to cry out for justice, simply chose to fully embrace their place in the Advent Story (they were not "woke"). More than anything, the call I issue for you the reader through these writings is for a renewal of exploration into these events, a call to find our place in the Story, inside the events that took place when God visited our planet. What was common experience in the 1st century is a lost art in the 21st century, for those in a world seeking to be "woke" are looking the wrong places to Awake from their slumber.

Purpose and Meaningful Destiny were a part of every first century Gospel. Matthew, In his Gospel, mentions a simultaneous event occurring around the same time Mary was visiting *Elizabeth* (Matthew 2:1-12). Imagine, around the moment Mary and *Elizabeth* were sharing a reunion as mothers to be, the Magi were looking westward toward a Star. The Magi following a Star was yet another powerful illustration of Authority and Purpose, just as was the birth of these two boys. Both events found their true meaning within the Purpose of God for Israel, the Purpose of God for the Nations, the Purpose of God for two Jewish Mothers, and the Purpose of God for all human history, including our time. The Magi did not follow a Star as we follow the words of an Astrologer. They were scientists. They were fully committed participants in the Science of their day to find meaning and purpose that transcended their temporary existence on the planet's surface. The Magi believed there was a *Metaphysical* Reality worth pursuing at the end *(telos)* of their journey, so they had been waiting and watching for this event for many years. Their entire lives.

This Star meant that the Creator had a plan that spanned millions, if not billions of years. The stars were set up to declare something of significance by a purposeful Creator who had something important to reveal. These *Magi* were not reading the sky like a horoscope, looking for a personal word for the day. Instead, they saw the night sky as a map of reality, a Word from the Creator, a purpose for their existence. What is Purpose according to Mary, *Elizebeth*, the Magi, Luke? They believed the answer would come from the One Who created this universe, this planet, human life, and our reality. It was simple for those whom Luke wrote about, so he shared His "Timeless Script" for those in search of the "Why?" Our two mothers and Luke found their answers. The Star points others to the answer they found as well. And all these point us past our problems to possibilities in our day.

Know this - Any Author who writes has a purpose for writing. In the same way, a Creator who creates has a purpose for creating. In the case of Luke's Gospel, we are wise to heed the intent of both. You see, we believe suffering is the enemy. Luke understood suffering as a sign of the Almighty in our midst, sculpting us into everything we are created to become.

"The Dawn from on high will visit us… Luke 1:78 (Amplified Version)"

I work closely with college students. Many of them are searching for purpose, and they see this as a hopeless and meaningless task. They have inherited their skepticism from us, the generations who came before them. They have watched us build our empires, drive our cars, own our houses, buy our stocks, break up our marriages, and neglect our children until we have forced them to wonder - "Is there a purpose to all of this?"

One of the reasons younger generations so easily dismiss meaning and purpose is because they have grown convinced that discomfort and inconvenience are barriers to finding such things. Somewhere in the recesses of their unconscious *psyche* they have grown convinced that life is supposed to be convenient, supportive, fulfilling, and void of discomfort. Somehow happiness is owed to us, so these things are to be avoided if happiness is to be found. "But a radical new body of evidence shows that people are at their best – physically harder, mentally tougher, and spiritually sounder – after experiencing the same discomforts our early ancestors were exposed to."[102] What a novel idea. The oppressed are blessed, and much of what we believe to be experiences to avoid are the very experiences that mold and shape us toward our full potential as human beings. There is no denying that Jesus taught this to his early followers, and never once categorized oppression or oppressors as the source or the atmosphere of evil. Instead, both were sign of God's Authority. The questions and the answers created by evil are more complicated than simple blame to suffice. Luke says it outright through the words of Simeon:

"Simeon blessed them and told His mother Mary - 'Indeed, this child is destined to cause the rising and falling of many in Israel and to be a sign that will be opposed, and a sword will pierce your own soul, that the thoughts of many hearts may be revealed'" (Luke 2: 33-35, Holman Christian Standard Translation). The Advent Story is a tragedy which created hope, and comfort and convenience were not part of the story.

Comfort and convenience can become the enemy of hope and faith. Consider the following. Let us suppose that in order to discover the depths of love one must first be challenged to love when love is not returned. I once saw a movie starring Nicholas Cage in which he had a twin brother - Charles and Donald in "Adaptation" (A 2002 Comedy). Charles is the most popular and successful brother, or was he? During one scene in this movie the two twins

---

[102] Michael Easter, "The Comfort Crisis: Embrace Discomfort to Reclaim Your Wild, Happy, Healthy Self", 2021. Rodale Books, Penguin Random House LLC, NY, NY. Quote from chapter titled "33 Days".

are hiding from their oppressor and having a conversation about their youth. Each expressed how much he respected and loved the other one (as we often do when we think we are about to die).

Donald, the unpopular brother, was adored and respected beyond what he understood by Charles. He did not know this, but it did not matter. During the conversation, an interesting event was discussed. Donald had a high school crush on Sarah Marshall, for which everyone made fun of him for. Especially Sarah. The popular twin believed his brother did not know. But he did. "I loved Sarah, Charles. It was mine. I owned it. Even Sarah didn't have the right to take it away. I can love whoever I want." "But she thought you were pathetic," said Charles. "That was her business, not mine. *You are what you love, not what loves you.*" His brother Donald had stumbled upon one of the most profound truths we can discover. Purpose and meaning in life, especially when it comes to us in the beautiful form of love, is not a thing that is void of suffering. It is the opposite. Love is not something which automatically offers comfort or convenience. It is not a "happily ever after" guarantee. The most beautiful things in this world come to us via risk, discomfort, inconvenience, patience, hard work, and a myriad of other things which we do not willingly seek. Giving love shapes and empowers us, even more than the love we receive.

God created a universe where love, faith, and hope must be tested to be real. Many of us would have done this another way, and certainly Gen Z would vote for a world where justice and equity always rule. However, this design would never survive the test of time, and would certainly never build the type of longing which resides inside the heart of humanity for a better world relative to the one we now know. Suffering brings motivation, desire, and faith all rolled up into one Being. And this Being is our only chance to make it through this life certain of a better and more fulfilling future. Without suffering there is no longing. Without longing there is no hope. Without hope there is no transformation. Without transformation there is no growth. And without growth there is no future. Suffering is the link in a long chain that leads us toward that which we all long to find - Meaning and Purpose beyond anyone's ability to dismiss. "We are what we love, not what loves us." This is the rule Jesus lives by. He delights in loving me and you, even if we choose to respond with indifference or disdain. Advent is the proof.

I have also noticed college students push back on tradition. Fortunately, it seems they are not satisfied inside hopelessness, which mindless tradition often creates. They desire to find meaning but have been robbed of the very foundations that make this search possible. Their surrender to a narrow purpose defined by personal preference exists primarily because our culture has robbed them of a reason to search beyond themselves. We neglected to teach them the most valuable things we inherited from centuries of faith. We emphasized the wrong parts of history and tradition for the sake of ease, comfort, and power. Far too many parents and teachers have forgotten how to connect, with each other, with our children, with our communities, with our fellow human beings from all walks of life, and yes, with our Creator. Loneliness, depression, and isolation are the natural result of the worship of social media, the single parent family, our constant uprooting toward greener pastures, the disappearance of the Community where we learn to thrive, the avoidance of church, and faith as an anchor in times of pain and need. Self-Help books cannot and will never replace the "Timeless Script" Luke left for us, but we have forgotten how to teach the cure he offered. Education was sacrificed on the altar of ideology, and Truth was replaced by propaganda selling the latest political agenda.

Education used to be one of the most important pegs of Christendom. Universities sprang from the human desire to understand the world of the Creator. "Monasteries spawned

Universities, and these Universities served as the model for Universities all over the world." Unity in diversity is embedded in the word itself - university (united within diversity). Public schools grew out of church schools, and although public schools have moved toward a more secularized worldview at their foundation, this has not changed the fact that Education as a concept is fundamentally a religious activity, an act of worship. Education leads to innovation, awe, and the betterment of the human condition, which is fundamentally a religious task. It is no coincidence that despite the separation of Church from State Schools, in principle as well as practice, that we still discover that "religious participation is positively linked to higher school achievement." Simply put, it still holds true - If you want to do better in school, go to church. There is a standing generational correlation between the two that just will not go away.[103]

Throughout all of this The Church is a primary culprit, for we are often so busy guarding our Traditions (By this I do not mean Orthodox Theology, but rather the music we embrace or the language we use or the morality we preach or the sins we accentuate), that we have forgotten how to connect with people outside our sanctuary. In many ways, we have become a culture of many religions but with little faith, just like Rome at the time of Advent. This subtle erosion of a love for Truth and Purpose does not happen in a vacuum. I am convinced my students do not want to live lives of indifference and skepticism. But they need a reason to believe otherwise, and we do a poor job of providing what they need.

However, I am fully committed to the idea that human beings can never get to a place of permanent indifference. Even if we claim we do not care, there are sure signs that we do. We are like

---

[103] Quote and information in this paragraph I owe to the research and writing of: Mary Poplin, "Is Reality Secular: Testing the Assumptions of Four Global Worldviews, 2014. InterVarsity Press, Downers Grove, IL. Part V, chapter 27

the people who say they are not trying to impress anyone, yet they shower and comb their hair anyway. Somewhere inside there is a desire to be embraced, recognized, received in a positive way. We are wired for such. Just as we are wired to find a passionate reason for "our" existence.

Human Beings are wired to desire more than "it just doesn't matter." The philosophers used to proclaim that humanity is made for immortality, which is probably why every ancient civilization had some sort of belief in the afterlife. More recently, Science has tried to convince us that there really is no purpose to this world other than the survival of living species, of which we are the most advanced. However, human beings when we hear this, instinctively shout "NO!" We are always pushing back on this notion. The pushback can be found in popular music, the movies we love, and the art we enjoy. Postmodernism developed as a pushback against "Survival of the Fittest." Human beings will never settle for simple scientific explanations of the reasons for life. Science caters to the "How," and avoids the "Why?" Humanity will never abandon the "Why?"

Individual human beings can get stuck along the way; the road so curvy that "Why" is not an option. "I'm trying to survive here, man!" And when survival consumes us, we can get stuck, and hope can disappear. Science seems the wise one. But it is not the ultimate reality. It is not true Truth. "Why" always breaks through. Hopelessness can be powerful, but it is the result of frustration during our tiresome search for meaning, nothing more. We do not abandon the search, even though we tell ourselves we have. Yes, hopelessness can create the illusion that it just does not matter. But renewed hope is always just a breath away. There is always an Advent on the horizon. So, we love until hope is revived, and this is what we call Faith.

I grew up in WV. Sometimes you can travel up a mountain so curvy that you cannot get moving over 30 miles an hour for the curvy nature of the road. You keep going up without making much progress. At the top of the mountain, you can stop the car and look down at the road where you were driving fifteen minutes ago. You just traveled 10 miles, but the road is less than a mile below where you stand in a straight line down. And those below you can look up a little way and see where they will be in fifteen minutes, without a clue they will have to drive ten miles to get to you. They can see you. They could throw you a baseball. They could play catch with you. But only because you have traveled the mountain they are yet to climb.

We are all traveling this road. We know there is a goal, the road is taking us somewhere, it ought to be easier to get there. But there is no tunnel or interstate on this mountain road in WV. We get car-sick, we cry out "are we there yet?" We blame our parents for taking us on this road, we ask to turn around, or we just close our eyes and go to sleep. I tried them all. But none of these solve the question of "Why?" The exits we take postpone the inevitable.........the end of the mountain road, the goal, the reason we drove this way to begin with. Human beings are creatures in search of meaning and purpose. Advent is the best answer we have for these Metaphysical Questions, and we have learned to stop asking them.

John the Baptist was in Luke's story to help point you toward the One with the answers you search for. Advent is the True Center of Human History and the Answer to the Question of Destiny. Advent is the "Why?" John's father proclaimed for all to hear the purpose his son entered the world – to prepare us for the Visitation of the "Dawn from on High." He was not the One, but he was there to hold up a sign pointing toward the One. If you find yourself in the dark and you are wandering up that WV mountain, finding yourself a little bit queasy, check Him out. He surprises me every day. He no doubt will surprise you as well. There is a gift wrapped with our name on it under the Eternal Advent Tree, just for me, just for you, and time is not a barrier, for it contains "a Timeless Script."

In 1999, we were treated to a *metaphorical* illustration of real-life challenges, compared to the story we tell ourselves or our culture tries to present. This movie was called *The Matrix. The Matrix* is the world of ideas that has been "pulled over our eyes, blinding us to the truth." *The Matrix* is a powerful illustration of our desire to escape the task of looking for the Truth because it is difficult, hard, uncomfortable, and inconvenient. It is always, always, better to live by Truth than to abandon the Real. Always. The Red Pill is the door to Truth, where we are empowered to meet "The One."[104]

Quoting Morpheus from the Matrix:

Morpheus: "There is a difference between knowing the path and walking the path."

Neo: "Are you saying I will be able to dodge bullets?"
Morpheus: "No, Neo, I'm trying to tell you that when you're ready, you won't have to."

Morpheus: "The Matrix is a System, Neo. That System is our enemy."

Morpheus: "Unfortunately, no one can be told what the Matrix is. You have to see it for yourself."

Morpheus: "You take the blue pill - the story ends, you wake up in your bed and believe whatever you want to believe. You take the red pill (the Christ pill) - You stay in Wonderland, and I show you how deep the rabbit-hole goes."

---

[104] Quotes are taken from "The Matrix: Morpheus' 10 Best Quotes, Ranked", Devin Meehan, Feb 4, 2022. CBR, cbr.com

Day 14

In the Spirit and Power of Elijah.... Luke 1:17

Setting the Stage: The Old Testament Prophet gives way to the New Testament Apostle.

THE OFFICE OF PROPHET WAS AN OLD TESTAMENT VOCATION, patterned after a guy by the name of *Elijah*.[105] Some refer to John the Baptizer as the last of the Old Testament Prophets. However, the activity of the Prophet was transformed into something even more powerful and significant, simply because the age of Messiah had arrived. A New office was born out of a distinct group of Jesus followers after the Resurrection - The office of "Apostle," The most famous of these Apostles was Paul, Luke's traveling companion and mentor.

For over 30 years Paul traveled some 10,000 miles (about 16093.44 km) across the Roman Empire, preaching in cities brimming with the poorest and most oppressed of people, who were desperate to hear a message of hope and everlasting life during an age of "spiritual poverty." Whereas Jesus spoke to Jews, primarily, Paul took his message to the world. His was a Gentile Targeted Gospel, as he reimagined Jewish Tradition and the Authority of the Law that he might emphasize Jesus' teachings for potential non-Jewish converts. Though himself a Jew, Paul

---

[105] Got Questions Ministries, "Who is Elijah?" (January 4, 2022). GotQuestions. org is the flagship site of Got Questions Ministries, gotquestions.org

understood that the message spoken in the Synagogues would not resonate with Romans and Greeks. This is one reason Luke's Gospel is so relevant today, for Luke understood Paul's strategy and adopted it in the writing of his Gospel. Do you get it? Paul pushed back on Tradition for the sake of his audience. Not Truth, but Tradition. And he taught Luke to do the same.

In Luke's mind Jesus was much more the Son of Adam than He was the Son of David. Both are important, but in a world opposed to the concept of A Divine Visitation in Human Form the Son of Adam had a more powerful voice. Some historians believe Paul's family were once Roman slaves who were later freed, and this experience made his message more believable for those who lived under Roman domination. We cannot know for certain. What we do know is that Paul had an enormous impact on Luke's life and therefore Luke's Gospel.

We also cannot say exactly how or when Paul died, but we do know that before his death he preached the Gospel of Christ throughout the Roman Empire. And as far as we can tell, Luke was always by his side. Paul's efforts led to the new religion called Christianity reaching the outer limits of the civilized world of his time. Eventually, Christianity would become the dominant religion in Rome, and this was made possible by the Apostleship of Paul.[106] His ability to reach the expanse of the Roman World with the Good News Jesus had introduced stands as one of the most amazing religious campaigns in human history. (Maybe surpassed only by Billy Graham.)[107] Without army or political power, no propaganda machine, and all status removed, Paul walked across Roman Roads with a message that would eventually make it to the home of the emperor. He was armed with nothing more than

---

[106] Information gathered from *"The Roman Empire in the First Century"* (2006), Devillier Donegan Enterprises. PBS.org
[107] Billy Graham is said to have preached the Gospel of Jesus Christ to more than 215 million people by Smaritanspurse.org.

a proclamation of Truth about a person who has now become the most famous individual on the face of the earth - Jesus of Nazareth. (Start with Time Magazine and adventure into any publication you choose you will find Jesus listed at the top of everyone's list. The name of Jesus cannot be surpassed, even by those who do not delight in Him.)

There was a powerful exchange that came with the arrival of Jesus. The Old Testament Prophet, John being the last, was replaced with a new kind of prophet with a new kind of message. No longer would Tradition and Doctrine be the magnet which drew people to God. It would now be The Gospel, what Paul called "the Power of God unto salvation" (Romans 1:16). *Elijah,* renewed through the ministry of John the Baptizer, had to decrease, so that the name of Jesus might be proclaimed throughout the land through the testimony of those who knew Him best. The name that continues to be proclaimed today through Paul's dear friend and companion, Dr. Luke. Let us lean in.....

In the Spirit and Power of Elijah.... Luke 1:17

Not only was John's destiny tied to the Messiah he announced, but his personality predated his birth. He came in *the Spirit and Power of Elijah. Elijah,* to say the least, was a larger-than-life kind of prophet. In his lifetime, he was part of restoring a dead son to his widowed mother. She fed *Elijah* in her home shortly before her son died (This story is in 1 Kings 17). He pronounced the miraculous in her midst: "Lord My God, let this boy's life return to him" (I Kings 17:21). Just as the prophet had pronounced an endless supply of oil and flower amid tremendous draught, God now restored life to a lifeless son amid a mother's suffering. These two miracles were even more incredible when considering that the widow was a lady of *Zarephath,* a non-Jewish woman who lived in that region. Jesus referred to her in Luke 4, stirring up the anger of those in Galilee, for both the events of the Widow of *Zarephath* and

Jesus' pronouncement in his hometown highlighted the fact that Messiah was a Messiah for Jew and Gentile alike. He is Messiah for all people. The *Spirit of Elijah* was the spirit of one drawn to the outcast, the impoverished, the "undeserving." These were a substantial portion of the people who migrated toward John the Baptist in search of hope.

A second miracle worth mentioning pertains to the draught in Israel during the time of *Elijah*. For more than 3 years the people of Israel, ruled by the unfaithful king *Ahab*, had been without rain (See 1 Kings 18). One can only imagine what this would entail - constant thirst, crops that would not grow, starvation, anger and frustration, the entire nation in "survive at all cost" mode. It is easy to draw a parallel between this time of draught and God's time of silence in Israel before the coming of Messiah. There was a spiritual draught in Israel at the time of Messiah's Advent. For more than 400 years there had been no rain in the form of a Prophetic Word from God's Spirit in Israel, no prophet in the Land, no voice, no spokesperson for God. Just as the land had lain silent in the days of *Elijah*, the nation of Israel was engulfed in silence in the days of John the Baptist.

Then someone came "in the spirit and power of *Elijah*." He spoke, and the draught was lifted. He was used of God to usher in a new beginning, where the prophets of Baal were no more, and the more than 3-year draught was ended. John the Baptist was this prophet in the 1st century, as the draught of God's Word ends with his voice. His birth signaled the beginning of a new era, as the Kingdom of God was to bring a renewal of conquest over godless kings and John's Testimony paved the way for a new beginning for all people. *Elijah's* name means *My God is Yahweh*. It is to this claim John the Baptist was born, it is to this message John the Baptist went baptizing, and it is to this purpose John the Baptist lived and died. The Spirit of *Elijah*, none other than the Spirit of *Yahweh*, rested upon him from conception. Just as the

Angel announced to *Zachariah,* "He will be filled with the Holy Spirit even before he is born........ He will turn the hearts of the parents toward their children and the disobedient to the wisdom of the righteous—to make ready a people prepared for the Lord" (Luke 1:15-17).

In addition to the miracles of Word as rain, John captured the spirit of *Ellijah* in at least two other ways, parallels we can draw between *Elijah* and John. (There are others.) Firstly, John lived at a time when the dominant politics of the day was not in line with the Will of God. During such times, the message proclaimed was consistently met with push back, powerful push back. Though Israel was a nation claiming to follow *"YAWAH,"* the hearts of the people were not acting in ways consistent with this confession, much like the postmodern world of our time. Our mouths say one thing, our lives say another, and consistency of thought and action seldom correlate. These cultural tendencies were a part of both the time of *Elijah* and the days of John the Baptist in the land of Israel.

There are a myriad of reasons for this. I will mention only two. First, God has major competition in America. The State. Even for those who are religious at heart, we find ourselves surrendering to the god we have created, *Nationalism.* "Responsibilities for education, healing and public welfare which had formerly rested with the Church devolved more and more upon the nation state. In the past century, this movement has been vastly accelerated by the advent (small "a") of the 'welfare state.' National Governments are widely responsible for and capable of providing these things that former generation thought only God could provide - freedom from fear, hunger, disease and want - in a word 'happiness.'"[108]

Today, if there is any entity to which ultimate authority is due, it is no longer The Church. The Authority some believe the Church

---

[108] In this passage we are borrowing heavily from: Leslie Newborn, "The Other Side of 1984: Questions for the Churches, 1983. Geneva: World Council of Churches. Pages 13-15

once had has been supplanted by The Nation State. In the name of the Nation State, we continually see religion revolt against religion, even within specific religions, in the name of the Nation State. The Bible refers to blasphemy as the unpardonable sin (Matthew 3:28-30). Today, the unpardonable sin is treason. There was never a better example of this than the horrors committed by the so called "religious Nation State" under Hitler, as people who called themself Believers supported genocide. It has happened other times, often in the name of the god we are calling the Nation State. It takes a superficial study of Rome in the 1st century to find the parallels between the power of the Roman government as supreme and the place our government claims today. The Covid Crisis highlighted this national trend toward empowering and surrendering rights to our government. Vaccine mandates for military and federal workers, university professors, health care providers, and other vocational entities, and the censorship encouraged by government officials upon social media, are primary examples of this trend. The Nation State has become a god for many, including people inside our churches. For many religious people, the traditional priority list of God, Family, then Country has become God/Country, Me, then Family.

A second reason our lives do not always consistently reflect our confession is because of a migration away from Theology as a legitimate avenue for discovering Truth. At some point in the 19th or 20th centuries a post-Enlightenment ideology took the throne. As a Social Scientist myself, I must admit that the most powerful player in this silent war was the Social Sciences. They offered the heaviest critique of religious life. Beginning with Auguste Comte, who leaned heavily on Darwin, we begin a period in which the social sciences begin to peck away at a Theological understanding of the world. I teach my students that the person who had the most influence on Psychology was Charles Darwin, who along with Comte seemed to misconstrue he nature of Theology. They both worked to set the two against one another, as if they could not co-exist - Science and Theology.

Theology is not rooted in Mythology. It is a different thing all together. Christian Theology, as are the theologies of the three largest world religions, is rooted in historical events. "God with us." Darwin and Comte decided that the "Why" question was not worth pursuing, the very question Theology intends to answer. Science tells us "what goes on and how it goes on. Theology tries to tell us 'Why' the whole thing goes on and 'Who' stands behind it."[109]

Charles Darwin was the person who opened the doors to the denial of faith as a primary means of discovering the Truth about the human psyche. Auguste Comte took over his mantel. Whereas Darwin introduced the concept of natural selection, which was nature's mechanism of insuring survival and growth, Comte took his theory a step further and applied it to human society. "Comte believed society evolved in a unilinear fashion: The Age of the *Theological,* The Age of the *Metaphysical,* and The Age of *Positivism.*"[110] This "Positivism" Stage gave birth to the *Naturalist,* who proposed we do not need God to explain reality. The primary problem with this supposition is that the *Naturalist* was never required to prove that God is not needed, it was simply assumed, then integrated into the theories of most early Social Scientists. For instance, Marx simply assumed God is not real, then proceeds to build his social theory. He never gives any evidence for his assumption; he simply states it and moves forward. In contrast, "it seems to me that in a pluralistic culture it is almost impossible not to reflect critically on where one should place one's trust ... It

---

[109] Stephen Evans, "Philosophy of Religion: Thinking About Faith, 1982. InterVarsity Press, Downers Grove, IL. Page 125

[110] "Darwin's Evolution and Positivism", Sky Kalfus, November 12, 2010. Science and Society, Science Leadership Academy @ Center City, science leadership.org. and also The Sociological Perspective, From the classes of Walsh Bedford, 2018-19. Social Science Libre Texts, socialsci.libretexts.org.

would be fallacious to infer that religious beliefs are false on the basis of an account of their sociological origins."[111]

The State and Social Sciences of the day often stand against religious accounting for the world. It is not new. As The King of Israel rejected *Elijah*, so did the political powers in John's Day reject him, for both Temple (the hub of religious social life) and Rome rejected God's Prophet. *Ahab* was a wicked King of Israel, just as *Herod* was a wicked King of Judea. Both Kings refused to embrace the will of God, and both were met with strong criticism by the Prophet of God for their time. Just as *Elijah* presented himself to *Ahab*, John presented himself to *Herod*. *Ahab* greeted *Elijah* with these words: "Is that you, you troubler of Israel (I Kings 18:17)? Herod's fear of John is revealed with these words: "Herod wanted to kill John, but he was afraid of the people, because they considered him a prophet" (Matthew 14:7). Matthew reminds us that *Herod* in fact did kill John, just as *Ahab* and his Queen attempted to kill *Elijah*. Both faced political persecution for the message they proclaimed. And both prophets predicted a devastating future for each Kingdom. History confirms these prophets were correct, for Israel and for Rome. In fact, throughout Old Testament history there were always consequences when leaders chose to ignore the prophets of God. This was not the simple "hammer of God," but more often natural consequences for the faithless, leading us to a second observation.

A second parallel was that both spoke directly to the authorities in Israel about an extremely specific area of life - Family. (You did not know the prophets were also social scientists, did you?) They warned these two kings of the consequences that would take place if each king were not willing to repent and turn to the God of Israel regarding family life (See Matthew 14, Luke 3:19,20). Both were granted a bit of leeway until they addressed the family structure adopted by the King. *Elijah* confronted King *Jehoram* for

[111] .Stephen Evans, "Philosophy of Religion: Thinking About Faith. Page 20, 127.

murdering his own brothers to maintain power (See 2 Chronicles 21). John confronted *Herod* who married his sister-in-law. Both were committing sins against their own family, and the nation was suffering due to their status in the Land. Family! In case you have not yet figured this out, God prioritizes family.

The Judeo-Christian Tradition has always held family in exceedingly high esteem. It is not coincidental that the present crisis in American families is noticeably correlated to the unprecedented decrease in the practice of family worship and family faith. Family has always been a priority in our Land.[112] So, what is happening in these United States? Where are we? A transformation is taking place. Though divorce rates are stable, fewer of our parents get married. No fault divorce, or divorce for any reason, reigns supreme as single parent homes have become half of all family units. We are often bystanders as the State tries to strip away parental rights and influence over our own children. There is an undeniable family crisis in our Country.

We are too frequently raising children we do not know or understand, and often dropping the ball in protecting our children's minds in our schools and across social media platforms. Preparation for God to do a new thing often begins with a Word for Rulers and a Word for Family, from Theology and Science. The Prophet of God in our day find themselves in the same place as these two prophets of old (*Elijah and John*)- Speaking to Kings and Rulers about The Family.

The one time of year we celebrate family more than any other is the Advent season, but this is not enough. It is time to

---

[112] For information on "Family Crisis" I recommend studying: "*12 Rules for Life*" by Eugene Peterson.; "*Family Revision*" written by Jeremy Pryor;; "*The Prodigal God*" by Timothy Keller; "*As for Me and My House*" by Walter Wangerin; "*The Family: A Christian Perspective On The Contemporary Home*" by Jack O. Balswick and Judith K. Balswick; Mooney, L. A., Clever, M., & Willigen, M. V. "*Understanding Social Problems (11th ed.)*". Also, search Family and Religion Articles on ncbi.nim. nih.gov and MDPI.com if you are genuinely interested in this topic.

prioritize our children, our brothers, and our sisters, far beyond a few weeks toward the end of each year. It is time to daily hear the call of God from the Prophet of God as we learn again to honor our commitment to family. It is time to extend a major theme of Advent into our hourly lives year-round. Our family of origin, our family in fellowship, and the family of God's children, all need us to heed the words of John in the "Spirit and Power of *Elijah*" - "He must increase, and I (what we desire and believe) must decrease" (John 3:30, parenthesis mine). If we continue down the route of self-fulfillment and personal autonomy primarily, family will end up as a relic of the past, as eventually will be the foundations this nation rests upon. It is not too late, but the cliff is edging closer in America in my view. Family life and our practices therein are at the core of almost all our issues as a nation. If we want to fix our Land, we must first fix our families. This has always been true.

Jason DeParle, writing in *Two Classes, Divided by 'I Do'* says: "While many studies have found that children of single parents are more likely to grow up poor, less is known about their chances of advancement as adults. But there are suggestions that the absence of a father in the house makes it harder for children to climb the economic ladder."[113] It is becoming clear to those who research such things that the family unit, most often made up of a mother and father who are working hard to have a quality marriage, is the environment most conducive to children growing up to become thriving adults. This is not a religious or moral proposition, but simply a fact discovered through research. Families are key, and the presence of an involved father is "key to the key."

Presently, we are highlighting and rewarding the very opposite of this idea. We have circled back once again to the question of Authority. Family is a major God priority. It is becoming less of a priority in our Land. If prophets are to be listened to in our day,

---

[113] Jason Deparle, "Two Classes Divided by 'I do'", July 14, 2012. MYSA. mysaantonio.com

they would need to incorporate the "Spirit and Power of *Elijah*," speaking to those in positions of power about the Authority of God as it relates to the American Family. In the words of one African American father, "When you believe in God . . . yes, the boat still gets to rockin' but [God] says, 'In me you can weather the storm'"[114]

From my Journal: *"Once upon a time I believed myself free from authority. I thought that if I could live as I want to live, without the inconvenience of being told what to do, I could find true happiness and fulfillment. The New World Order had freed me to live as I desired. I did not realize I had simply transformed the meaning of freedom to fit my own self-centered motivations. I thought freedom meant no fences, no constraints, no barriers, and no chains. It was only the consequence of choice that caused me to reassess my paradigm. I discovered that some authority, not all, was put in place for my protection. I discovered that being a child in some things would help me to learn to be an adult in other things. I learned that fences protect me, constraints embrace me, barriers insulate me, and the chains that gripped me were of my own doing. True freedom is not freedom from Authority, but it is the choice to surrender to an Authority which is owed my devotion and my allegiance. Only in surrender can freedom be experienced. And only through surrender of my will to One greater than myself can Truth be found. The question is not will we serve, for we all serve something or someone. The question is - Who or What will we consciously choose to serve."*

---

[114] For Academics, a good starting point for research is Sociology of Religion, Oxford University Press. 2021 Autumn. *"Transmission of Faith in Families: The Influence of Religious Ideology", by Jesse Smith.* Published online 2020 Dec 8. doi: 10.1093/socrel/sraa045.
For those who are curious about this topic you might read Jeremy Pryor, *"Family Revision: Ancient Wisdom to Heal the Modern Family" (2019).* Published by Jeremy Pryor. ISBN: 978-0-578-52612-6

*Each of us chooses to live under the Authority
of Someone or Something. And you?*

(LAUGH WITH ME...)

I knew a fellow named Otto Kahn. He was a very rich man, and his close friend was Marshall P. Wilder, who was a hunchback. They were walking down Fifth Avenue, and they passed a Synagogue. Kahn stopped for a moment and said, "You know, I used to be Jewish." Wilder responded, "Really, I used to be a hunchback." (Groucho Marx)

(Bill Scheft is known to say) "I'm from a very liberal Jewish family. My parents believe in the Ten Commandments, but they believe you can pick five."

Day 15

"Greetings, you who are highly favored" ... Luke 1:28

Setting the Stage: Do you believe in Angels?

IN JUDAISM, CHRISTIANITY, AND ISLAM, GABRIEL IS AN Archangel. Without limiting the power of this Archangel, Gabriel had a particular task we need to take note of in all three of these world religions - "The Messenger" of God's will for human ears to hear and obey. We know *Gab* brought powerful messages to Daniel. And we now hear him bringing great news to both *Elizabeth and Mary*. Gabriel stands in comparison to Michael the Archangel, the Warrior Angel (See Daniel 10). Traditional religions teach that Angels are spiritual creatures which exist in a realm beyond our own but are allowed to assist and communicate with human beings for special purposes. Hebrews 1:14 describes them as "ministering spirits." They have two primary responsibilities within the Christian faith - worshipping God at God's throne (See Isaiah 6 and Revelation 4 for two examples) and taking care of human beings when God's plan is at stake (See 2 Kings 6 for one example). They are the invisible army of God that sometimes becomes visible. In the Bible alone there are 108 references to angels in the Old Testament and 165 references to them in the New Testament, and the entire Bible contains 273 references to angels.[115]

---

[115] *"How Do We Know That Angels Are Real?"* Written by Glory Dy, content creator for Christianity.com. Posted on April 8, 2022. Fact checking: Salem Web Network.

For over three millennia the people who practiced the faith attributed to Abraham (3 world religions) have wholeheartedly embraced a belief in the existence of Angels.

My mother used to teach me that each of us has a Guardian Angel. If so, I certainly hope it's the Soul of my dog Sassy. Or my sister. We can stretch this out for sure. However, humans do not become angels inside any Biblical evidence I can find. Or dogs. Therefore, Guardian Angels are speculation at best. There are times when Angels intervene, so it is highly likely they have come to our aid a few times, maybe more. I am certain this has happened in my life during some very sticky moments.

"Ministering Spirits" had a huge role in the Advent Story, and they are quite excited about the event in Luke's telling of the Story. Luke told us what is at top of mind on this day as the Angels proclaim in Unison: "Glory to God in the highest, and on earth peace to those on whom God's favor rests" (Luke 2:14). A huge host of Angels celebrated the birth of Jesus. And the Shepherds could see. Who would settle for a single Guardian Angel when the likelihood is a multitude comes to our side when needed the most? They seem to delight in ministering to human beings. Luke did not hesitate to introduce us to the transcendent Truth we come to know because of Advent.

Whether we believe in Angels is already determined for us, depending on the worldview we ascribe to. I will introduce you to four primary worldviews a bit later, but even as I do you will not instantly recognize the one which describes your worldview. This is because few of us have taken the time to investigate why we believe what we believe, to test the consistency and the foundation of our thinking. Luke spoke to us from a *Monotheistic Perspective*, which means he was open to the possibility of Angelic Visitation.

For additional information on the topic of Angels please consult *"Best Books About Angels [Top 10]"* [Update 2023]. Posted by Rubin Alaie. https://happyrubin.com/book-lists/best-books-about-angels/

For Luke, this event was part of his reality. For many today, it would not be, and the only choice they have left would be to read this story as a Myth. My hope is that upon reading this book you will at least be finding yourself ready to challenge the boundaries of your own thinking, willing to open yourself to alternative ways to see the world and trusting Luke's effort enough to explore the possibilities of what he left for us to read. Luke wholeheartedly believed what he wrote. For this reason alone, it is well worth our time and consideration, notwithstanding his brilliance in doing so. His is a "Timeless Script" indeed.

"You who are highly favored" … Luke 1:28

What does it mean to be "highly favored"? I have often been curious about this greeting from the Angel *Gabriel* to Mary. *Gabriel (Gab)* wanted her to know this, to have her understand that God's blessing rested upon her in a way that was extremely specific and quite unusual. My mind is set to wondering – "was she better than other women, was her genetic make-up somehow superior, was her family line prominent, did her mother teach her stuff that normal women do not learn, was she more equipped for the suffering she would go through, was it all or none of these"? I wish I could interview Mary, which Luke no doubt had done. I would have a few questions for her: "What did *Gabriel* look like? Was there ever a time you thought it was all one big hallucination? When you tried to explain this to your mom, did she call the local 1st century Shrink to your house? Did Jesus ever look lost in thought when making or eating bread? Did you ever think you caught him in a lie only to find out later you were WAY OUT OF LINE? Did you ever offer thanks to him before a meal? Did he have your eyes, or His Father's eyes?" I could easily overwhelm this page with my questions.

However, Mary was not "Highly Favored" because of herself, but because of her Child. I understand this will not sit well with some of you, for Mary has been a hero of faith for longer than we can remember. For those of you who are doubting me at this point, please consider. She was the "Highly Favored one," not because she was perfect, but because she was chosen. A servant of God, a child of God, just like anyone who has been adopted into her Son's family. It was the blessing of God that rested upon her. No matter whom God had chosen, it would take a special over shadowing of God's Blessing and God's Grace to prepare His mother for what was to follow. I have no doubt that Mary was special indeed, that she was especially prepared and equipped for what was to follow. But the Living Atonement that was to be carried in her womb was the sole reason for her blessedness, the sole basis of her favor. It was not "a something" in Mary; it was "the something" in Her Son - God's Son. She was to be the vessel from which all blessings would flow. She was to carry the very heart and hands and feet and eyes and mouth and love of God inside her body, and the blessing that flowed from her womb would overcome any shortcoming inside of Mary. The favor is from God, and God places it upon Mary, just as God now places favor and blessing on all of us who receive her Son (And in some way, upon those who do not).

There are two times in the New Testament that this word for "highly favored" *(caritovw* in Greek or transliterated as *charitoo)* is used. The first one, of course, is here, as *Gab* wanted Mary to understand that God's grace is upon her in abundance. The second is found in Ephesians 1:6: "His glorious grace.... which He has freely given us." His "glorious grace" is the same Greek word used for "highly favored" in reference to Mary. Paul, Luke's traveling companion, wholeheartedly believed that the same "highly favored" blessing that Mary received is also placed upon people when God's grace is given through Jesus Christ. From this we can deduce - The highest form of favor came to Mary as God graciously chose her to be the mother of the Messiah. In addition, this same "highest favor" rests upon the entire family of God as

God invites us to become part of the family of God and blesses us through the same Child placed inside Mary's womb with the same *charitoo* that Mary received. Jesus was God's gift to Mary, a vivid sign of God's grace at work in her life. Jesus is God's gift to us, the most vivid sign of God's grace extended to those who believe.

So, why was Mary able to hear, but so often we are not able to hear how "Highly Favored" we are? Imagine two men are walking through the crowded streets of a city bustling with activity around Christmas time. So much noise, as a young man walks with his father during the dad's first visit off the farm to his son's new home. As they walk together dad stops suddenly and tunes his ear to a sound on the street. Mind you, there are cars screeching, people laughing, songs playing, children crying, parents scolding, salespeople working and the like. He walks over to a rock on the sidewalk, lifts the rock, and out pops a cricket this farmer dad had been hearing. The son is amazed. "Dad, how in the world did you hear this?" "Son, it's all about what we have been conditioned to listen for. Are you so far from the farm you have forgotten? I'll show you." Dad pulls from his pocket a handful of coins and drops them on the street where they stand. The same noisy street. Every head turns, every eye is focused on the sound of these coins. "You see son, we hear what we are listening for." Listen for the sounds of Advent: Mary and me and you - *The Highly Favored Ones*...........[116]

---

[116] χαριτόω (from *xárisma*, "grace," see there) – properly, highly-*favored* because receptive to God's *grace*. (*xaritóō*) is used twice in the NT (Lk 1:28 and Eph 1:6), both times of God *extending Himself* to *freely* bestow grace (*favor*). This note is taken from Strong Concordance reference number 5487, 2021 from Discovery Bible, listed on "biblehub.com".

"Every time we love, every time we give,
it's Christmas." (Dale Evans)

"If Christmas is just a nice legend, in a sense you
are on your own. But if Christmas is true, then
you can be saved by grace." (Timothy Keller)

"Ironically, our culture's rejection of absolute truth is stroking
an unprecedented hunger for truth." (Tullian Tchividjian)

"The Christian church testifies that in the actual
events of this finite, contingent, and yet rational world
of warped space-time there are words and gestures
through which the Creator and Sustainer of the world
has spoken and acted."[117] (Leslie Newbigin)

---

[117] Leslie Newbigin, "Foolishness to Greeks," page 88

Interlude

A Postmodern Gift to our understanding of Advent

*"Freedom of speech is not just another principle, it is the
mechanism by which we keep our psyches and our societies
organized and we have to be unbelievably careful about
infringing upon that because we are infringing upon the
process by which we keep chaos and order balanced and
if chaos and order go out of balance then all hell breaks
loose and the situation is not good." (Jordan Peterson)[118]*

ONE OF THE BARRIERS THAT WAS PLACED BEFORE CHRISTIANITY,
and religion per say, was the belief within the *Modern Naturalistic
Worldview* that truth can only be discovered through the Scientific
Method. However, faith is dependent upon subjective and
objective reality. Those who wish to dismiss the subjective when
discovering Truth are dismissing the heart and soul of religious
belief. In a culture which often embraces the idea that answers
about the nature of things are discovered via science only, the most
important mechanism of faith is dismissed before the conversation
even begins. A bit like pushing Trump off the ballot in Colorado,
ensuring people *cannot even think about* moving in his direction at
the ballot box. Pure and simple, both above are mechanisms used

---

[118] "Jordan Peterson on Freedom of Speech," Jordan Peterson, 2017. A quote from
Conversational Leadership, an online book by David Gurteen: https://conversational-
leadership.net/video/video-jordan-peterson-on-freedom-of-speech/

to restrict people from thinking in ways that differ from those who believe they are entitled to restrict such things. Often such a view of reality "pinches the possibilities" that religion, philosophy, and traditional thought opens to us. This is the very heart of Jordan Peterson's claims about restricting speech on college campuses. In his view, restricting speech is to restrict thought and dismiss freedom altogether. The result is major harm to our search for Truth and for Society in general. If I can effectively dismiss your right to speak in ways that contradict my version of reality, then I can control the way you think. When it comes to Truth this is precisely what many in political and scientific communities attempt to do. If we can relegate the discussion to the arena of facts, as defined by those holding the cards (scientists and politicians), then we can effectively control what you believe about that which is "true" moving forward. "Away with your open Universe, you religious types! We declare the facts – The Universe is Closed! There is no room for God in our Laboratories. There is no place for Theology in our conversations. We will control the thinking of future students by making sure they are not exposed to your inappropriate words in our classrooms, determined of course by us."

This commitment to a closed universe is usually determined by an elite person or group who believes they have the power to suppress truth through objective declaration and a denial of subjective possibilities on the part of less sophisticated and less educated individuals. (Never mind that this belief itself is very subjective.) The *postmodern* worldview cleared the path for pushback against this "pinching of possibility" that *Naturalism* mandated. It must be noted, however, that a commitment to believing truth only comes through scientific research, what the *Naturalist* calls "facts" as opposed to "values," is in truth an act of faith. *The Naturalist* cannot prove there are no values which are in fact "facts." It is simply assumed. It is a faith commitment based on their interpretation of the evidence. In fact, "No-one seriously believes we can observe life with no preconceptions."[119]

An important gift of *Postmodernism* is the door provided to escape the chains wrapped around us by a complete surrender to the Scientific Method. Our minds are open for business once again, free to explore and ask questions about the spiritual and the transcendent. But this does not justify the dismissal of rational thinking and evidence-based belief systems. *Postmodernism* ideologues would have us embrace the idea that any idea is a promising idea if it is sincerely held. Though we can certainly celebrate a revival of the power of autonomous belief and the courage on display in expressing personal preference, we cannot simply allow personal preference to define Reality. True faith is never blind faith. We still need to question the facts and follow the evidence, even if the evidence is of a type we are not accustomed to. That which we call "spiritual" cannot be void of evidence and consistency. We must allow meaningful exchange of ideas as we explore that which is real. We need to find commonalities, search for evidence, ask the right questions, open doors to the traditional and new ways of thinking, all in the name of trying to discern if what we believe is, in fact, "True Truth."[120] (In case you have yet to notice, this is exactly what I am attempting to do in this book as we explore Luke's magnificent Gospel).

A "necessary" question to ask in the 21st century would be: *How does the believer know that Christianity is true?* "In 2022, around 31.6 percent of the global population identified as Christian. Around 25.8 percent of the global population identified as Muslim, followed by 15.1 percent of global populations which identified as

---

[119] Earl Babbie, "The Practice of Social Research, E 14", 2016. Cengage Learning, Boston MA. Page 133.

[120] I will suggest again a groundbreaking discussion of the concept of "True Truth", written by my good friend Dr. Art Lindsey, "True Truth: Defending Absolute Truth in a Relativistic World, 2004. IVP Books, Illustrated Edition.

Hindu."[121] My question above is specific and should encourage an important discussion. Given that Christianity has survived the worldview challenges presented by both *Naturalism* and *Humanism*, this question warrants discussion on the global stage. The *postmodern* mind may attempt to redefine the environment in which we discuss this question, but the discussion must take place none-the-less, according to this worldview. From a *Monotheistic Perspective*, which emphasizes a commitment to spiritual reality, the answer I might give goes something like - "We know Christ is real because of the self-authenticating witness of God's Spirit and because of the trust we place in the credibility of the Biblical account of past events."[122] The Spirit is the primary mechanism of assurance, followed closely by a reasonable investigation of the suppositions of our Faith, the latter being complimentary to the former. Spiritual transformation is of primary importance.

There are some things in life that simply cannot be described adequately short of the actual experience of said thing. Most *postmoderns* believe this, for they will always emphasize experience over and above theory. For example, describing the inner witness of the Spirit of God is kind of like describing what it's like to hit a game winning home run to a person who has never hit a game winning home run, or what a chocolate brownie tastes like if you have never had one, or describing biscuits and gravy for breakfast to a person who knows nothing of gravy, or describing what it's like to be a bride to one who has never been a bride, or feeling the love of your own child though you never had a child. Some things cannot be comprehended without having the experience. Advent is about a *Transcendent Metaphysical Reality becoming*

---

[121] Share of global population affiliated with major religious groups in 2022, Published by
Einar H. Dyvik, Oct 13, 2023. Statistica, 2024. Statistica.com
[122] For a fantastic discussion of the role of the Holy Spirit within the concept of Faith see especially: William Lane Craig, "Reasonable Faith: Christian Truth and Apologetics", E-3, 2008. Crossway Books, Wheaton, IL. Chapter 1.

Existential Experience through the undeniable activity of God's Spirit, in the world and in our lives. There is no experience that can substitute for this experience and there is no way to acknowledge the result of this experience without having it in the first place. This is not circular reasoning, for we can easily establish that some things need to be experienced to be understood (see above). I can account for evidence for faith all day long, but none of this means anything without the affirming presence of God's Spirit to validate the reality of the Living Christ in our own heart and psyche. Once we know, we know. And if we have never known, we simply cannot know until we know. It is impossible to persuade a person into this experience. We might be able to provide the address (Luke's Gospel) and we might be able to open the door (The Advent of God through Jesus), but we cannot walk through the door of the address provided for another person. And we cannot describe the experience of walking through this door adequately enough to persuade them. In this decision, each person stands alone with their own choice to make, and not making a choice is a choice. Adversely for many, this choice always involves a degree of surrender to a possibility beyond what science can acknowledge.

This Holy Spirit, Who is described as "overshadowing" Mary in Luke 1:35, is the same Holy Spirit that John wrote about when he repeated these words of Jesus: "But the Counselor, the Holy Spirit, whom the Father will send in my name, will teach you all things, and bring to your remembrance all that I have said to you" (John 14:26). In addition, this is the same Holy Spirit Luke mentioned in his second volume, Acts 1:8, as he described how the disciples will be empowered to witness throughout the Roman Empire. This is the same Spirit of God that Paul described when he wrote about the connection between Spirit and Life: "You, however, are not in the realm of the flesh but are in the realm of the Spirit, if indeed the Spirit of God lives in you. And if anyone does not have the Spirit of Christ, they do not belong to Christ. But if Christ is in you, then even though your body is subject to death because of sin, the Spirit gives life because of (His) righteousness. And if the Spirit of him who raised Jesus from the dead is living in you, he who raised Christ from the dead will also give life to your mortal bodies because of his Spirit who lives in you" (Romans 8: 9-11). You see it, right? This is a "if then" phenomenon.

In plain language, we can discuss Jesus in the 3rd person all day long, just as we might discuss any person behind his back believing we capture the essence of the person we discuss. However, the discussion always falls short of the presence of this person at the moment of our conversation. And even this would fall short of living with this person. Being with this person is always superior to our 3rd person discussions about this person. This is the role of the Holy Spirit, for this is the Person of Jesus in our midst. The Holy Spirit is Jesus entering the room as we discuss Him, entering the conversation in our hearts and minds in the 1st Person Triune. This is the transcendent mystery of the Gospel. The Advent Miracle enters our life each day through the Person of the Holy Spirit, and the miracle of Advent becomes our story as well, as we are transferred into the actual Life and Mind of Jesus Himself – *God with Us*. The Holy Spirit is the Person who makes the Gospel of Luke a "Timeless Script."

There are countless examples of the role of the Holy Spirit highlighted in the pages of the Bible. I can make no apology for the belief that the Holy Spirit is the mechanism by which God draws people to GodSelf. The thinking person would understand this necessity, seeing that we are speaking of a Being Who is not limited by or confined to the 4 dimensions of our creation. It would be like human beings introducing themself to the two-dimensional beings that exist on our computer screen. We need an "in," a mechanism by which we can communicate with beings that cannot grasp our four-dimensional reality, simply because they are who they are - two dimensional creatures. The Holy Spirit bridges this gap, "hovers" within our space (Genesis 1:1), can enter our being (Genesis 2:7), and by this way alone can God's Spirit testify to our spirit that we are now a part of God's family. Just as family is both an objective and subjective reality in this world, entering God's family is a subjective experience before objectively realized in God's family as well. A baby subjectively understands the special connection they have with Mom and Dad before they ever understand how this connection is defined and maintained. The human child is embraced by the spirit of the family, beginning with Mom. The child of God is embraced by the Spirit of God, and this before objective proof for faith is validated. The objective truth alone will never convince the child of God, just as an absentee biological dad will never be embraced as "father." Without subjective reality, research means extraordinarily little when it comes to religious faith. Unfortunately, much of the scientific community is in denial of vast amounts of evidence before ever considering this evidence.

Now the "catch 22," for lack of a better term to describe it. One must first believe, connect with God in what we might call the Soul (*Psyche* in Greek), to be able to truly experience the reality of The Living Christ. This is a Spiritual Connection. At one level this makes perfect sense, for why would we expect to embrace (or be embraced by) a Transcendent Being based on research in a "human laboratory" alone? One would expect that an Eternal Being surpassing our comprehension would have to become apparent to us in ways that transcend human experience and measurement devices. The instant that the scientist denies the possibility of God simply by making claim to a system which has no room for God is the instant that science stops doing science. Science was born out of a belief in God. Science was the natural consequence of the exploration and understanding of Creation. The beginning of the scientific journey never excluded faith, it simply tried to compliment what we call "revelation." The Advent

Story is a unique Event with religious relevance validated by early scientific investigative skills. Believing in The Spiritual does not dismiss the importance of scientific inquiry. But the incredible task of scientific inquiry does not disprove Spiritual Reality.

John B. Haught authored a book called "Science and Faith: A New Introduction."[123] In his first chapter he proposed three separate ways of considering the relationship between science and faith. First, *The Conflict Position*, whereby science has made all religious claims untenable and unbelievable. Second, he identified what he calls *The Contrast Position*, whereby there is a claim that science and religion are not in competition, and therefore cannot be viewed as viewpoints opposed to one another. At the end of knowledge, they must exist in harmony. (Once again, a pre-supposition.)

The third system is what he called *The Convergence Approach*. In this system of thought science and religion are in a conversation, working in cooperation with one another to investigate and discover truth claims. Science and Religion are two distinct ways of investigating the same Reality. This is a bit like what we find in the story of Joseph in the book of Genesis (chapters 37-50). Joseph, sold into slavery by his brothers, had both a subjective and an objective reason to despise his brothers and cry out for justice. The events that truly happened to him are events that make for a great tragedy in Hollywood. However, he did not consider objective reality alone. Joseph believed that God was using the circumstances and experiences of his life to write a miraculous history in the life of his brothers, who became the twelve tribes of Israel.

As it turns out, he was correct. Actual human events, often horrific events, were the very mechanism used by God to preserve the nation of Israel. This was *Convergence* in historic detail. Many, including this author, believe that Science and Faith converge

---

[123] John R. Haught, "Science and Faith: A New Introduction" (Paperback), January 2, 2013. Published by Paulist Press, Mahwah, New Jersey. www.paulistpress.com

with one another and work together to tell the same story, the history of God's "relationship with humanity." This was Luke's worldview. It is also mine. Science is just as dependent upon unproven assumptions as what we find in theological discussions. These assumptions may not be as obvious, but they are certainly there. Even as I type these words, I have just finished reading an article about an observation revealing the universe is expanding at different speeds depending on where we look and measure. If true, Cosmology could be shaken to the core with this discovery. Science is a search for truth based on less-than-certain commitments, just like faith. For this reason, I presently embrace *The Convergence Approach* as I attempt to understand Luke's Gospel Narrative.

The Monotheistic Worldview will include the knowledge brought by science into theological conversations, in fact, will welcome the scientific voice; but will never embrace the idea that Truth might not transcend scientific inquiry. However, *The Naturalist* will always dismiss the Theologian as not relevant in their search for Truth. Therefore, a virgin birth, which I am about to discuss, can never be more than a metaphor for *The Naturalist,* no matter the historical evidence we find. According to *The Naturalist,* history is not allowed to contradict science. During this period of *postmodern* pushback, scientists are beginning to expand their thinking. In fact, one prominent Social Scientist says it thusly: "Our research would have shown that their (speaking of researchers of "genocide") is not single answer to the question. That alone represents an advance in our understanding of reality."[124] He refers to such research as a "more sophisticated understanding" of the phenomena being researched.

Two prime examples of what I am discussing have happened in recent days. First, America witnessed a Total Solar Eclipse in 2024, the first since 2017. I witnessed the 2017 event, and there was one

---

[124] Earl Babbie, "The Practice of Social Research, E 14", 2016. Cengage Learning, Boston MA. Page 131,

thing about the eclipse that took me to a place beyond AWE. Of course, I was struck by the utter darkness, the silence of the birds, the glow of the Sun's corona around the edges of the Moon, the sheer other worldly subjective experience of an event set in motion since the creation of the Solar System. But it was the perfection of the moment which grabbed me most. If you have seen one, you may know what I am speaking of. The Moon fit exactly inside the Sun. The Size of the two heavenly bodies and the distance between them set up for Earth observers to see the Moon and the Sun fit together perfectly, leaving only the Sun's corona for us to observe. This fit is so perfect that we can look toward the event without eye protection, for the Moon is our protection, though we never lost sight of the remnants of the Sun directly behind the Moon. It is a Cosmic Miracle. This cannot be an accident. This vision is put there for Earth dwellers to see, as if the Creator of the Universe is writing a Silent Song for all of us to learn and dance to. Those of you who believe this an exceptional coincidence require more faith to believe this than it takes for me to believe a Creator is painting this Cosmic Portrait for us to enjoy.

The second example was on display during the recent Covid Pandemic. The beauty of a natural event like an Eclipse is tragically matched by the horrors of the Covid Pandemic. I lost two beloved family members to this Virus. Many of you share in this experience of loss. Friends. Family. Familiar Faces. No longer with us because of a Pandemic we did not anticipate or prepare for. In those early days we looked to science and faith. We had nowhere else to go. We prayed for a vaccine, faith and science working together to find a solution. But even as answers were proclaimed by those in charge, people continued to die. Some countries protected the elderly and the vulnerable, not even closing their schools. Other nations closed every door and quarantined every symptomatic person. States within our Union took different strategies, all claiming scientific reasons for doing so. Meanwhile, we developed Tests and two

Vaccines at a record pace. One day we are told the Vaccine is ready. Next, we are told the Vaccine would stop the spread. But people continued to die. Then we were told that the Vaccine cannot control the spread, but it will save lives. Then we are told that children are not susceptible, but they should be vaccinated anyway. Next, we are told that the vaccinated are also dying. Presently, scientists are still debating the evidence, trying to learn what is true and what is not true. The bottom line, we got much wrong, both scientifically and politically, beginning with the science and the politics that birthed the Virus to begin with. My desire for each of us, theologian or scientist, is to open our minds to the fact that we got much wrong, and still do. Science often creates more questions than answers and we must open ourselves to Truth that does not come from the Laboratories we have learned to blindly trust.

How do we decide on the truth? Twentieth Century philosopher Sir Karl Popper felt the deepest reason for the fallibility of humans is our constant search for truth.[125] Popper argued that we cannot entertain finding absolute or certain truths, only repeated tests. "Knowledge consists in the search for truth…. It is not the search for certainty."[126] It is striking to me that one of the results of twentieth century postmodern thought is the belief that science does not have all the answers. We are left with a shared question - *Who should we trust?* Who has the best chance of offering us Truth? Science was given this mantle in the late 19th century. However, the 21st century is pushing back. Whether we believe the answers come from Science, Faith, or a unique combination of both, we are at least beginning to understand that we are talking about an

---

[125] Wired to Doubt: Why People Fear Vaccines and Climate Change and Mistrust Science, Geoffrey P. Dobson, Review Article, January 28, 2022. Frontiers, frontiers.org.

[126] Dobson GP, A chaos of Delight: Science Religion and Myth and the Shaping of Western Thought, 1st Edition, 2016. Routledge: London.

issue of *Trust.* "Who do we trust?" is another way of asking "How do we decide on Truth?"

We cannot hold onto religious beliefs that have no basis or objective foundation to build our knowledge from. Of course not. However, we cannot rule out religious beliefs simply because they have no basis in *The Naturalistic Worldview,* for this would mean we are assuming there is no other way to understand Reality itself. It is not rational to close out the exploration of possibilities beyond scientific thought, if in fact the search for Truth is our primary goal, no matter where this search might take us. Without such an understanding of an objective convergence between science and faith, the description of *The Virgin Birth* which follows will fall on deaf ears and closed minds. I am hopeful of more from you, for this purpose Luke wrote.

"The ability to understand and embrace the Virgin Birth of Jesus requires an openness to the spiritual and the transcendent that the 20th century scientist worked to root out of each of us." (From the Journal of Dr. Rick Farmer)

"Archaeology has in many cases refuted the views of modern critics. It has been shown in a number of instances that these views rest on false assumptions and unreal, artificial schemes of historical development...." And "The excessive skepticism of many liberal theologians stems not from a careful evaluation of the available data, but from an enormous predisposition against the supernatural.[127] (Millar Burrows)

"By attempting to exclude supernatural explanations from scientific consideration, these *Naturalists* demonstrate a bias equal to that of young-earth and IDM (Intelligent Design Model)

---

[127] The quote is a direct statement from outstanding Yale professor Millar Burrows as cited in Josh McDowell, *Evidence that Demands a Verdict,* 1972. Arrowhead Springs, CA: Campus Crusade for Christ, p. 66.

proponents. They insist the natural realm has no Creator. They assume a priori that an atheistic perspective is the only possible basis for doing scientific research and education." (Hugh Ross)

"If in fact there is a Creator, as much scientific, theological, and philosophical evidence seems to favor, and if this Creator had the ability to create *something from nothing*, what is the big deal about *A Virgin Birth?*" (Rick Farmer)

Day 16

The Virgin is with Child ...Luke 1:35

Setting the Stage: God's Best Idea is Mom

"MOTHERHOOD WAS AN EXPECTATION FOR ALL FEMALES IN THE Greco-Roman world, regardless of their social class. Yet, only free women were culturally acknowledged as true mothers and matrons."[128] One of the key comparisons made in the 1st century Greco-Roman culture was the comparison between male and female. Does it surprise us that the male was considered complete, while the female (and all things deemed feminine) was dubbed inferior, especially if they did not culturally succeed in terms of marriage and bearing children? Roman women were free, which meant they had opportunity to raise and instruct their children and were held in even higher esteem if they nursed their children as well. Non-free women were usually slaves, and therefore could not own property or give birth to "legitimate children," but simply could add to the number of slaves by becoming a biological mother. Though slaves would often serve as "wet nurses" and often raised more children than they bore, it was in service to others rather than service to the children or their own families.

Jewish women in the 1st century also highly valued motherhood and were defined in Jewish Culture by marriage and childbirth as

---

[128] *"Motherhood in the Greco-Roman World"* by Alicia D. Myers (2023). Bible Odyssey. BibleOdyssey.org

well. However, the value of women in Jewish Culture far exceeded that of the Greco-Roman tradition. Women were viewed as created in the "image of God" (Genesis 1:27), and therefore equal in value to men. This was an imputed creational norm, which is not embraced by every culture. However, equality of sexes in Jewish society has always been the goal to which they aspired. "The role of women in traditional Judaism was not as lowly as many have understood; in fact, in many ways, the position of women in Jewish law that dates to the biblical period was better than the position of women under American civil law as recently as a century ago. Those ancient ladies had the right to buy, sell, own property, and make their own contracts, rights which women in some Western countries did not have until the early- to mid-20th century. From earliest biblical times, Jewish women have stood shoulder-to-shoulder with their male counterparts in times of feast and famine, peace and war, comfort and persecution."[129]

For example, the woman in Proverbs 31, a much-dreaded text by radical feminists, owned both a vineyard and a garment business"[130] She was a businessperson, a working mother, wife, and volunteer rolled into one woman. I once had an ultra-conservative friend in the church specifically tell me that my wife was living an anti-Christian existence because she worked as a full-time teacher. I pointed out to him that Old Testament women were full time workers, often solely responsible for the household franchise and certainly the primary agent of teaching young daughters how to serve the family business. Every person in the family contributed to the livelihood of the family. What he was referencing was the postindustrial family, where mother remained in the home and raised the children while father earned the paycheck. No such family existed in ancient Israel. All worked, father, mother,

---

[129] *"Mary: A First-century Jewish Woman"* (2023), Rev. Cheryl L. Hauer International Development Director. Bridges For Peace, BridgesForPeace.com
[130] Once again, see Mary Poplin, "Is Reality Secular?", chapter 27

children, and extended family. And they all contributed to the financial stability of the family. There was no dichotomy of innovation and responsibility in Israel. Though such distinctions existed in Greek and Roman culture, they did not adapt these habits from Hebrew Culture, for in Israel the family that lived together worked together. Women were an especially important and intricate piece of the overall survival and wealth of the family.

The Virgin is with Child.......

Western Culture highly values scientific knowledge and achievement. It is exceedingly difficult for us to buy into things that defy the laws of physics or contradict our scientific understanding of the known world. So, when we deal with claims like *The Virgin Birth* there are many who balk at Dr. Luke's testimony. I have mentioned Luke discussed these things with Mary during his investigation of the facts. Why wouldn't he? He certainly had access to her. He spent at least two years with Paul around the Jerusalem area while Paul was kept under guard in Caesarea, which was a mere 70 miles from Jerusalem. While there, Luke, Paul's traveling companion, would have remained to minister to his needs. We read about Paul's travails in Acts 22 and 23, and most certainly Luke was with him this entire time. This would have left Luke considerable amounts of time in and around Jerusalem to do his investigative work, which would have included interviews with some key witnesses. Luke told us this in the first lines of his Gospel. Mary would certainly have been one of these witnesses. We can discern from Luke's writing style, his propensity to validate facts and pinpoint history, and from his desire to accurately represent details, a systematic and scientific approach to his Gospel. This being the case, how in the world could Dr. Luke have adopted a belief in a *Virgin Birth?*[131]

Some would say that *The Virgin Birth* goes too far, that we cannot embrace something as fact that never occurred before (or since). Others insist that other virgin births are scattered throughout history. Although virgin births were sometimes connected to gods and major leaders and kings in ancient religions, there was only one such event that was predicted hundreds of years before the birth occurred. In other words, the virgin conception was not only a historically witnessed event recorded by Luke in his Gospel, but it was anticipated and predicted in several Old Testament passages:

---

[131] In the Hebrew Language *virgin* is highlighted using two different words: 1. The Hebrew word ʿalmāh refers to a "young woman of childbearing age". This is the probably the Hebrew word Luke is transliterating in his description of Mary. It must be noted that this word literally means "young maiden", most often a reference to a young unmarried girl. Luke uses the Greek equivalent, which is παρθένος or *parthenos,* meaning "virgin". 2. The purest word in Hebrew for "virgin" is *betulah,* which is used most often in the Old Testament. However, it is quite clear from the context of Luke's Gospel that the *alma* of Isaiah 7:14 is being transliterated as *virgin* in Luke 1:35. For a great discussion of these two terms see: Arthur W. Kac, *The Messianic Hope: A Divine Solution for the Human Problem,* 1975. Baker Book House, Grand Rapids MI, chapter 2.

Genesis 3:15,16, Isaiah 7:14, and then amplified by Pauls' words in Galatians 3:15.

For those who are skeptical of the possibility of a virgin birth, consider this. There was a time when no human had flown. There was a time when no human foot had ever stepped onto the moon. There was a time when near death experiences were undocumented. There was a time when no child had been born outside the womb. There was a time when the Cubs could not win a world series. There was a time when not one person would believe in a Resurrection from the dead, much less such an event being witnessed by more than 500 people. There was a time when the Universe had not yet been born, yet here we are. Believing a thing is not possible does not mean a thing is not possible. Miracles are nothing more than possibilities that cannot be explained by our present level of knowledge. But we live in four dimensions of reality only, whereas some physicists theorize there are at least eleven dimensions of reality to one day discover.[132] What if "Virgin Birth" is a possibility attached to dimensions beyond our own present reality, and God can invade our existence from beyond our existence?

The point here being - Things that human beings once thought impossible do become possible. Is it unwise to believe that we will accomplish a complete understanding of reality through the Scientific Method alone? This is one of the major contributions of our *Post-Modern Age* - science is not the end of inquiry. All these miracles are interpreted differently depending on our world view, which we discuss in more detail on another day. For now, let it suffice to say that the *Scientific Worldview* is not the end of the matter, but a single paradigm for understanding reality. The open-minded knowledge seeker is willing to consider possibilities entertained by other worldviews, which opens for us many

---

[132] For one example of such a theory: 11 Dimension, Robert Sheldon. Tech Target, What is? Techtarget.com

possibilities when exploring various issues, including the open womb. If of course we are open to such open-minded exploration. (I love the word "open"). The important thing to know at this point is that a *Monotheist Worldview* incorporates and integrates knowledge from all other worldviews, tested of course through theological reflection and Biblical authority. Other worldviews are not so integrated and are often closed when it comes to ideas outside their adopted principles. Monotheism is the most open to integration of new knowledge, for we are trying to understand an infinite number of possibilities flowing from an Eternal Being.

Consider the greatest miracle of all – Life! Once there was *nothing*. Now there is *something*. For a Creator who can bring something from nothing, why all this fuss about a Virgin conception? I once heard this question during a philosophy course: "If there was ever a time when nothing existed, what would exist today?" The answer is obvious. There would be *nothing*, for *something* cannot come from *nothing*.[133] There must be an Eternal Something, or Someone. Would we not expect that if The Eternal God were to become human this would come about in an abnormal or non-ordinary way? Even a miraculous way? Especially considering all this "Seed" came to earth to accomplish.

Genesis 3:15 announces that the Enemy of God will one day be destroyed by "the Seed of the Woman." This phrase, *Seed of the Woman (Seed* is masculine singular in the Hebrew Text), is explained in detail by Paul in Galatians 4: 4,5: "But when the time had fully come, God sent God's Son, born of a woman, born under Law, to redeem those under Law, that we might receive the full rights of children." Paul thoroughly believed the Old Testament narrative pointed to a singular person, coming from a

---

[133] For further study on the philosophical arguments for the existence of God as Eternal Creator of all things see: Internet Encyclopedia of Philosophy: *"Western Concepts of God". Article authored by Brian Morley. This is a Peer Reviewed Site.* https://iep.utm.edu/god-west

future woman, who would obliterate the Serpent who had deceived Eve. The fantastic imagery of this event is recorded in Revelation 12. Metaphor or not, there is no denying that Paul understood Genesis 3:15 as a reference to and prediction of the Virgin Birth of Jesus. Genesis 3:15 was an obvious diversion from the typical way of referring to children in the Old Testament Text, for children were always referred to as the "seed of the man" (See for example Jeremiah 31:27 and Genesis 38:8 for two examples). The Warrior King, the Child who destroys evil, the birth which will overcome the mistakes of our first parents, according to Genesis 3:15, will come from "Woman" and "Woman" only, as her "Seed." Not women (plural), but a specific Woman, will bare *The Seed* (1st person singular).

Remarkable. God made us aware of how we might recognize this Child thousands of years before it happens, so we might not miss this Child upon arrival. Those who read this in Genesis would no doubt have sent it to the editors for correction, had it been written in our time. But Genesis declared that which it intended to declare, to be clearly understood in future generations - "The Seed of the Woman." Our adoption into God's Family is linked to *The Virgin Birth.* It is one thing for Luke to relay the story of *The Virgin Birth.* It is quite another thing to relay this story and have this miracle predicted hundreds of years before it occurs.

Luke, who wrote to a non-Jewish audience, did not emphasize this type of prophecy, but he did accurately record the event. There is little doubt that *The Virgin Birth* of Jesus led to incredible suffering for both Mary and Jesus. There is little doubt that few would have believed such a report, and that Jesus would have been seen as a child born from what appeared to her community as immoral circumstances. Yet, Mary bore witness. Her husband Joseph embraced them both. And Luke reported a truth which could only point to the activity of our Creator.

As I mentioned, a scientific worldview does not easily allow room for such a miraculous conception. *The Virgin Birth* tests the limits of our understanding of reality. But this is only true if we live in a closed universe. The possibility of *The Virgin Birth* is a likely event if God is God and unfolded within a Universe created by God. I would suggest that such a miracle would make perfect sense in a Universe created by God. If God genuinely wanted to come to us as One of us, why would God do this in an ordinary way? If God genuinely wanted to come to us as One of us, why would God not want to transmit God's own Personhood into the human God becomes? If God genuinely wanted to come to us as One of us, would God not want us to recognize God the human upon arrival? *The Virgin Birth* accomplishes all of these - A miracle to announce His coming to family and eventual followers; A Father that transcends Humanity just as Moses and Isaiah predicted; A continuation of the intimate connection with the Father that Jesus had always enjoyed before He was born as Jesus. *The Virgin Birth* makes perfect sense, if in fact Jesus is the Son of God. For if Jesus is the Son of God, as Luke claimed Him to be, why would we expect anything less than a miracle from conception forward? Though Science cannot explain it, faith can, and so did Luke.

> "If Christmas is just a nice legend, in a sense you are on your own. But if Christmas is true, then you can be saved by grace." (Timothy Keller)

> "He who has not Christmas in his heart will never find it under a tree." (Roy L. Smith)

> "Our Generation is crying out for something different, something higher, something beyond this world." (Tullian Tchividjian)

Day 17

"He will reign over Jacob's descendants forever" .... Luke 1:33.

Setting the Stage: The New Temple of God

AT THE TIME OF JESUS' BIRTH THERE ARE ONLY TWO IDENTIFIABLE thriving tribes in Israel - Judah and Benjamin. In Genesis 49 Jacob outlined a fate for his sons. One of his sons, Judah, was given a glorious future in this prophecy. Genesis 49:10 declares: "The Scepter will not depart from Judah, nor the ruler's staff from between his feet, until He to whom it belongs shall come and the obedience of the nations shall be his" (Genesis 49:10). The older sons would bow to Judah; the younger sons would serve His cause. "The ten 'lost tribes' are the ones that inhabited the kingdom of Israel but were exiled by the king of Assyria, who conquered Israel in 721 B. C."[134] Upon the return of the tribes of Judah and Benjamin during the rebuilding of Jerusalem described in Ezra and Nehemiah, these ten tribes migrated back from areas of captivity and were absorbed into the nation of Israel through Judah and Benjamin, which became Israel surrounding Jerusalem in the days of Jesus. The others incorporated into various people groups who were not considered part of the" pure" people of Israel.

---

[134] *"Whatever happened to the 12 Tribes of Israel?",* Almanac (August 10, 2023). https://www.almanac.com/fact/whatever-happened-to-the-12-tribes-of

For example, the Samaritans[135] were viewed as a type of half-breed, because they were born from Jewish people groups who had intermarried with people groups from non-Hebrew nations. In today's world the Samaritans are one of the purest races on earth and have diminished to below 200 of them because of the refusal to marry outside those who are Samaritan. Ironic. It is only recently they have begun to marry outside of their own people group in the name of survival. All this is to say that those who were considered true Israel at the time of Christ were an exceedingly small group of people from only two tribes in Israel.

When *Gabriel* spoke these words to Mary, that her Son would reign, her mind would immediately be brought to the promise found in the blessing of Jacob. "How can this be, since I am a virgin?" (Luke 1:34) There was but one answer - the Holy Spirit was moving in the Land. This same Spirit prophesied through Jacob. This same Spirit guarded over and protected the tribe of Judah. This same Spirit continued to place the hope of Messiah in the hearts and minds of the Prophets. This same Spirit now brought to pass the prophecies of old – The Messiah from Judah was conceived in Mary's womb. "The Holy Spirit will come upon you, and the power of the Most High will overshadow you..." (Luke 1:35). Judah gave us Jesus, Benjamin gave us the Apostle Paul, and the other ten tribes melted into Jewish history. Symbolically, these 10 tribes are you and me, a New Dwelling Place for God, and God's people.

It occurs to me that one reason the Temple has never been rebuilt is because The Temple has been replaced. That made of brick and mortar is now made of flesh and bone. That which was a temporary home for God, confined by stone in a specific place for a specific time, has been replaced by living, breathing, loving souls miraculously transformed into an Eternal and Indestructible

---

[135] History & Society, "Samaritan, Judaism". Written and fact checked by The Editors of Encyclopaedia Britannica, Last Updated: Jan 18, 2024. https://www.britannica.com/topic/Samaritan

House of God. God's people used to worship inside a building. Now God's people worship wherever and whenever, for they are now the House of Worship living and moving among us. The Destruction of the Temple marked the beginning of a House that can never be torn down. This was God's purpose all along. A House built by Jesus Himself.

House of God (by Rick Farmer)

There was a Temple.
Dream of King David, Heart of Solomon
Smoke rising from the God who is One
Fashioned for sacrifice, home of the Priest
Temporary door through which sin is released
House of God.

There lay a Man.
Seed of the Woman, Gift from our Dad
Growing and Learning like any good lad
Fashioned for sacrifice, Love in His eyes
Tear down the Temple and watch Him arise
House of God.

Here sits a Steeple.
Tied to her Founder, Framed with Living Stone
In front lay an alter where the lost find a home
Fashioned for worship, Praise fills her halls
Open the Door for He's torn down the walls
House of God.

Here lives a Body.
Filled with His Spirit, birthed through His death
Mouth, eye and hand are moved by His breath
No standing or status for a Servant is King
Into all nations His glory to Bring
House of God.

"The amazing thing about the Christian Faith is that it was never meant to be a stagnant never changing faith. Faith is the root of change and change is what we are chemically designed for. Christianity was born a Living Faith. What began as a fertilized egg in the womb of a Virgin grew into a boy who worshipped and cut wood, cried, skinned his knee, and took care of his little sisters. This boy became a man who became a Teacher, A Servant, A Miracle Worker, A Friend. From there He became a Savior and then a Risen Lord. He did not stop there. Soon after, He lived in a new way inside His followers via The Holy Spirit. This is when The Body really takes off, as we experience millions of people later, all part of the Living, Breathing, Body that we call the Invisible Church. Christianity was always meant to be a People belonging to God and a People through which Jesus Christ lives. Know this, to look into the eyes of another person is to look into the eyes of the place Jesus chooses to call home" (A Blog written by Rick Farmer).

**"He will reign over Jacob's descendants
forever" …. Luke 1:33.**
Mary, and Jesus

Could He be Messiah?

Mary was a daughter of Judah through the lineage of King David. There is no escaping the significance of this fact. Matthew's Gospel gave us the lineage of Jesus through the line of Joseph and points us to the legal and seeming biological right Jesus had to the throne of Judah promised to a son of David (See Genesis 49:10, 2 Samuel 7:16, and Psalm 2). Mary's lineage, traced for us in Luke 3, deviated from Matthew's accounting. This was because Luke, using Mary's lineage, displayed for the Gentile world that Jesus came from the blood line of David all the way back to Judah, and then beyond. Notice the phrase Luke chose to identify the line he was tracing for us - "He was the son, so it was thought, of Joseph" (Luke 3:23). *So it was thought* is a clear indication that Luke knows something about the relationship between Joseph and Jesus that is not apparent to all. He had just told us why in chapter 2. Clearly Luke was pointing us away from Joseph, which leads us to conclude the differences in his genealogy follow the human line of Jesus through Mary. Why would Luke take such time in Luke 2 to highlight the Virgin Birth only to then trace His lineage through Joseph, who Luke believed was not his biological father? He would not. He goes all the way back to Adam, and then calls Him the Son of God, to emphasize both the divine Sonship and Jesus' human lineage, which could only be traced through the genealogical line of Mary. A Kingly line in Matthew, a Human line through Luke, both pointing to Mary and Joseph as the children of David.

The coincidental occurrence of such a truth was mathematically explored and allegorized. The number is astronomical, so I will not pretend to have it memorized. But I can give you an approximation, taken from a book called *"Science Speaks"* by Peter Winebrenner Stoner (Author) and Robert C. Newman (Collaborator). If we pile silver dollars across the state of Texas two feet deep, then mark one silver dollar and drop it from a helicopter flying somewhere above Texas, we create a hidden treasure indeed. Let us then choose a random blind man in Ohio, deliver this blind man to Dallas, alone, and direct him to set out on foot from Dallas in any direction. We will ask him to stop at some point of his own choosing to reach down to pick up the one silver dollar among all those spread across Texas which was marked beforehand and dropped from a helicopter. One silver dollar out of 100,000,000,000,000,000? (Opps, I said I would not try the number. My bad. Back to Texas).

You get the picture, right? It is understood that Texas is a big state. It further is understood that we have no clue which way the blind man will walk when he leaves Dallas. The simple truth - finding the coin will never happen by accident. Never! This is an allegorical representation of the odds that Mary and Joseph simply meet and marry by coincidence within the lineage they share. Luke established a profound Truth. Jesus is this coin. Jesus is this event. Jesus, the One expected from Judah through David on his mother's side and his earthly father's side, is no Accident. Not a chance! He is the One. He qualifies in a way others cannot. He is the One born to rule over Jacob, as a child of Judah through his mother and his earthly father, straight from the lineage of King David.

For now, Luke wanted us to know He was a most probable candidate, and he outlined this through a tedious list of generations in his Gospel. Do you understand why he took the time to do so? A master historian would not have wasted time writing about a candidate who was disqualified at birth. Instead, he points to the location of a Silver Dollar scattered among the millions of sons of Israel and tells us where to find the One human being Who cannot be disqualified. Luke wanted the world to know he found the Marked Texas Silver Dollar.[136]

(Simeon contemplates Jesus' identity in Luke 2:29: *"Sovereign Lord, as you have promised, you may now dismiss your servant in peace. For my eyes have seen your Salvation, which you have prepared in the sight of all nations: a Light for revelation to the Gentiles, and the glory of your people Israel).*

---

[136] Peter Winebrenner Stoner (Author), Robert C. Newman (Collaborator), *"Science Speaks: Scientific Proof of the Accuracy of Prophecy and the Bible"*. *1969 MOODY BOOKS PRESS (3rd Revised Edition) PAPERBACK.*

Was Luke correct? Could He be Messiah? When answering such a question there are several things to consider. First, does he meet the criteria outlined for Messiah in the writings of the Old Testament? Second, is there a better candidate that we simply do not know about? Third, is it possible that Messiah is yet to come, and the future holds the key?

Does he meet the Criteria? There are several qualifications that the Jews were (and are) anticipating when it comes to identifying Messiah. The Messiah would be a Hebrew man (Isaiah 9:6) born in Bethlehem (Micah 5:2) of a Virgin (Isaiah 7:14), a Prophet akin to Moses (Deuteronomy 18:18), a Priest in the order of Melchizedek (Psalm 110:4), a King (Isaiah 11:1–4), and the Son of David (Matthew 22:42). All these requirements are met with Jesus of Nazareth, and few historians have questioned the validity of most of these items. Even the Romans marked Him as "King of Israel" during his death. As we have discussed, the Virgin Birth is controversial, but there is no denying this was predicted, and Jesus's followers claimed that it was fulfilled in Jesus born of Mary. Even Islam embraces this doctrine. Jesus is certainly not eliminated when we answer our first question, and many would suggest a compelling case can easily be made.

Is there a better candidate for Messiah than Jesus? This question is more difficult to answer, seeing that we do not know all the candidates there may be in human history. We can only investigate those who have become a part of the historical record. However, we might expect that any Messiah candidate would be talked about and written about, since the Jewish people were expert historians who daily discussed the coming of Messiah. Isaiah 53 is an enormously powerful and amazingly specific description of Jesus of Nazareth. Jewish Theologians most often discount this chapter's application to Jesus by claiming it is not a prophecy about Messiah. Instead, they tend to describe this chapter as relating to the nation of Israel in general, not a specific person. You can read Is. 53 for yourself to determine what you think. My caution about finding a better candidate than Jesus can be summed up in the words of an atheist writer whom I respect, Tim O'Neill, when he writes: *"Anyone researching this subject should beware of some of the wild and unscholarly online claims about "Messiahs who parallel Jesus" based on supposed similarities between the gospel stories and stories about various ancient gods and demigods like Dionysius and Mithras. Firstly, "Messiah" has a specific meaning unique (even in its Christian forms) to the Jewish tradition. We cannot just consider any old godman or demigod as a "Messiah" because we choose to. Secondly, most of these so-called parallels are highly contrived, based on dubious interpretations or (in the case of most of the notorious ones claimed about Mithras) totally invented and without any evidential foundation at all. These "parallels" are beloved by kooky New Agers and by atheists who really should know better (yes, I'm looking at you Q and you as well Bill Maher), but they are pseudo historical nonsense (sic)."* [137]

Is Messiah yet to arrive? The third question is a bit more subjective in terms of trying to find a satisfactory answer. If you are Christian, you already embraced Jesus as The Messiah. So, of course we do not expect another, though most of us are anticipating His return one day. If you are Jewish, you have either given up on the hope of Messiah coming or are holding out for someone other than Jesus. Our religious worldviews decide how we answer question three, but it is Jew and Christian who emphasize the role of Messiah. Given the Jewish belief that Messiah is yet to arrive, the total rejection of Jesus as either Messiah or Deity has never been a central issue for Judaism. Thus, I am declaring that most of us answer question three subjectively before we ever begin thinking

---

[137] Tim O'Neill is an atheist who has studied the scholarship on the historical Jesus, his Jewish socio-religious context, and the origins of Christianity for over 25 years. This quote is taken from Quora.com, where he is a well-established voice on this platform. http://www.livius.org/men-mh/messiah/messianic_claimants00.html

through the question. Not a wise course of action, but none of us wants to get kicked out of our church or synagogue for asking the wrong question. It is interesting to note that The Vatican recently proclaimed that Jew and Christian alike are both right, for they are both waiting for Messiah, one for His first coming, the later for His second coming. They proclaimed that both would recognize Jesus as Messiah when He arrives.[138] Interesting philosophy indeed. Even so, "Come, Lord Jesus" (Rev. 22:20).

> "Science reckons many prophets, but there is not even a promise of a Messiah." (Thomas Huxley)

"I am a messiah. Ask anyone on the Internet."[139] (Warren Ellis)

---

[138] "Vatican Says Jews' Wait for Messiah Is Validated by the Old Testament", By Melinda Henneberger. New York Times, Jan. 18, 2002, NYTimes.com
[139] See Brainy Quote/Messiah. BrainyQuote.com

Day 18

"He will be called the Son of God" .... Luke 1:35

Setting the Stage: Jesus through the eyes of other religions

IT IS INTERESTING TO CONSIDER WHAT THOSE WHO PRACTICE Islam believe about the one they call "Jesus, Son of Mary." For instance, Muslims believe that Jesus is "The Son of God," but not the "begotten Son of God," as Christians believe. Though there is a special bond between God and Jesus, there is not a shared kinship between the two, according to Islam Orthodoxy. According to Islam, Jesus does not have an earthly father, but is not conceived of the Holy Spirit as Christians proclaim. Instead, they teach that Jesus is spoken or commanded into existence inside the womb of Mary by the Power of the Word *be* or *kun*. ("Be, and it is" - *kun fa-yakūnu* - is a phrase that occurs several times in the Quran, referring to the act of creation by Allah). God commanded the angel *Gabriel* to "blow" the soul of Jesus into Mary, thus conceiving Jesus. For Muslims, Jesus is the Christ (Messiah) sent to the people of Israel as a prophet and messenger from God (Allah), whose mission was to lead Israel into a *New Revelation* (Arabic word for the Gospel).[140]

Who do Jews believe Jesus to be? The easy answer is to

---

[140] These statements can be checked against references found in: The Oxford Dictionary of Islam, p.158; "*Surah Al-Ma'idah[5:72]; Surah Al-Ma'idah [5:75]: Surah Ali 'Imran [3:59], Surah Al-Anbya [21:91].*"

say a Jewish prophet in the 1st century, with no special claim to Messiahship. For some Jews, the name alone is synonymous with *pogroms* and Crusades, charges of deicide, and centuries of Christian anti-Semitism. More recently, other Jews have come to regard him as a Jewish teacher. This does not mean, however, that they believe he was raised from the dead or was the Messiah. The last century has seen an inclusive movement where Christians and Jews interact, share a respect for one another in terms of the commonalities of faith, and recognize a general sense of sadness and regret as to the way Christians have treated Jews since the time of Jesus. However, "anti-Semitism" still exists and is the consequence of the exaggerated belief that the Jews had a role in the crucifixion of Jesus.[141] (As I type these words Anti-Semitic protests are occurring throughout our country. However, these are not commonly organized by Christians in our time, but rather are a part of the Israeli/Palestinian Conflict. They have more to do with the struggles of the Palestinians and Jews in the Land they both occupy and claim as their homeland.)

History tells us that Jesus died for primarily two reasons, one of them Theological and the other Political: 1. God had ordained and ordered it to pay the sin debt humanity bore; 2. The Roman Empire saw Him as a threat to the "peace of Rome" (*Pax Romona*). Jewish leadership had no power to sentence any person to death and could not have done so even if they had wished to. Rome alone had this authority.

In recent times a rising sentiment has grown throughout Christendom and the West. Jews and Muslims are our brothers and sisters within this shared human experience. There is much Truth that we share in our Traditions. Love and mercy, the high esteem of family and community, a love for the Law of God in our

---

[141] *"What Do Jews Believe About Jesus? How Judaism regards the man Christians revere as the messiah."* BY MY JEWISH LEARNING in 2022. See https://www.myjewishlearning.com/articlc/what-do-jews-believe-about-jesus/

societies, and a commitment to Tradition and Testimony as an act of faith, to name a few. May we embrace our Jewish brothers and sisters as descendants of the Chosen People of God as we proclaim the Gospel of Jesus to the World, especially during a time of a need for peace in the Middle East. And may we find a path toward reconciliation with our peace loving and truth-seeking Muslim neighbors and friends who share with us a religious heritage descending from the seed of Abraham.

(LAUGH WITH ME...)

Probably the worst thing about being Jewish around Christmas time is shopping in stores, because the lines are so long. They should have a Jewish express line: "Look, I'm Jewish, it's not a gift. It's just paper towels!" (Sue Kolinsky)

A Priest and a Rabbi went to a prizefight in Madison Square Garden. One of the fighters crossed himself before the opening gong sounded. "What does that mean?" asked the Rabbi. "Not a thing if he can't fight," answered the priest. (Belle Barth)

My mother is Jewish, my father is Catholic. I was brought up Catholic ... with a Jewish mind. When I went to confession, I'd bring a lawyer with me ... "Bless me Father, for I have sinned. I think you know Mr. Cohen?" (Bill Maher)

Rabbi Greenberg is sitting alone in the sanctuary of his synagogue crying. He is clutching his prayer book and holding a written sheet of paper. A letter. Tears streaming down his upturned face, his chest heaving as he sobs. "Why Lord?" he cries out. "Why did this have to happen. My son! My only son! Why would he destroy me like

this? My only son converting to Christianity!!" At once a
booming voice speaks from heaven: "YOURS TOO?"

"He will be called the Son of God" …. Luke 1:35

Why do we believe Jesus is not just an ordinary man, created by
historical editing as many critics believe? Why all this commotion –
prophecy, the Virgin Birth, the trip to Bethlehem, the Angelic
Visits, the shepherds, and the Magi, and for heaven's sake, why
do we need four Gospels to tell us His story? I suggest that the
simplest answer for all the questions begins by considering the
genealogy Luke recited in his Gospel in Luke chapter 3. In Luke
3:37 he traced Jesus all the way back to the very beginning. After
informing us that his lineage is traced through David, through
Nathan's line (no doubt the line of Jesus through his mother Mary,
the bloodline), Luke then informed us that Jesus was "the son of
Seth, the son of Adam, the Son of God" (Luke 3:37) Jesus, the son
of the first human, is also the Son of the Divine Creator. Jesus is
The Son of God.

This was precisely what the Angel said to Mary with the words:
"he will be called the Son of The Most High" (Luke 1:35). The need
for excitement and the four Gospels is traced to the child's identity.
It is this type of repetitive testimony that forces us to look deeper
into the Gospel accounts of Jesus. The expectancy of the people,
the incredible fulfillment of so many prophecies, the record of his
life and words and actions, and the circumstances surrounding
his death, are each made more powerful when considering his
ancestry along the line of David. It would not be logical to have
the Son of God come to earth without creating a stir.

It would not be wise to have seen his life before our very eyes
and not find a way to tell the world about Him. The most famous
person who ever lived arrived in a day without social media, texting,
or the internet. Luke's narrative was the beginning of a fame which
the world now embraces, so he took great strides to be very precise

about his human existence and the purpose for his coming. The name of *Jesus* is the most known name on the planet, the most significant person in all human history, this according to Time.[142] If the Son of God visited earth, it would be amazingly reasonable to tell the world of the miracle and significance of His coming. This was precisely what the Angels proclaimed, and very much what the Gospels intended to tell us. Luke, therefore, connected all this evidence to the blood line of Messiah, which is a major reason we can consider the rest of the story of primary importance. Messiah was expected, so Luke made sure we understood that this man meets all the criteria from ancient writings which created a universal expectation on the part of the Jewish Community. At the same time, God had also insured Messiah was not just an expectation of Israel, but of the world. A flesh and blood Messiah in the line of David that would become a Savior for the entire world. He was real and he was anticipated, just as Luke declared.

Archbishop Fulton Sheen made a case that the non-Jewish world also expected Jesus:

"Turn to pagan testimony. Tacitus, speaking for the ancient Romans, says, "People were generally persuaded in the faith of the ancient prophecies, that the East was to prevail, and that from Judea was to come the Master and Ruler of the world." Suetonius, in his account of the life of Vespasian, recounts the Roman tradition thus, "It was an old and constant belief throughout the East, that by indubitably certain prophecies, the Jews were to attain the highest power." The Annals of the Celestial Empire contain the statement: "In the 24th year of Tchao-Wang of the dynasty of the Tcheou, on the 8th day of the 4th moon, a light appeared in the Southwest which illumined the king's palace. The monarchs showed him books in

[142] "Who's Biggest? The 100 Most Significant Figures in History, A data-driven ranking by TIME People of the Year". By Steven Skiena and Charles B. Ward (Dec. 10, 2013). *Steven Skiena and Charles B. Ward are the authors of* Who's Bigger? Where Historical Figures Really Rank, *Cambridge University Press, 2013. The views expressed are solely their own.*

which this prodigy signified the appearance of the great Saint of the West whose religion was to be introduced into their country." The Greeks expected Him, for Aeschylus in his Prometheus six centuries before His coming, wrote, "Look not for any end, moreover, to this curse until God appears, to accept upon His Head the pangs of thy own sins vicarious." The Fourth Eclogue of Virgil recounted the same ancient tradition and spoke of "a chaste woman, smiling on her infant boy, with whom the iron age would pass away." Not only were the Jews expecting the birth of a Great King, a Wise Man, and a Savior, but Plato and Socrates also spoke of the Logos and of the Universal Wise Man "yet to come." All these were on the Gentile side of the expectation. What separates Christ from all men is that first He was expected; even the Gentiles had a longing for a deliverer, or redeemer. This fact alone distinguishes Him from all other religious leaders."[143]

Jesus, the Son of God, walked and talked among us. Consider the names used to identify Him in Luke/Acts alone – Christ of God (9:20), Consolation of Israel (2:25), Dayspring (L 1:78), Holy Child (A 4:27, Holy One (A 3:14), Horn of Salvation (L 1:69), The Just One (A 7:52), Lord of All (A 10:36), Prince of Life (A 3:15), Savior (L 2:11), Son of God (L 3:37), and Son of the Highest (L 1:32). As *Christ,* He was the longed-for Messiah who delivered God's people from sin and death. As *Consolation,* He brought comfort to those who mourned and hope for those who were lost. As *Dayspring,* He gave light to a people in darkness and paved the path for those who sought after God. As *Holy Child,* he walked, talked, learned, and lived as one of us, though all the while was more than us. As *Holy One,* He fulfilled the demands of the Law on our behalf and qualified as the spotless sacrifice that God demanded. As the *Horn of Salvation,* the Power of the Almighty was in Him to carry out what was needed for the salvation of God's people. As

---

[143] ArchBishop Fulton J. Sheen, *"The Life of Christ" (November 1990).* Image Books. Information found in chapter 1.

the *Just One,* He spoke justly and walked righteously as He taught the world the heart and the will of His Father. As the *Lord of All,* He brought true worship into the hearts of everyone He touched and established His Kingdom on earth for all eternity to come. As *Prince of Life,* He displayed God's purpose and intent for living and showed us the way of love and mercy. As *Savior,* He laid down His own life on the Cross to give all His followers' forgiveness from sin and grant them life everlasting. As *The Son of God,* He was the very presence of God among us in human form so that the invisible God might be someone we could touch, and love, and come to know. And as *Son of the Highest,* He bowed low to be exalted as highest, surrendered His life to bring resurrection and exaltation to all who trust in Him. No wonder Luke spared us no detail to prove his case, including a tedious detailed genealogy of the human lineage of Jesus. *Thus, the Hoopla. Thus, the written record. Thus, The Son of God.*

"Our Christian conviction is that Christ is also the Messiah of Israel. Certainly, it is in the hands of God how and when the unification of Jews and Christians into the people of God will take place." (Pope Benedict XVI)

"We modern people adore personal power above almost anything else. Our society, in brief, is built on the presumption that the good society is that in which each person gets to be his or her own tyrant (Bernard Shaw's definition of hell: Hell is where you must do what you want to do). ("Resident Alien," page 33)

Day 19

"May your word to me be fulfilled" .... Luke 1:38

Setting the Stage: Did Daniel know the time and the season?

DID 1ST CENTURY JEWS EXPECT A 1ST CENTURY MESSIAH? IT would seem to us that if Messiah were expected around the time Jesus was born, there is truly little reason not to consider Jesus as a legitimate candidate. So, how about the timing of it all? Is there any reason to believe that we can pinpoint a period which drastically narrows the list of candidates, as if there is such a list? As it turns out, there is important Old Testament evidence which causes us to pause and consider, and there were certainly a large enough number of Jewish eyewitnesses to consider his life work and his teachings. Let us ask, was Messiah expected around the time Jesus came?

There is a complicated formula in the book of Daniel that seems to point to the answer being "yes". In fact, the predictions were so precise and so amazing that many have suggested Daniel must have been written much later than some Biblical Scholars claim, for he was so incredibly accurate with his predictions pertaining to Babylon, Persia, Greece, and Rome. However, even if one dates the book of Daniel later than most do, the predictions about Messiah were still extraordinary. I will only summarize them here, but you can expose yourself to a more thorough examination of the sources I leave for you. "More than any other book of the

Hebrew Scriptures, the writings of the prophet Daniel confront us with evidence of the time of Messiah's coming—evidence that many people would rather not see. But it is there, and it cannot be ignored."[144]

In Daniel 9 we find a prophecy that theologians call "The Seventy Weeks of Daniel" prophecy. Daniel proclaimed: "From the time the word goes out to restore and rebuild Jerusalem until the Anointed One, the Ruler, comes, there will be 'seven sevens, and sixty-two sevens.' It will be rebuilt with streets and a trench, but in times of trouble. After the sixty-two sevens the Anointed One will be put to death and will have nothing. The people of the ruler who will come (Most likely Rome) will destroy the city and the sanctuary (obvious prediction of 70 AD).........In the middle of the 'seven' He will put an end to sacrifice and offering "(Parts of Daniel 9:25-27). I will not pretend I can outline all the elements of this text for you here, for it involves knowing the dates connected to various decrees we can trace in history, specifically edicts to rebuild Jerusalem clear through to the time of Jesus Himself. Because the book of Daniel is a Hebrew document, we will count time according to the Jewish Calendar[145] to summarize this prophecy.

---

[144] "The Messianic Time Table According to Daniel the Prophet," Arnold Fruchtenbaum, April 20, 2018. Published by Jews for Jesus. JewsForJesus.org

[145] The normal year according to our Calendar is 365 days, 366 during a Leap Year. We do this because a day is a bit over 24 hours when we calculate using the earth's rotation and the moon as markers. Therefore, we add a day every four years to adjust. However, the Hebrew Calendar is 354 days. Therefore, they added a second month after Adar I called Adar II. This came to be after the Israelites in ancient times had to account for the imperfections of the Lunar Calendar. To correct the inaccuracies, they produced 19-year cycles that a month every third, sixth, eighth eleventh, and nineteenth years of the cycle. Considering the cycle is how we account for Adar II. The corrected accounting also helped establish the number of days in each month. Using the Jewish Calendar, after listening to Daniel's "seventy sevens" prophecy as 490 years, we would calculate from the edict to rebuild Jerusalem until the death of Jesus in 30 A. D.. We find ourselves smack in the middle of the 70th week of Daniel on April 7 AD 30. There are others

We also would need to study the reason Old Testament prophecies like this one are literally "weeks of years" symbolized by "seven sevens and sixty-two sevens," with one last seven as it pointed to the time of the Messiah (*seventy sevens*). Sabbath Law in the Old Testament often set the clock for 7-year periods for the Hebrew people. Daniel most likely is referring to 70 periods of 7 years, totaling 490 years split into three distinct groups - the 49 years it took to rebuild Jerusalem after the edict was given ("seven sevens"), 434 years from this completion until the time of "Anointed One" ("sixty-two sevens"), and then a final 7 that marked the beginning of Jesus' ministry and the acceptance of the Gospel by the Gentiles in Acts (The 70th seven). Daniel predicted that amid the last "seven" the "Anointed One" would be "cut off" from the people and would instigate a "New Covenant" (The New Covenant is spoken as prophecy in Jeremiah 31:31-34, right here in Daniel 9:26,27, described in detail by the author of Hebrews in Hebrews 8:6-13, and established by Jesus Himself in Matthew 26:27-29, and many other places). Striking!

If we measure from the edict to rebuild and the time of the crucifixion, we will anticipate the "The Anointed One" arriving in Jerusalem around 27 A.D., given that the rebuilding of Jerusalem began in 457 B. C. under Ezra. (Remember to subtract one year from 1 B. C. to 1 A. D., since it is 1 year not 2). If Jesus arrived on the scene around 27 or 28 A. D., adding the 3 years recorded in the Gospels for Jesus' period of teaching around Jerusalem before his crucifixion, this would date the crucifixion around 30 or 31 A. D. Is this the right time? "If Jesus died on Nisan 14, the Day of Preparation, then we need to ask in what years during the prefecture of Pontius Pilate in Judaea (AD 26–36) did that

who argue against this date and choose instead to date the Christ event ending in 33 A. D.. Either way, the accuracy of this prediction is astounding, considering it was made around 600 years before the time which Jesus taught in and around Jerusalem. See also https://www.gotquestions.org/seventy-sevens.html

day fall on a Friday, since Jesus was crucified on a Friday? Using astronomical data, Humphreys and Waddington have calculated that there are only two dates during this decade that a Friday Passover could be celebrated on Nissan 14: either April 7, AD 30 or April 3, AD 33".[146] From such a prophecy it is easy to guess that those who knew of Daniel's Word would have been looking for the birth of Messiah sometime around 10 B. C. to 5 A. D., precisely within the period Jesus arrived as a baby.[147] If in fact Messiah was not only expected, but expected within the actual period of Jesus' life and ministry, we are left with incredible evidence in support of the case Luke made that Jesus' birth was very likely be the birth of Messiah (Of course, Luke was certain of this, which is an important detail given his status as a contemporary of Jesus and an educated historian).

"May your word to me be fulfilled" …. Luke 1:38

Gabriel announced to Mary that the child she was to conceive would be called the "Son of God." I cannot imagine how Mary would have felt at this moment. Not only was she a virgin, but she was a poor peasant girl from a small village in Galilee. She had no claim to royalty, no riches untold, no famous uncle on her dad's side, no special gift we are aware of, no reason to believe that of all the women in Israel she should be chosen. Yet she was. She was to become the mother of Jesus, the very Son of God. Her response was understandable. "But how will this be, since I am a

---

[146] "Dating the Crucifixion" (1983) by Colin J. Humphreys and W. G. Waddington, *Nature*, 306, 743-746

[147] For further study on this prophecy please consider: *"What are the seventy weeks of Daniel?"*, Got Questions (2023). GotQuestions.org. Also consult: John Walvoord, *Daniel: The John Walvoord Prophecy Commentary (2011)*. Edited by Charles H. Dyer and Philip E. Rawley. Moody Publishers. For an additional reference for understanding the Jewish Calendar as it relates to the death of Jesus you can see "The Date of the Crucifixion" (1985) by Colin J. Humphreys and W. Graeme Waddington, *Journal of the American Scientific Affiliation*, 37, 2-10

virgin?" (Luke 1:34). When an angel comes to you and tells you that the impossible is to become possible, that a thing that has never occurred is about to occur, you have questions. Mary did. I would. You would.

I was once told that I had been chosen to be interviewed by the local TV station about the upcoming rivalry game for my high school football team. I did everything I could to get out of it. Begged my coach. I pretended to have laryngitis. Begged my friend *Fish*. I did not want the job. I was nervous and afraid (My students would testify today as to how time has changed me). In the end I ended up saying everything *Fish* told me he was going to say. I panicked. When it was time for *Fish* to speak, he simply stated: "I really don't have anything to add to that." Of course not! I stole his entire routine. The only reason I was not left speechless is because of "pretend preparation." The preparation was not my own, and there was no evidence here of a witness ready to speak. I simply repeated what I heard, and mindlessly recited words not my own. I am afraid this has become a metaphor for our time. I cringe when I hear my students say: "Do we need to know this for the test?" This is one reason I give diverse types of tests and focus on learning via digging for answers and discussion over and above memorizing notes for a test. I desire that my students learn the art of critical thinking, to grow accustomed to thinking through their positions, to find a way through this world utilizing more than a recantation of what they have been instructed to believe.

I fear for this Generation, considering the deemphasis of critical thinking skills. I am fearful we have too many people asking *Fish* what to say, because we have little clue what to say for ourselves. Group think is the kind of preparation we most often use in our time. We see this vividly amid political discussion, where post-Truth thinking requires a person to recite the latest slogan of our time without asking ourselves if this information is true, tested, or trustworthy (My Triple T for Critical thinking: Truth, Test, Trust).

We "feel" our way. We believe ourselves to be intelligent if we can recite the latest slogan we heard across the internet, regardless of whether we have deeply considered the truth of this slogan. If we believe a thing sincerely enough, we believe we are to be heard and honored for our thoughts. Sincerity matters more than being correct. Memorize the latest slogan, embrace the ideology of my political party, recite my feelings, BS my way through a question which requires genuine time and study, and I am a modern intellectual. In our world today, one's ability to celebrate a "yellow school bus" becomes a sign of intelligence and prestige. Knowing such things may even get you elected inside a post-Truth electorate.

I was prepared for my answer in high school because I cheated. *Fish* had a plan. I had a friend with a plan. But I stole his plan and made it my own. Mary was prepared for the unexpected precisely because her faith was her own, her life had prepared her for this moment, and she did not need someone to teach her what to say and do in the moment. She had been taught through a lifetime of faith, a faith that guided her reflections and gripped her heart.

I fear the life of faith is slipping into the crevices of history as New Generations in America redefine spirituality. This may be a major reason we were not prepared for the Pandemic and ill prepared for the political division we are now experiencing. Luke was writing for such a time, for the Romans allowed free-thinking if it did not threaten allegiance to the State.[148] This means Luke was also speaking to us, for we are in theory a free-thinking people. However, our thinking often leads us toward recitation over and above critical thinking, especially when it comes to Faith. Our "group" tells us what to think. Our agenda controls our choices. And our prophets have their own Social Media followers. We have little clue what it means to ask real questions about foundational truths, for there is no longer the need for foundational truths, so we surmise.

Mary asked, "how can this be?" Notice, she never dismissed the notion; she never disrespected the source, and she would not rule out the possibility that what was thought impossible was about to occur. At the core of her question was her faith, and a person of faith recognizes that the once impossible can indeed become possible. Mary's faith allowed her to embrace the Angel's word: "May your word to me be fulfilled" (Luke 1:38).

For certain, one cannot prepare to be a virgin with a child in the normal sense of the word. How could Mary be prepared for such a thing as this? No friend to advise, no warning of what was coming, no history to consult, nothing but the faith she had been practicing her entire life. She had no friend named *Fish*. I wonder, was Mary afraid? I wonder, was she confused? I wonder, was she at least a little bit nervous? Her response was one of faith, not fear. Her words reflected surrender, not confusion. She had to be shocked and amazed, yet she willingly accepted her destiny. God had in fact prepared her as only God could. I have no doubt God

---

[148] For a brief history of the way religious thinking was tolerated under Roman rule you might read: 1. *"BRIA 13 4 b Religious Tolerance and Persecution in the Roman Empire"*, **Teach Democracy, 2023. crf-use.org or 2. The discussion on Quora.com under the discussion titled, "What was the ancient Roman concept of freedom or free will?"**

had already been working in her. She was chosen long before *Gab* paid her a visit. She was prepared as much as faith would allow. Messiah was dear to her heart long before she knew He would come from her body.

Where might she have found her answers? There is a strong probability that the Scriptures served as her guide. Consider things she would have heard since the beginning of her childhood: "The Lord Himself will give you a sign: The Virgin will conceive and give birth to a Son and will call him Immanuel" (Isaiah 7:14). She would name him. What circumstances would have created a situation where a 1st century Jewish mother suspected of impropriety was allowed to name her son? Luke took us back to the days of Leah and Rachel in Genesis 29, where a barren woman gave birth to a miracle.

A virgin conception? "For to us a child is born, to us a Son is given, and the government will be on His shoulders. And He will be called Wonderful Counselor, Mighty God, Everlasting Father, Prince of Peace. Of the greatness of His government and peace there will be no end" (Isaiah 9:6,7). We know that the Gospel writers connected these passages to the birth of Jesus. The fulfillment was at hand: "All this took place to fulfill what the Lord had said through the prophet: The Virgin will conceive and give birth to a son, and they will call him Immanuel (which means *God with us*)" (Matthew 1: 22,23). She had already come to know God as The Faithful God throughout the history of her people. She had already come to know God as the miracle working God through all she was taught from childhood. She had already experienced God at work in her life in response to her own prayers, certainly having taken part in the prayers of her people for the coming of Messiah. Why not believe? Why not trust? Why not respond as one who knew? Mary experienced an *Existential reality* resting upon a *Metaphysical understanding of Truth*,[149] something we are

---

[149] Existentialism is a 20th century phenomenon yet has now captured the minds of many people in the West. You can begin to understand the concepts of

not accustomed to doing in the 21st century. (I will say more about this later). Mary handled the news as a True Servant, embraced the plan God had for her, for a Divine Plan often defies what we define as "possible." Yet still, imagine….

Mary's response does not discount the enormity of the task, however. *"God's Son is going to grow up in my house. Should we look at Him when we say grace? Should I ask his permission when I send Him to His room? Should we tell his brothers and sisters to protect him at school? Should we get all panicked when he comes down with a cold? Should we let him name all the animals? God's Son In my home!!!! Wow!!!"* I wonder what Mary thought the first time Jesus bloodied his nose or the first time someone mistreated him at school? I cannot imagine being put in such a position in life. I felt the full impact of being a pastor each day, being held responsible for things I could not control and being given credit for things I had nothing to do with. The position breeds enormous responsibility. For all responsibilities preparation is key. But to be

---

Existentialism and Metaphysics by seeking various articles sited here, a couple of which I will post. This is but the beginning. It is my belief that the college students I teach on the modern college campus are captured by the philosophy of Existentialism (believing it to be just the way we are supposed to think), with little concern for an understanding of Metaphysical Truth. This leaves them ill equipped to tackle the questions of ultimate reality beyond their own individual experiences. This is a major reason Advent is now embraced as a Existential Experience rather than a Metaphysical Reality. See: 1. *Existentialism As Metaphysical And Philosophical Concept.* (2021, September 09). Edubirdie. Retrieved November 6, 2023, from https://edubirdie.com/examples/existentialism-as-metaphysical-and-philosophical-concept/ and 2. Philosophy, Volume 28, Issue 107, October 1953, pp. 342 - 347. DOI: https://doi.org/10.1017/ 3. If you ask an AI to explain the difference you get something like (which is ironic seeing an AI does not have a subjective reality to draw from): "One of the key philosophical ideas of existentialism is the concept of "existence precedes essence." This means that human beings do not have an inherent, predefined essence or nature, but rather their essence is shaped by their experiences and choices. In this way, existentialism emphasizes the individual's freedom to create their own identity and meaning in life." (https://www.classace.io/answers/metaphysical-of-existentialism-and-its-epistemology#google_vignette)

the parent of God's Son? To be trusted to raise the Messiah? Mary, you are our hero. Blessings upon you for doing such a wonderful job with Jesus, and for accepting a responsibility so many of us would have chosen to avoid. Thank you, Mary, for receiving into your body and into your life the Son of God.

"The good news of great joy changed the course of every silent night to come." (Alicia Bruxvoor)

Day 20

"With God nothing (is or ever) shall be impossible...." Luke 1:37, Amplified Translation

Setting the Stage: True Truth[150]

MOST PEOPLE WHO STUDY THE HISTORY OF KNOWLEDGE (epistemology) acknowledge at least two types of Truth. Before I name the two, let us consider a presupposition that many, including myself, embrace. In the words of Leslie Newbigin: "All statements that claim to speak the truth about realities external to the speaker are affirmations of faith to the which the speaker commits himself."[151] In my view, this is what he means - Every speaker of truth has a Lens (Worldview) he peeks through, which she had chosen (or inherited without choosing) to embrace before she began investigating reality. It could be religious, scientific, a gift from their parents, contemporary or traditional, political, there are many possibilities as to the Lens. However, we all have one (or more). *Christians embrace Authority in terms of Truth as belonging to the One who called Himself Truth: "I am the Way, the Truth, and the Life" (John 14:6).*

---

[150] For a brilliant discussion of the idea of True Truth see: Dr. Art Lindsley, *True Truth: Defending Absolute Truth in a Relativistic World*, April 8, 2004. InterVarsity Press, Downers Grove, Illinois.

[151] Lesslie Newbign, *"The Open Secret: an introduction to the theology of mission,"* 1978 and 1995 (Rev. Addition). Eerdmans Publishing Co., Grand Rapids, Michigan. Chapter 2.

I confess I begin with Jesus as my Lens. He is the glasses I wear to see reality. Without my glasses it is difficult for me to find my way around. Every now and then I forget them and try to drive to various places without them. I inevitably miss a sign, misread a street name, and end up lost. Without my set of lenses, I find it difficult to navigate this world. This is the test of a Worldview. I affirm that we all have a Lens, conscious or unconscious. If we are thinking people, we own a Worldview.

Mary Poplin identified four foundational, or primary, worldviews. They are: *Material Naturalism*, which is foundational to the belief in Science as the ultimate source of truth, and begins with a commitment to a closed universe, with little room for Metaphysical Reality; *Secular Humanism*, which highlights the innate goodness of the Human Being and the power of Human Agency in determining both individual and collective futures, and defines morality as a historical and cultural phenomenon that is the result of human experiences, reason, and of course science; *Pantheism*, which teaches that everything in our world is connected and originates within the framework of Universal Spirit, a nonsecular idea which entertains a concept of the divine, but only as impersonal life force similar to "The Force" in Star Wars Lore; *Monotheism*, which teaches there is a Personal Divine Being who created and interacts with the world, is responsible for Life as we know it, and opens up history to the certain reality of *Metaphysical* Truth through oral, written and natural revelation.[152]

Poplin teaches us that each of us interprets reality through one or a combination of more than one of these Worldviews, which will determine what we come to embrace as Truth before we ever begin to consider the evidence. For example, if we operate with a *Naturalistic* Worldview, discussion about the "Virgin Birth" of

---

[152] Mary Poplin, Is Reality Secular? Testing The Assumptions of Four Global Worldviews, 2014. IVP Books, InterVarsity Press, Downers Grove, Illinois. Chapter three.

Jesus would be meaningless, unless we can first define virgin birth as a metaphor or symbol of something that cannot occur. This presupposition would precede any consideration of the evidence for the *Naturalist*.

Through our Lens (Worldview) we search for primarily two types of Truth as we investigate reality. First, we observe that which is called "Objective Truth," or factual Truth. This is Truth about Reality which applies to everyone, no matter what we choose to believe (*Naturalists* exclude *Metaphysics* as a legitimate category for discovering Truth). Examples are things like the source of gravity and the reality of the Sun, 2 plus 2 always equals 4, X or Y chromosomes determine biological sex, and the necessity of oxygen for life on earth. All of these might lead us to analyze the concept of "intelligent design," something which flows from the evidence that is apparent to all. This would be an exploration of Objective Truth which transcends opinion or personal preference. We do not always get these truths right, but we do believe that once determined, they apply to everyone.

Second, we embrace what we call "Subjective Truth," which is a truth decided by personal preference, emotional commitments, or self-proclamations of reality (*Existential Truth)*. Examples of this type of truth might be love, friendship, parenting style, sexual identity, or whether you like this book. These are truths which are decided by the individual or group using a mechanism found in the human soul or psyche. Somewhere in the history of Truth whether I prefer *Captain Crunch* to *Cornflakes* became a matter of reality. These two types of Truth go by other names: scientific fact vs. personal opinion; laboratory truth vs. practical truth; what we can know vs. what we believe; scientific truth vs. truth decided by values; universal truth vs. contextual truth; and others. The core foundation of the two distinct types of Truth comes down to the determination of Ultimate Authority. Is the Authority behind Truth in the hands of the autonomous individual, the skilled scientist, the government, my religion, God? One's Authority will impact one's Truth. One of the most disturbing details lost in this discussion is the fact that if Subjective Truth, defined in our culture as personal preference in need of nothing more than that a person believe it, becomes the primary source of ultimate reality, then Truth becomes both unknowable and unsustainable, which is really no Truth at all. We cannot simply define reality as that which is left up to the private truth of each individual, without needing reasonable investigation to confirm. This type of belief system dominates the political agenda of those we deem "far to the Left, as well as those who are so far into Conservative Fundamentalism[153] that they are unable to allow their views to be challenged."

The reason this question of Ultimate Truth and Authority is so important in this discussion of Luke's Gospel is because the concept of Truth we embrace will determine the future of Christianity, or any other religious movement for that matter. "If

[153] Conservative Fundamentalism has several arms which help us identify and understand this movement in Theology. Many of these arms are traditional and have been embraced by The Church for centuries. However, there were new arms that sprung from this system of thought, especially as it relates to Dispensationalism and End Times Prophecy, which developed in the late 19th and early 20th centuries. Suddenly, Theologians combined the idea of the Authority of Scripture with a particular understanding of prophecy and end times. Those of us who have entered discussions with those of this system of thought have found ourselves quite frustrated that there seems to little for discussion, for many of these Theologians seem to have more knowledge about the return of Jesus than Jesus Himself claimed to have (Luke 17:26-37). The bottom line is this: Those on the "far right" and the "far left" are often characterized by an unwillingness to enter conversation about the reasonableness and the evidence for their particular view, simply dependent upon their version of Subjective Truth which requires nothing more than sincerity of thought to be valid. Without evaluating the content of their beliefs, I am here critiquing the system by which they arrive at their thinking. (For a great discussion of the definition of Fundamentalism see: "Christian Fundamentalism: American Protestant Movement", Written by Ernest R. Sandeen and J. Gordon Melton, Fact-checked by The Editors of Encyclopaedia Britannica, Feb. 14, 2024. Britannica, britannica.com)

what matters about religious belief is not the Objective Truth of what they affirm, but the sincerity with which their beliefs are held, if religious belief is a matter of personal inward experience rather than an account of what is objectively the case, then there are no grounds for thinking that Christians have any right - much less any duty - to seek the conversion of their neighbors to the Christian faith."[154] However, if a religion is objectively True, and not simply True because people subjectively believe stuff, then sharing such Truth with our neighbors would be of primary importance. Luke wanted us to know that God's Revelation is a series of objectively true propositions, not just an inward spiritual experience he was having.[155]

"When Henry Ford decided to produce his famous V-8 motor, he chose to build an engine with the entire eight cylinders cast in one block and instructed his engineers to produce a design for the engine. The design was placed on paper, but the engineers agreed, to a man, that it was simply impossible to cast an eight-cylinder engine-block in one piece. Ford replied, 'Produce it anyway." (Henry Ford)

Mary said to the Angel, "This cannot be, for I am a virgin." The Angel said, "God said, 'Do it anyway'" (Paraphrase by Rick Farmer).

"With God nothing shall be impossible...." Luke 1:37
Not exceedingly long ago we lived in a world governed by

---

[154] Once again: Lesslie Newbigin, "The Gospel in a Pluralist Society."

[155] Our reading for today will also include the introduction of a new stage in the Truth discussion - The Post-Truth Era. This is a time we have already entered, in which relationship and circumstances are granted ultimate authority in the determination of truth. Emotion and personal belief are the tests given for the power of such truth and reliable information becomes a tricky thing to find. I am writing more on this in my book on Advent from the Gospel of John. This is a significant Generation Z Truth Movement.

the theories and propositions of science. We were governed by mathematical principles, scientific explanations, and political agendas which often came down to that which guaranteed the desired outcome, both in politics and in education. We calculated, postulated, and investigated until we were locked into boxes of our own making. We were not sure how to handle the miraculous, scrutinize the spiritual, and rationalize the impossible. In such a world "near death experiences" were postmortem hallucinations. Spontaneous healings were vitamin C induced. And transformation of a person's psyche was all about achieving chemical balance in the brain. Those of us who appeal to a Transcendent Being who is intimately involved in the details of our lives were seen as irrational and superstitious by the scientific community. Even if we presented our case as being one based on sound research techniques, reasonable conclusions, and legitimate documented evidence, religion was delegated by many to the part of life that simply is not testable, and therefore not knowable. This was the Post-Renaissance World, the Modern Age.

We have now entered a new era in knowledge, where it is acceptable to say: "Humbug *to the nay sayers!!" Postmodern* Worldview has delivered us from the clutches of *scientific truth or no truth.* We have been given permission to "push back," to question authority, to reexamine tradition, to metaphorically "slap" the scientist for being so close minded, to disobey our parents, to cohabitate without sacrificing family, to hold paradoxical views, to worship without going to church, to question sexual identity, to mistrust government, to legally smoke Weed, to skip out on college, to redefine intelligence, and to do a myriad of other new and creative things in resistance to classical science and technology. Thus, the Worldview of the Post-Modern Mind is becoming dominant.

For now, we will assume the Post-Modern Mind is giving way to a Post-Truth Mind, which will eventually add a third dimension

A TIMELESS SCRIPT FROM A 1ST CENTURY DOCTOR

to parameters of the Truth we investigate. Objective Truth and Subjective Truth will be joined by "Post-Truth" Truth. This is the conquest of a *Humanistic and Pantheistic Worldview,* working as allies against both *Naturalism and Monotheism,* though too few realize this battle is occurring in our political and educational institutions. If you have ever used the phrase, "that may be true for you, but for me...this is my truth", you are a participant in the war being waged by a Postmodern and Post-Truth worldview.

The irony undergirding this battle is that the conflict between Worldviews is a necessary occurrence if we are to move forward in our discovery of knowledge and Truth. We open possibilities by attempting to shut down dissenting voices, for attempts to silence some will inevitably create in us new ways to speak. There will always be an "Elon Musk" in our midst. There always has been - MLK, Rosa Parks, W. E. B. Du Bois, J. F. K. and Robert Kennedy, Maya Angelou, Malcolm X, Harriet Tubman, Medgar Evers, Jackie Robinson, Gandhi, Nelson Mandela, Winston Churchill, Mother Teresa, Abraham Lincoln, George Washington, the list is endless. Rising above all of these was the name of Jesus, who so transformed the world that we dated the calendar in honor of his day. The one thing these all had in common is they continued to speak Truth even when those in power tried to silence them. As we discussed earlier, silence is often the very evidence that something amazing is about to occur.

We were lost inside a strictly *Naturalistic* Worldview. But a closed universe is really no universe at all, for it assumes Transcendent Reality is either not real, or not important enough to consider. The Postmodern pushback, which began in the late 19th and 20th centuries, was a crucial step forward, opening for humanity a resurrection of knowledge which is discovered outside the "laboratory." Within this intellectual environment Luke has a voice, Jesus has a place, and religion offers meaningful insight into our search for Truth.

189

All three of these systems of Truth are yet to finish their course. They will be transformed in our future, this much is certain. However, for this writer's purpose, we are where we are as we explore Advent from a Truth perspective. I have tried to touch on all three types of Truth as I write. My presupposition is that we cannot fully discover Advent afresh if we do not recognize the gap between Luke's world and ours, his Worldview and ours, due to advancements in knowledge and the transformation of the concept of Truth. It is important to understand where Luke was coming from in comparison to where we are today as we search for relevant contemporary meaning within the Gospel Luke left for us. Luke was highlighting the fact that the impossible was in fact possible, that the way we understand Truth is not so simple at times.

All this is to say, "It is difficult to fully comprehend Advent without first understanding our view of Truth" (Dr. Farmer's view). Allow me to discuss a couple of assumptions which give rise to Truth pertaining to the miracle of Advent. First, Science offers no solution to the problems of ultimate origins (*Metaphysics*). *Naturalism* cannot explain or discount the existence of God. This is simply not a question the *Naturalist* entertains. Exploring *Metaphysics* is a philosophical debate which always ends in speculation, the *Naturalist* says, and will add nothing to our investigation of "the real." But what if their tendency to reject Metaphysical and Religious questions is a mistake? What if this decision alone guarantees they will never discover ultimate Truth as it relates to the "Why" question, "why" are we here, "why" do we exist, "why" do this thing and not the other thing? Scientists can take us backward in time through carbon dating and fossil records, but they are left admitting that any conjecture they offer about how it all began, and why life exists on this planet, are as much a faith stance as any view held by a religious theorist. What if the *Naturalist* is intentionally rejecting a legitimate form of Truth that human beings cannot exist without – The Spiritual Dimension of Human Life?

Fortunately, Science does not exclude the possibility of *we do not know yet.* This is my second assumption. In fact, Science is built on the proposition that there is more to learn and much we do not know. Why else would we continue to investigate? One day there may be scientific evidence for the possibility of a *virgin birth* we have not yet discovered. Someday there may be a rational explanation for the overwhelming evidence which exists for the anthropic principle (The belief that this planet has An Intelligent Designer with human life in mind from the beginning).[156] One day there may exist a science course that teaches a student the complimentary relationship existing between Science and Faith as something more than a philosophical concept. Science itself would not deny such possibilities, for they would be the first to tell us - "we must go where the evidence leads us." What are we to do as increasingly scientific evidence leads us to the likelihood of intelligent design, pointing toward an Intelligent Designer? The more thoroughly researchers investigate the history of our planet, the more astonishing the story of our existence becomes. The number and complexity of the astronomical, geological, chemical, and biological features recognized as essential for human existence have expanded explosively within the past decade. The importance of this added information cannot be overstated."[157]

When the Angel said to Mary, "nothing will be impossible with God," we bore witness to a statement that not a single thinking person on earth can dismiss. If we assume that God does exist, and

---

[156] If interested you can find an incredibly good discussion of the Anthropic Principle in: 1. Michael Denton, *"The Miracle of Man: The Fine Tuning of Nature for Human Existence" (2022)*, Discovery Institute. 2. Hugh Ross, *Improbable Planet: How Earth Became Humanities Home (2016).* By Reasons To Believe, Published by Baker Books.

[157] Hugh Ross, "Improbable Planet: How the Earth Became Humanities Home" (2016). Chapter One.

we certainly have lots of circumstantial evidence to support such a claim, then this statement was very logical to make. What is the big deal about a *virgin birth* for a Being that created something from nothing? What is so impossible about a *Resurrection* for a Being who created life from the Big Bang? What is so hard to believe about a God who manages to keep the stars in their place, the earth on its axis, and the forces of nature consistent across time and space? It seems to me that the Angel which spoke with Mary may have had some insight into things we are not privy to, no matter the extent of our scientific or religious knowledge.

So, what would such a Truth mean for you and me? It would mean that Advent is a season of possibilities, that the birth of Jesus is about the impossible becoming the possible, that December is a month of unexpected Joy, that the problems we face are not insurmountable, that the bills we must pay can be figured out. Advent declares that the separation between us and loved ones can be bridged, our unforgiving hearts can be melted away, and the lack of hope you know today can be replaced with the promises of God for tomorrow. *Gabriel* spoke to each of us – "*Nothing will be impossible with God!*

"The discovery of ignorance for Socrates was the beginning rather than the end of the philosophical task, for only through that discovery could one begin to the overcome those received assumptions that obscured the true nature of what it was to be a human being. Socrates conceived it his personal mission to convince others of their ignorance so that they might better search for a knowledge of how life should best be lived.....In Socrates view, any attempt to foster true success and excellence in human life had to take account of the innermost reality of a human being, his Soul or *Psyche*." (Richard Tarnas, *The Passion of the Western Mind,* page 33.)

"All things are possible until they are proved impossible and even the impossible may only be so, as of now." (Pearl S Buck).

Day 21

At that time Mary got ready and hurried to a town in the hill country of Judea, where she entered Zechariah's home and greeted Elizabeth. .... Luke 1:39,40

Setting the Stage: I wish I understood women

As a Psychology Professional I have always been interested in differences between men and women. I admit that I do not understand women. They seem to be from a different planet. One psychologist suggested "Venus" as a metaphor. However, research has revealed some very real differences, which may account for why *Mary and Elizabeth* visited without *Joseph and Zac* involved. Here are some documented male/female differences:

- Boys develop the left side of their brains faster than girls: visual-spatial-logical skills, perceptual skills, better at math, problem solving, building, and figuring out puzzles.
- Girls develop the right side of brain faster than boys, which leads to talking, vocabulary, pronunciation, reading earlier, and better memory.
- Women use both hemispheres of the brain at the same time; the corpus callosum is thicker in women because of all the traffic in her brain from left to right and back again.
- Up to age 2, mothers tend to talk to and look at their daughters significantly more than they do with their sons

and make more eye contact with the daughters as well. Mothers show a wider range of emotional response to girls than boys. Girls are more social, and better able to interpret emotions than boys.

- Fathers use "command terms" with boys more than girls; and more than mothers use. Girls use more terms of endearment than boys.
- Boys get away with more aggressive antisocial behavior in school and at home than girls do.
- More girls survive the first year of life than do boys, though slightly more boys are born than girls. This means by the end of the first birthday, males are outnumbered on this planet. In fact, more males die at every age from birth to average age of death.
- Boys talk about things and activities - what they are doing and who is best at the activity. Girls tend to talk about other people, share secrets to bond friendships, communicate more at school, and share wishes and needs.
- Teenage boys talk about sports, mechanics, and the function of things (and of course girls). Teenage girls talk about boys, clothes, and weight.
- At ages 12-18: Biggest event for girls is to have a boyfriend. At ages 12-18: Boys are equally interested in sex, cars, and sports.
- A man's sense of self is defined through his ability to achieve results, through success and accomplishment. To feel good about himself, men must achieve goals by themselves.
- Men rarely talk about their problems unless they are seeking "expert" advice.
- Men are more aggressive than women; more combative and territorial.
- Men's self-esteem is more career related.

- Women value love, communication, beauty, and relationships.
- A woman's sense of self is defined through her feelings and the quality of her relationships. Personal expression, usually displayed through clothes and feelings, is especially important. Communication is important.
- For women, offering help is not a sign of weakness but a sign of strength; it is a sign of caring to give support. Men are more logical, analytical, rational.
- Women want empathy, yet men usually offer solutions. Women are more intuitive, holistic, creative, integrative.

- Men are more at ease with their own angry feelings than women are.
- Women are in touch with a much wider range of feelings than men.
- Men tend to be more functional in approaching problem-solving; women are aesthetically oriented in addition to being functional.

- **The most frequent complaint men have about women: Women are always trying to change them.**
- **The most frequent complaint women have about men: Men do not listen.** [158]

There you have it. All the stuff in my brain was transmitted into those bullet points through education and experience. Can I call this understanding? Can I now claim to understand women because I can spout a few facts garnered through education, observation, and research? I think not. Nor can I fully comprehend the event I will discuss today – two Women of Faith gathering to discuss the day the world changed forever!!! Notice the men were not invited......since they would not have listened anyway. We can have all the details, take all the right measurements, design perfect research, but still not be aware of all we need to know to reach complete understanding of *the woman*. Why? Because science has limits, knowledge is always growing, and the most wonderful idea God ever had (the woman barely edging out coffee) is a biological, psychological, and spiritual reality.

Mary visits *Elizabeth*.... Luke 1:39

We are not told what prompted Mary to visit *Elizabeth*, but we can assume it had something to do with the Angel's proclamation that *Elizabeth* was with child despite her age. I am wondering if confirming the miracle inside *Elizabeth's* womb would not help Mary to begin to embrace and understand the miracle inside her own body. Modern male/female research suggests that men tend to focus on success, whereas women are driven toward a focus on relationships. This story is but one more confirmation of this. Mary needed relationship as she processed this miracle growing

---

[158] These are some differences from my own notes. For even more differences you can consult: "25 Fun Facts About What Makes Men and Women Different", Ask The Scientists (2023). Askthescientists.com

inside of her. What better place to find this than her aunt, the "grandmother mother to be" of a miracle child conceived well beyond childbearing age?

There is a tendency for people going through extraordinary events to migrate toward people who share like events. AA meetings and support groups that center around particular tragedies or single parent gatherings and even reunions all point to our need as humans to be around other people who have in some way experienced what we have experienced. We tend to share the circumstances of our life with those of like circumstances. Thus, Mary found *Elizabeth.*

A story is told of two men who hated shopping. They shared this hatred with passion. As their wives sat out to shop one day in December, these Florida retirees decided to take the boat out on the Lake and do some "real men stuff" (fishing) while their wives shopped. However, they had not done their homework, for if they had they would have noticed the storm headed in their direction. The rain was a downpour, the wind was beyond compare, the temperature dropped unexpectedly, and it was not long before the boat was stuck on rock and debris in an unfamiliar part of the Lake. The men jumped from the boat, pushed, and tugged, and did all they could to unlock their boat from its shallow prison, as the rain and the wind and the water beat against their face and skin. They were making little progress and seemed hopelessly stuck, as one man looked to the other and uttered the phrase they both were thinking - "Sure beats shopping!" Endurance alone can be unbearable. Sharing our burdens can become a Miracle.

Mary needed a companion. She needed a woman who understood her fears, could wrap her mind around her questions, and help carry her burden. She was to face gossip, ridicule, shame, and rejection. She was to endure the hardship of mothering a Son who would never be fully understood by his family or his community. And she was to endure the utter nightmare of having to release her Son into the world that would one day try to destroy His life. Mary needed a heart and an ear as she prepared to face a miracle that would change her life forever, for better and for worse. And so, Mary went to the only place that made sense to her at the time – *Elizabeth's* house. Each one of us could use an *Elizabeth* or two in our life.

Because another Advent is always approaching, another Visitation is always possible. It may be a walk across the street to the widow's house, a long overdue nursing home visitation, a second invitation for that son or daughter too busy every year, a plane ticket to see the grandchildren, a day alone with a forgotten father, reconciliation with an estranged sibling, an extra place setting for a lonely priest, or the lonely person in your life. These are the real events of life, celebrated each Advent. Mary visited *Elizabeth. Elizabeth* blessed Mary. And the world is transformed by the blessing she shared within the context of a simple intentional visitation.

Day 22

"The baby leapt in her womb" …. Luke 1:41

Setting the Stage: Human Life before Birth

I HAVE ALWAYS BEEN INTRIGUED BY THE ABILITY OF A FETUS TO sense or respond to the outside world. Research on this question has grown exponentially in recent years. Scientifically, we want to figure out the amount of conscious awareness the unborn have. It is easy to understand that such knowledge would have a major impact on the abortion debate, our understanding of Fetal life, and potential Fetal learning before birth. Recent studies suggest "the newborn infant exhibits in addition to sensory awareness specially to painful stimuli, the ability to differentiate between self and non-self-touch, sense that their bodies are separate from the world to express emotions, and to show signs of shared feelings."[159] As more and more evidence unfolds, we are discovering a "world within a world" as we sneak a peek inside the home to the Unborn. In this case Luke hinted of an emotional response from one cousin to another.

　　We cannot consider the consciousness of the Unborn without touching upon the issue of Abortion. Abortion is an intensely

---

[159] *The Emergence of Human Consciousness: From Fetal to Neonatal Life"* (March, 2009), Hugo Lagercrantz & Jean-Pierre Changeux. Pediatric Research. nature. com Also read for more information: *"Windows to the Womb: Revealing the Conscious Baby from Conception to Birth"* (Paperback – January 15, 2013), by David Chamberlain and *"Origins: How the Nine Months Before Birth Shape the Rest of Our Lives"* (Paperback – July 5, 2011) by Annie Murphy Paul."

personal and very controversial topic in our world today. We tend to decide on such matters by appealing to our adopted frame of reference, our Worldview. *Naturalists* do not hold to a particularly moral view of the intrinsic value of human life, for they have no frame of reference to do so. We are left to understand our humanity as part of the natural processes of evolution, so our decisions are often determined by what seems best for the people in our lives, the culture at large, and of course our ability to live happy and fulfilling lives as defined by us. The *Naturalist* sees the Fetus as a combination of nerves and cells and growing organs that has not yet achieved measurable consciousness. Abortion is not a moral dilemma for the *Naturalist*.

The *Humanist* takes a simple approach to the issue of abortion. Each person has free will. Each person has innate goodness within. Each person has the right to use free will and innate goodness to make the best possible decision a person can make for their own well-being. The Fetus cannot yet choose and has not achieved the status in our community where its own well-being is paramount. We need to do what seems best for ourselves when faced with the choice of giving birth to a child. Abortion is a moral issue for the *Humanist*, but morality is about the free will choices of the pregnant mother and the rights of the mother, not the Fetus.

The Pantheist is complicated to understand on the issue of Abortion. In a sense Abortion does not end a life, for the life of the Fetus in never isolated from the Collective Spiritual Oneness of the Universe. Therefore, the Fetus will not cease to exist, but instead will be transformed into another form of existence serving the Unity of all things. However, many *Pantheists* oppose abortion for religious reasons, since they are a religious people, though for them God is an impersonal force not a Personal Being.

For example, for the Hindu, if a Fetus is aborted, the soul within it suffers a major *karmic* setback. It is deprived of the opportunities its potential human existence would have given it to earn good karma. The life force within the Fetus is returned immediately to the cycle of birth, death, and rebirth. Thus, abortion hinders a soul's spiritual progress, but does not end its being (This according to the BBC's interpretation of the Hindu Faith taken from a discussion of Abortion found on bbc.co.uk). As you can see, the issue is more complicated when we consider Metaphysical concepts.

As you work through this issue from a *Monotheistic perspective* there are clear indicators of vital details that other Worldviews do not consider relevant. For example, Christians believe the life inside the body of a woman is *The Image of God* and represents an ongoing creation of God which has been given life for the purpose of enjoying God and God's creation. Abortion robs a human being of this opportunity. Christians also teach that Fetal Life is Human Life, and places direction in ancient texts for the protection of said life. Exodus 21 clearly deals with what some deem a Fetus that is harmed. Exodus 21 does not indicate if the injury inflicted upon the unborn baby leads to death. However, the clear implication being, for both the mother and prematurely born child, the death penalty is in place for those who cause either of them to die.

It is important to note that Scripture is not silent on the issue. However, this passage was about a prematurely born baby, not necessarily a non-viable fetus. So, what are we to think about the Fetus? Some of us believe that biblical writers held to the obvious and common belief of the time, so why discuss a question everybody agrees upon? It is called the "argument from silence." We do have considerable evidence that the Early Church opposed Abortion, which no doubt gives credence to a belief that early followers of Jesus did not believe Abortion an honorable moral choice to make.[160]

Personally, I find myself increasingly interested in the discussion arising in Psychobiological circles about the concept of human consciousness in the growing mind of the Fetus. The

---

[160] "What the Early Church Believed: Abortion", Catholic Answers, 2004. Catholicanswers.com

brain ignites somewhere around day 15. However, consciousness is achieved at some point thereafter. Luke declared John the Baptist was conscious inside his mother. Long before he could articulate the source of his joy, he experienced joy. I believe this area of research will have much to teach us about Fetal Life.[161]

The positive thing about the interaction of worldviews is that we can combine evidence from different declarations of Truth to work toward understanding and consensus. This is the beauty of the American system. We are blessed with the opportunity to discuss. I discovered that the *Monotheistic Worldview* encourages this discussion and incorporates different ideas from all differing worldviews. Exponentially more than the other three can interact and integrate. The *Naturalist* speaks to me, as we explore things like consciousness in the Fetus and the reality of pain at some point in Fetal development. I can incorporate the thinking of the *Humanist* as we weigh the rights of Women in comparison to the rights of the Human Fetus. I can understand the *Pantheist* as they remind us of the concept of shared Humanity and the striving of all people groups toward Unity. As a follower of Jesus, I can speak on this issue with compassion, forgiveness, and a desire to understand the psychological pain of Abortion from a variety of angles. The conversation must continue, and each perspective needs to be heard if we are ever to come to a place of understanding within the context of supreme value for all Human Life.

As for this Author, I cannot move forward without mentioning the interconnectedness of Humanity emphasized in the Christian faith, whereby all Life is sacred, and we are called to protect the Living, especially those who are most vulnerable. There is no human life more vulnerable than the Human Fetus.[162] Jesus held

---

[161] The first study I read on this topic: *The Emergence of Human Consciousness: From Fetal to Neonatal Life,"* Hugo Lagercrantz & Jean-Pierre Changeux, March, 2009. Pediatric Research. nature.com

[162] The Fetus in Biblical Law: Does Exodus 21 Support the Practice of Abortion, Ron du Preez, D.Min. September 1992. Ministry Magazine, ministrymagazine.org

an exceedingly high view of taking care of children. However, many make the argument that the Fetus is not yet a child, worthy of the same kind of consideration we give to our children. Be this as it may, it does seem an arbitrary line to draw, often for convenience's sake, given that we can all agree that a Fetus is at the very least a *potential Human life.* It is also very striking to me that every mother immediately and instinctively begins to protect this *potential Human life* the very moment she learns this life is growing inside of her. Human mothers have a Fetal protection instinct built into the core of their being. Though we cannot make a case that this is scientific truth, I wonder, is this not clearly Metaphysical Truth?

My point in these few paragraphs is to open all of this to the idea that our Worldview directs our beliefs about this and other issues. The things we believe are often tied to the time in which we live and the dominant Worldviews of the time. The challenge is to recognize this and go further. We will never be able to communicate productively about such issues until we understand that we often restrict ourselves inside the intellectual avenues we choose to travel when searching for Truth. The interaction of two unborn children recorded by Luke is only possible if we look beyond the *Naturalist View of Reality* in the hearing of this event.

"There are three stages of man: he believes in Santa Claus; he does not believe in Santa Claus; he is Santa Claus." (Bob Phillips)

"The baby leapt in her womb" …. Luke 1:44

The thought of John the Baptist having leapt in his mother's womb when *Mary* entered the house is astounding. The mystery that leaps forth with this statement leaves me wondering and questioning Luke's intent for mentioning this. What was he trying to communicate? Was he merely recounting something revealed to him in an interview, leaving all readers to make their own deduction? Was he trying to tell us something about the work of the Spirit in our lives long before we realized the Spirit's presence within us? Was he pointing to a pre-birth cousin connection between John and Jesus that defied explanation? Was he trying to teach us that the reality of Advent is so mysterious, so amazing, and so utterly unpredictable that we should expect the miraculous to be commonplace for those who long for Jesus? All these questions, and more, occur to me as I try to wrap my mind around an Unborn Child leaping inside *Elizabeth's* womb as Mary entered.

My son captured my world from the moment of conception. I believed him to be a girl. I named him "Sarah," my favorite feminine name. I used to read to him, sing to him, tell him jokes, and even discuss the Cubs with him, all the while calling him "Sarah." I remember thinking that I was the most blessed man on earth, a beautiful bride carrying a much longed for child as we celebrated our last Christmas as non-parents the winter of 91. We had little clue how much Sarah/Josh was about to change everything in our lives. My wife would not allow pictures, ensuring we could not use a six-month pregnant body against her at some time in the future. By now he was kicking, and man did he kick, push, shove, leap. Our baby was a highly active pre-born child. He seemed to respond most to music, and to this day he moves to the rhythm of rap music with the best to them. He is also very habitual and ritualistic, just as he kicked and moved at precise times during both day and night during pregnancy. He is stubborn (like his mom of course), and he showed this by taking his good old time during the birthing process. After a day and a half of labor and six hours of pushing, he finally decided to visit us. The birthing experience was both a test of patience for his dad, and a blur of pain and exhaustion for his mom. This is still the case for both of us, as it is for most parents.

I can honestly say that parenting my son is the most joyful event of my life, while also being the thing I have failed at the most. The advent of my son ended all questions in my mind about the nature and power of God. The One who promises, the One who protects, the One who delivers, The One who chooses, The One who holds the destiny of each child in Hand, faithfully delivered the gift that ruled my heart and mind for eight and a half months. *Josh*, not *Sarah*, was born, and I leapt for joy at his coming. Christmas, the Advent season, is at the core a unique celebration of life, and in the case of John the Baptist he was celebrating the most unique Life birthed in human history before he could understand or articulate the significance of the event. He chose to celebrate his cousin in the only way he could – "he leapt inside the womb."

Advent is about at least these two things: anticipation and birth. God chose to promise a Child unlike any other child, and the birth of this Child marked the beginning of a New Phase in Human history. The Age of Messiah was promised and born. Advent was the miracle of miracles. This was no ordinary birth. Clyde Reid wrote in *You Can Choose Christmas (1975)*: "To anticipate Christmas is to decide now that miracles are possible, and that some are going to happen." If a person has experienced a miracle, she quite possibly understands the depth of such an event. Unexpected, other worldly, and forever transformative, a miracle comes to us like water in the desert or sunshine after a hurricane. Miracles change the way we see life. Miracles change the way we see ourselves. Miracles change the way we define reality. For those who do not believe in miracles I can only suggest that you are not looking for them, for they are all around us. The new baby in your family, the air that we breathe, the love that we have received, the song which inspires us, the poetry that touches us, the photograph that reminds us, the sun that warms us: these are all miracles. Advent is a continuous miracle if you allow yourself to see and understand.

In contrast, I have always hated the day after Christmas. For some reason, it seems the air changes, the atmosphere of life becomes ordinary again. My wife at once starts thinking of getting the tree down. (In my bachelor days I once kept mine up until March). Shopping is a mad house as people look to exchange unwanted gifts or wrong size clothing. I stopped shopping after Christmas in 1998, after someone almost knocked me down trying to get at the latest Nintendo. The bank account is empty, the family has gone back home, all the presents are unwrapped, Christmas Music seems out of place, and leftovers just do not taste the same. The letdown follows Joy. It is natural. It is inevitable.

Christmas time is a reminder of what can be, not simply what is. On December 26th we return to reality, left to wait another year for the reminder of the Miracle to arrive again. *Advent* is a perfect word for this time of year, for it is the hope of arrival, the joy of anticipation, and spirit of the Christmas Coming that communicates to our hearts the possibility of the miraculous. "I feel you, John in the Womb!" You were celebrating Advent, that first Advent, before you could understand what it meant. You were a miracle anticipating an even bigger miracle by miraculously leaping in your miracle Mom's womb because the miracle of miracles just entered the room. "I feel you, John!" You were reminding us to expect the miracle of Advent, and to never allow the mundane and the commonplace to dampen our celebration of the Coming of the Christ Child. Every year God gives us this reminder. And every year we need this reminder. Soon the Miracle of Advent will be upon us once again. Expect a Miracle and prepare to leap for Joy in life's womb. "We feel you, John!"

Joy cannot be contained!!!!!!

Day 23

And Mary said, "My soul glorifies the Lord, and my spirit rejoices in God my Savior, for He has been mindful of the humble state of His servant........" (Mary's song, God takes a side) .... Luke 1:46

Setting the Stage: What is Gen. Z teaching us about Faith?

"According to the Pew Research Center, younger generations, namely Millennials and those from Generation Z, are less religious than their Generation X and Baby Boomer counterparts."[163] Pew defines Baby Boomers as individuals born between 1946 and 1964, Gen Xers between 1965 and 1980, Millennials between 1981 and 1996, and Gen Z as those who touched the Earth for the first time between 1997 and 2012. Gen Z was the first Generation born with a cell phone in hand. No Generation has been more consumed or addicted to modern technology and social media than is Gen Z. What radio was to my Generation, social media on cell phones are to this one. Baby Boomers learned about Jesus, whether they wanted to or not. "Zoomers" learn about Charlie D'Amelio and Emma Chamberlain, whether they want to or not. In my generation "The Beast" was spoken of in Revelation 13 and was to be feared. In Gen Z, "The Beast" is "MrBeast," a dominant YouTube voice who entertains millions. Our attention

---

[163] *Why are millennials and Gen Z shying away from religion? (July 28, 2022),* Written by Conner O' Neil. Published by KARE 11. KARE11.com

seeking mechanisms have been completely transformed over the last four Generations, and The Church has failed to keep up.

While about half of all Millennials in this nation describe themselves as "Christian," around 40% fit into the category called "nones" (do not affiliate with any religion). Though many of these 40% label themselves as "spiritual," they are not using this word in a traditional way. Millennials and "Zoomers" (Gen Z) are changing the landscape in America, where church affiliation and church attendance are no longer part of the spiritual landscape. Simply put, for more than half of those in these two generational categories religious life is simply not a priority. The American Survey Center reports that around 22% of American young adults were not raised in a religion, compared to 3% of senior adults (>55).

Millennials and Zoomers prioritize helping people and showing compassion; they just do not tend to connect this as service to the Divine. Instead, for many of them the church symbolizes pain, condemnation, and is responsible for harming many marginal population groups in our society. I am not suggesting that some churches do not reach out to and create community for these groups. They certainly exist. People harm people, inside and outside churches. In many ways the Church gets an unfair rep, but in other cases it is well deserved.

However, there are many who believe that young adults are leaving the church more because of the "relevance" issue than the "condemnation" issue. If this is indeed the case, then churches can recover, but only if we are willing to move in new directions in terms of how we practice community and worship. The Mega Church movement and the growing church attendance in charismatic congregations gives cause for hope, if in fact mainline denominations can learn from them and implement better strategies toward becoming relevant to the needs of younger Americans. Although more than half of all people who attend church on Sunday are still attending smaller congregations, the average age of these attenders is above 45. Overwhelmingly, younger adults are not there.

If churches of any faith are to reach young adults and youth today, religious leaders must become relevant leaders, striving to reach people at the point of need rather than pushing younger people into becoming a "cookie cutter" congregant. This is not to say theology or orthodoxy must be abandoned. This line of thinking simply means that unnecessary tradition needs to be abandoned in favor of a more contemporary agenda. HAUMC's Associate Pastor Laura Hannah added that "Gen Z and millennials desire authenticity, honest questions that may not have a clear answer and a clear articulation of what religion means for their personal lives." I find this to be true in the college classroom while serving this age group.

Mary's song, God chooses a side…. Luke 1:46

One of the comments I often hear from people who are amid dire circumstances is the phrase: *"that's not fair."* In this DEI environment in which we live, the concept of "equity" is tossed around all through the public sphere. For example, it is part of the purpose proposed by the Institution where I teach. "Equity" seems like a grand gesture on the surface. We are a nation founded on "equal" justice for all, "equality of opportunity" for the rich and the poor, "equity" in the sense that public resources and opportunities are offered to anyone in need of them. The problem arises when we dig deeper into what various groups mean when they use the term "equity." Without an agreed upon definition of our terms, it can become difficult to identify exactly what we should be offering in the name of justice.

It has become obvious that many in the political arena have made "equity" and "justice" synonymous. I think some people in our *Postmodern World* believe that the necessity of fairness is somewhere written in the Cosmos. We often convince ourselves in the church God works within this unwritten rule of fairness, where good people ought to get the best, and bad people ought to get the hammer. However, when we look around this world, we find a consistently unfair reality which often confuses, disappoints, and frustrates our sense of justice. Terrible things do happen to "good people." Disease attacks life, the poor stay with us, and children are often born with ailments they certainly do not deserve. "Life is difficult. This is a great truth, one of the greatest truths. It is a great truth because once we truly see this truth, we transcend it. Once we truly know that life is difficult-once we utterly understand and accept it-then life is no longer difficult. Because once it is accepted, the fact that life is difficult no longer matters."[164]

Those who have adopted a scientific understanding of the universe have already adopted the concept of an unfair universe. Science does not lead us toward a hope for fairness and justice; religion does. The *Naturalistic Worldview* can never accept "equity" as a goal, for this would interfere with Nature's desire to practice "natural selection." We simply cannot devise a plan to protect the weak within a system that emphasizes Nature's desire to weed out weaker pieces of a species.

This is one reason Gen Z is beginning to reject the modern worldview of the Enlightenment. They stand up for justice quite often because they know the current power structures do not often work toward justice for all. This was inevitable once science and reason began to conquer minds and universities, eventually spilling over into cultural thoughts and patterns. In his book *The Gospel in a Pluralistic Society* Lesslie Newbigin writes: "To teach that human beings exist as the result of the successful elimination of weaker species by those which have accidentally inherited superior strength or skill is allowed. To teach that human beings

---

[164] M. Scott Peck, "The Road Less Traveled: A New Psychology of Love, Traditional Values, and Spiritual Growth," 25th Anniversary Edition. Simon and Schuster, NY, London, Toronto, Sydney. Section 1.

exist to glorify God and enjoy God forever is not allowed. Yet both beliefs refer to what is believed to be true for all humans. They are both - if true - extremely important."[165]

The Kingdom of God is a Kingdom built upon the concept and principle of Grace, which is the only permanent solution within a universe full of injustice. True justice would lead to consequences for all of us, even those of us who call ourselves "good people." This is the heart of the Gospel. None are good enough. Justice would eventually take us all down. Therefore, without Grace, we are in a perilous situation indeed. Mary's song displays this environment powerfully. Listen to her words in Luke 1:48: "He has been mindful of the humble state of His servant. From now on all generations will call me blessed, for the Mighty One has done wonderful things for me...." (Luke 1:48).

Evolutionary Theory can offer no explanation for the likes of Mary. It is interesting to me that Mary did not share the high view of herself that many have of her today. She did not see herself worthy or special, only blessed and underserving. Evolution would not have chosen Mary to be the mother of The Son of God. We must find a different explanation beyond that of "Mother Nature's" choice. In Vs. 51 we read: "He has scattered those who are proud in their deepest thoughts." This is a primary reason fairness will not work from God's perspective when we view God's activity in the world. If in fact God exists, it is a simple step forward to believe God sees what we cannot see, that God knows what we cannot know. Verse 52 announced: "He has brought down rulers from their thrones. But He has lifted the humble." Mary was singing to us that God has taken sides in the struggle. God has chosen the poor and the lowly. "He has filled those who are hungry with good things...." (Luke 1:53).

God responds to need. God loves the unlovable. God notices

---

[165] Leslie Newbigin, "The Gospel in a Pluralistic Society," 1989. Wm. B. Eerdmans Publishing Co., Grand Rapids, Michigan.

the unnoticed. Mary's song was not a celebration of fairness but instead delved deeply into issues of Justice. Her song was a celebration of God's desire to right wrongs, to lift the fallen, to bless the humble.......in time. Zoomers find themselves in agreement with Mary's Song, without realizing they do. The fight for the marginalized and the environment that pervades young people today is the fight introduced by Mary in her 1st Century Song - *Mary's Song is a song about Justice where Justice is needed most.*

Pause and consider for a moment all the people this message is relevant for in our world today. Gen Z is indeed teaching us what Mary seemed to know. However, the problem with the framework is apparent. Zoomers have no foundational reason to fight for the cause of the weak. Since there is no God for this generation, there is no Metaphysical reality that we call "justice." We are left to our own devices to define the terms we choose to employ. Without a proper foundation, Human movements will eventually fail, no matter how just they might be. History has taught us this. Without a solid foundation, houses crumble in times of crisis.

(Quotes pertaining to Foundations)

"Capitalism thrives in a climate where 'rights' are the main political agenda. The church becomes one more consumer-oriented organization, existing to encourage individual fulfillment rather than being a crucible to engender individual conversions into the Body." (Resident Aliens, page 33).

"The Very idea of treating religion as a subject that can be put into a list alongside physics, history, and literature is itself an assault on the foundation of belief."[166] (Lesslie Newbigin)

---

[166] If you are a follower of Jesus, I recommend that at some point soon you read the book
"Foolishness to the Greeks" written by Lesslie Newbigin. I have mentioned and quoted this book several times. In chapter 6 - *The Call of the Church* - he gives

"Whatever we may say about the religious neutrality of the State, the experience of passing through school and university is shaping the minds of young people in a certain direction. It is not and cannot be religiously neutral." (Leslie Newbigin, Foolishness to the Greeks, page 140)[167]

"Though religious beliefs have often been used to justify social oppression, they have also frequently provided the motivation for those who stood up against oppression - the abolitionists in nineteenth-century America being a good example." (C.Stephen Evans, page 128)

If believers sometimes show a deep psychological need to believe in God, nonbelievers sometimes show an equally deep psychological need to reject any authority over them

one of the best discussions of the relationship between public and private faith I have read personally. In this chapter, he challenges all religious people to consider the public discourse of religion and the necessity of this task from Enlightenment Thinkers. Without doubt, one of the greatest gifts of the Enlightenment and the Postmodern worldview is the importance of public discourse which takes us beyond the idea of religions as a private matter only. Advent Truths have been lost to us precisely because the Church has done such a poor job of making public this "Timeless Cosmic Event."

[167] The debate around the issue of public institutions' openness to offering religious content is a worldview debate. Are we better off as a society when we leave discussions of Transcendant Truth out of our educational institutions, focusing instead on Scientific knowledge and individual autonomy, which is our emphasis today? Is this a positive direction for our country? Is it better to discuss this issue as a part of our work for a good and secure future, or should we emphasize the right of the individual for freedom of expression, even if this includes censoring critique of certain individual beliefs as off limits for the Critic? One place this discussion could gain some merit in the public arenas is to study what those who founded this country had in mind when the separation of Church and State was wrtten into the Bill of Rights. A couple of helpful articles to get your started on such a discussion might be- Rose, The Founders and Christian Education, Madelyn Rose Craig, February 19, 2018. TLC; The Lutheran Column, thelutherancolumn. com and Thomas Jefferson and Religious Freedom, John Ragosta, 4/16/19. The Jefferson Monticello, Thomas Jefferson Encyclopedia, monticello.org

and to assert themselves as the own lords and masters. (C.Stephen Evans, Philosophy of Religion, page 130)

"Words could indeed distort and deceive, giving the impression of truth when actually they lacked solid foundation. But words could also point, as to the precious invisible mystery, to something genuine and enduring. To find one's way to that genuine reality was the task of confronting the philosopher." (Richard Tarnas, page 34)

What is important to remember from the above quotes is the undeniable knowledge that the ideas that guide our thinking and living in this world have come from traditional sources, and this whether we realize it or not. There is truly "nothing new under the sun," but instead we are re-evaluating and re-stating ancient conversations repeatedly with our questions and discussions in the modern world. This is certainly ok, unless we choose to willingly disconnect from the roots of the core beliefs that guide us, losing valuable opportunities to critique our beliefs and learn from critiques offered in the past for earlier versions of postmodern ideas. The only exception to this would be Transcendent Revelation of some sort. Know this – What we believe today is not a new understanding of reality, but instead a new way of stating a previously discussed exploration of that which is Real. Simply put, if a "Word" is not considered to be Revelation from a Transcendent Source, then this leaves us little choice but to deem it recycled human reflection. (Dr. Rick Farmer)

Interlude

Read at your own risk: Church People vs. Christ People

Allow me to speak about a community I understand well - the institutional church. Having served within her for over 30 years, I have watched firsthand the worldview conflict that has influenced the way we do church. Our conflicting theological identity is one of the major reasons young people in America are running away from our churches at an alarming rate. Too many of our people, at least within the Baptist Tradition (I suspect within other traditions as well), have chosen to be church people rather than "Christ People." "Church people" and "Christ people" have a completely different take on Advent. The following is taken from this Author's (Rick Farmer) Journal notes:[168]

From the Author's Journal: *"I write amid Quarantine. I wonder what God is doing among us as we trust our representatives to come*

---

[168] For the purposes of my writing: *"Church people" a*re those who focus on the church as an institution, where the priorities become the church building, the boards and committees of the church, the traditions of denomination or local church, conservative values often not taught in Scripture, and an over abundance of attention about things like reputation and the appearance of religious morality. *"Christ people"* are those in our churches who will always choose loving people over church tradition, emphasize theological views which are consistent with the Gospel of Christ, practice grace and mercy over and above judgment and condemnation, and identify with the marginalized in a given community or culture. I am presently working on a book on this topic for publication soon.

forward with a plan to curb the spread of Covid-19 while somehow dealing with the economic crisis which has already begun. It is sad when we realize we are trusting a Congress that somehow forgot they were elected to serve the people's needs. Especially when we realize they often cannot agree on even the most basic priorities in a time of dire crisis. Although it leads to tremendous frustration, it also causes me to ponder the basic nature of human beings. We seldom place the needs of others above our own. We seldom make our neighbor our priority, especially if this might cost us something we are attached to. And our ideologies often get elevated over genuine human need. People are dying around us, will soon be starving and homeless around us, and all we have to offer are statistics, debates, and a thirst for power.

For more than 30 years I have watched the same mentality as a Pastor in a mainline denomination. This crisis has highlighted for me the crisis which exists in congregations around America. You see, a virus is invisible, internal, and often very lethal. Much of the time we are oblivious to the cure and have no desire to work on a vaccine, at least in the church. We would rather die waving the flag of Tradition than bring life to those in need. We would rather preserve the King James Bible, argue about how much water we need in the baptismal, fight about the color of the carpet we are about to buy, and give without limits to repairing our steeple, wherein all the while drug addicts die in our streets and children are left to figure out life without Jesus. While this is happening around us, we make certain we have the right kinds of people beside us in the pews. We might agree to buy a bus for children in our neighborhood if they do not have to worship with us on Sunday. We may be okay giving a room for an AA meeting if we do not have to be friends with the participants. We may be ok with ministering to Opiate Addicts, as long as their children do not learn the Scriptures arm in arm with "our" children.

I have seen the above. I have watched in amazement, trying to minister to recovering addicts, while Boards and Committees argued about allowing cigarette smokers on our grounds. I have seen overdoses destroying families, while people inside the safe church sanctuary simply respond: "They got what they deserved." I have watched church leadership argue about a theological interpretation of a difficult passage with passion, while not showing one ounce of this same passion for the lost and the least in their community. I have witnessed gifted evangelists come home from mission trips abroad proclaiming joy for the 50 people they shared the Gospel with (through a translator of course), while not choosing to share the Gospel a single time for the next year, waiting for the next Mission Trip to hit their calendar so they can come back to us with even more stories of their love for people without Jesus. I have watched people quit churches because of issues that are almost laughable and never occur to 95 percent of the congregants worshipping there. I have seen families that have joined 5 churches in 6 years, each time promising this new congregation they are here to serve and minister with them as brothers and sisters in Christ, lifting hearts in condemnation for those among us who are divorced from our spouses while they divorce yet another congregation. I have watched life-long church members refuse to take communion from a deacon because he was an alcoholic 15 years ago, or refuse to sit in a pew beside a man who was accused of adultery by his wife, or vote to expel a brother because he experienced bankruptcy, or refuse to attend a Sunday School Class because the teacher did not read from the King James Bible, or completely reject a fellow congregant who was seen drinking a beer at the golf course. I have seen these firsthand in churches I have served. These are all symptoms of the virus, the invisible killer that has all but destroyed the church in America as far as our youth are concerned. Even now there are readers who are feeling defensive rather than alarmed.

We are losing a generation for the sake of our rules and traditions, which have extraordinarily little to do with sound theology. And we *are running out of time. Within another generation it will be too late. We are about to become a remnant. The Baby Boomers, of which I am one, are dying off. We are aging. We have carried the church forward in America for two generations, and because we have not understood our own shortcomings and come to truth about our viral tendencies, we will take main line churches in America with us to our graves. We are a present-day threat to the future of the Church in the West. We are running out of time.*

*There is a vaccine. There is! It is the same vaccine that has erupted in revival for 2 millennia in the church. The vaccine is The Gospel of Jesus Christ, brought to life within the power of the Resurrection, for each new generation in our world. The Word is not a stagnant, dogmatic, scientifically written document that is meant to be carried like any other book we have read. The Gospel is a living, breathing, eternally resurrecting Person who will never fit into our boxes or become content to live primarily in our sanctuaries. The Gospel burst open the walls of tradition and the chains of human bondage. The Gospel is not dependent upon our ability to understand it, it is dependent upon our willingness to live it. It is not what we know of Scripture which matters, it is what we Live of the Gospel that transforms the lives of people around us. God declares for all to hear: **"I am a God who has chosen the least, the last, and the lost,"** over and above those who believe themselves the chosen and the elite in our churches. The Gospel loudly proclaims this Truth – God has taken sides in the struggle, and the types of people we often migrate toward are not the ones Jesus sought out and embraced."* [169]

Mary's Song is a Gen Z song, for they have also taken sides in the struggle, fighting verbally and politically for the devalued and marginalized in our society. If the Church is going to survive it will

---

[169] Dr. Rick Farmer is currently writing a book on the topic of the modern Church, with the help of some of my students: *Church People vs. Christ People in the 21st Century.* Stay tuned.

be because we have taken up the banner being waived by Mary and "Zoomers," figuring out a way to unite this modern movement with the Gospel once again. Mary's Song, an Advent Song, must become our theme song for the Modern Church, as we learn to celebrate the heart of Advent every day of the year, living as true Children of Faith once again.

Day 24

Zac's song - "The oath He swore to our Father Abraham: To rescue us from the hand of our enemies, and to enable us to serve Him without fear...." Luke 1:73, 74

Setting the Stage: Do the "Maji" belong in our Story?

I GREW UP IN TWO SEPARATE CONGREGATIONS. ONE WAS BAPTIST and the other was Pentecostal (they had church basketball). In the Baptist tradition we had a saying that captured our lack of attention to the Holy Spirit when referencing the Trinity[170] - "Father, Son, and what's His Name ...." In my Pentecostal Church it was more like - "The Spirit has a daily Word for the fathers and sons in here...." However, there was one activity both traditions shared - "The Children's Christmas Pageant." This is the Sunday Evening Service which happens every December in every Christian congregation known to Humanity, focused on retelling the Advent Story through the acting talents of children. This pageantry is Universal, as we celebrate the Advent Event even if we do not stop to consider everything that it means. (I never got to be Joseph.

---

[170] The doctrine of the Trinity means that there is one God who eternally exists as three distinct Persons — the Father, Son, and Holy Spirit. Stated differently, God is one in essence and three in person. These definitions express three crucial truths: (1) The Father, Son, and Holy Spirit are distinct Persons, (2) each Person is fully God, (3) there is only one God.

The closest I ever got to fame was acting as one of the so called "Wise Men").

My role as one of the "Wise Men" sparked an interest in me about the identity of these characters. Allow me to share what I have discovered about them. *Magi*, as we formally frame them, were not kings at all, and were never referred to as "three." There were likely more, but we say three because of the three gifts. They likely came from the area that was once the Babylonian and then the Persian Empire, and there is a good chance they belonged to a school of study that grew up after the writings and teachings of Daniel were left behind. They studied the Scriptures of the Old Testament and other writings from the Empires that ruled before they were born. Kings were a topic of their study. The Stars were a point of emphasis.

In the case of Matthew's Gospel, the *Magi* put together heavenly beings with an earthly Being who was to be born a King. They read the "prophetic sky" and found the Sign of Signs, a Star pointing them eastward. They were people of great wealth and power, given the gifts they brought according to Matthew chapter 2. "They are called *Magi* in the Greek, which was a term that referred to a kind of subclass of Persian priests. But they have come to be known as "The Three Wise Men." Their orientation was much more in the area of what we might identify today as science."[171]

Babylon was famous for its astronomers, considered the scientists of their culture and time. It is important to note that traditions grow and change with time. But we can always return to the time and the text to discern some foundational truth. And this is the primary Truth in the story of the *Magi* - People were watching for and longing for Messiah, including some astronomers from Babylon (or Persia) who came to share in the celebration of the greatest gift ever given.......

---

[171] "Here's What History Can Tell Us About The Magi", Olivia B. Waxman, December 29, 2020, Time Magazine Online. time.com

I saw a commercial the other day where the narrator said: "Nature painted a colorful portrait when we look at the color of our food." Seemingly harmless statement, except it cannot possibly be true. "Nature" is not a person, therefore not an artist, and therefore cannot paint anything. The *Naturalistic Worldview* leaves us without explanation for the Artistry of the Cosmos, the color of our food, or the positioning of the Stars. The *Maji* understood that the positioning of stars was an intelligent and purposeful act performed by a Transcendent Personal Being of immeasurable power. It is the Deity that colors our food, a Person who has both the power and the creative energy to make the food we need and position the stars we gaze upon. This is why the *Magi* connected the positioning of stars with a Word from the Divine. The modern Scientist trying to explain such things by crediting "Nature" with abilities nonpersons cannot possibly possess has closed themself off from the Truth these *Magi* embraced. They would rather believe a nonperson created color in food rather than learn from the *Magi*. These ancient scientists read the ancient scrolls, watched and measured the stars, and it led them to where the new King lay.

Zac's song, "the oath God swore to our Father Abraham" …. Luke 1:73

John's father *Zechariah* "was filled with the Holy Spirit, so he prophesied." When we last saw him, he was silenced because he did not believe. What a word for us today. What do you think would happen if we made a rule in our churches that we are not allowed to speak without faith? What would our Board Meetings and Business Meetings be like if the rule of order were that unless we are speaking a word of faith guided by the Holy Spirit, we are to remain silent? I once pastored a church that tried something like this. We all agreed that as we spoke, we would say a prayer aloud before we shared our views (Thank you Dr. Mark). It was quite effective, for a while. It tapered the tone of the speaker. However, this new practice did not last long. After all, if you have 100 Baptists in a room you will have 103 different opinions and another outlier. We soon returned to the customary practice of listening to ourselves spout our own opinions rather than taking a moment to speak with God.

Our words and opinions are often *moot*, but like *Zac*, we do not like being *muted* when we wish to speak. *Zac*, however, was made *mute* because his words were *moot*. *Zac* was silenced because his faith was silent. *Zac* was not allowed to speak his doubt into the Community of Faith, not until he was ushered into the presence of the God who makes all things possible. Within our culture of noise, we value speaking more than silence, which is a primary reason that what we say often has little thinking behind the words we use. To speak without thought is like driving to a new City without preparation. There are many ways to get lost along the way. Silence breeds thought, thought breeds critical thinking, and critical thinking breeds a well-spoken word. Of those who spoke of Advent and what it means for us, few can surpass Dr. Luke, if any. *Zac* was silenced for the good of the people, and for the good of future generations who would share in his story. If we learn nothing else about Advent from my thinking in this document, please learn this - it is not wise to push away a Timeless Script without offering the Doctor a chance to introduce the very cure we need. Fifteen years of deep thinking and consuming conversation has led me to what you are reading right now.

We can easily find ourselves inside the Holy of Holies within a Temple[172] without being in God's presence, and not understand

---

[172] The "Holy of Holies" is the place inside the Temple where a designated priest enters once a year in order to offer prayers and the blood of animal sacrifice to intercede for the people. This year and on this occasion *Zacharias* was assigned the task. It was his turn to enter, one of the many historical events that lay under the Sovereignty of God during this first Advent. The result of this encounter changed his life forever, in many ways.

where we stand and what we are missing. In my field we call this "in-attentional blindness," missing what is right in front of us because we are distracted. I believe *Zac* spent his nine months of silence pondering, praying, and perceiving. He was brought into the atmosphere of God's Grace by the Spirit of God who would not abandon him, but rather taught him. Transformed by silence, *Zac* learned to pray before he ever spoke again. And when he finally did speak, he had something of tremendous value to say, something which transcended his smallish Worldview which he held to even as a priest. His worldview had boxed him in, his vision had been suppressed, his understanding of Glory had been covered over, and drastic measures were needed that he might be opened to a "Universe of the Miraculous." Nothing will keep us from seeing the miraculous more than a faulty Worldview. Luke wrote to unplug the faithless from the traditional religious Matrix of his time. In doing so, his Gospel can also unplug each of us.

By the time his words began to flow, he had become a different man. "Praise to the Lord.........because He has come to His people and redeemed them. He has raised up a horn of salvation of us.......to remember His Holy Covenant...." (Luke 1:68-72). *Zac* arrived at a place where he could grasp that the promises of God are sure and the activity of God on our behalf is unstoppable. His words were now bathed in a renewed understanding of God's promises to *Abraham*, whereby God acted faithfully on behalf of the people. No matter where we find ourselves, no matter the problems we are experiencing, God is able. We cannot discover the fascinating connection of Advent, through the unlikely line of David, to the outrageous promises God made to Abraham, and walk away unchanged. This remains true even if we choose to investigate from a historical scientific perspective. There is just so much "coincidence" as to deny that it is coincidence at all.[173]

---

[173] I found a neat little book online that serves as a beginning of exploration for such an investigation: Dr. David Reagan, "Christ in Prophecy." Format: Paperback

The difference between living with this belief and without this belief is the difference between living with hope and living without hope. Hopelessness surrounds us. Usually, a lack of hope takes two distinct forms, which our eyes do not go a single day without observing. First there is depression, which is dominant in our time. And there is rage, which dominates our roads, our city streets, and our domestic relationships. If the future depends on the will and planning of Humanity, as opposed to a Powerful, Purposeful, and Passionate Deity, then we are to be pitied as a species. But if God is real, as Luke entertained, the future fits within a Grand Design that can only leave us wanting for more. *Zac* had forgotten this. *Zac* had hidden his hope heartlessly. *Zac* needed a refresher course. As we read these Advent thoughts together, can we say we are all that different? Why not take some time for silence today with the goal of rediscovering the Truth about our destiny tomorrow? Listen to the Text before arguing with the Text. Enter your Holy of Holies. And if you are without one, create one. We no longer need a Temple, for we live in the day of *Immanuel,* "God with us."

My mother used to say to me, *"if you don't have anything good to say, don't say anything at all."* As an adult, I know this is to be an impossibility. However, the principle hinted at is pointing us in the right direction. We waste lots of time and energy flooding our faith communities with tainted words of disbelief. Hebrews 10 declares: "Since we have a great priest (not Zac) over the house of God, let us draw near to God with a sincere heart and with the full assurance that faith brings.......If we deliberately keep on sinning (he speaks here of the sin of unbelief) after we have received the knowledge of truth, no sacrifice for sins is left" (Hebrews 10:21-27, parts of). The Author of Hebrews is speaking of *Zac's* sin.

Book or Downloadable Book.
See also *Applying the Science of Probability to the Scriptures: Do statistics prove the Bible's supernatural origin*, David Reagan. Lamb and Lion Ministries, christianprophecy.org

Zachariah the priest ought to have known better. He lived in the place of God's presence within the Temple. He was standing for the people as their representative, and if anyone ought to have known that this visitation was the Word of the Lord coming to him, he should have. His response was one of distrust, lack of faith, and full of doubt. He spoke, but not from faith. He showed his hand. *"Do I really believe God can do this thing he is promising to do?"* But this was nine months ago. Silence has forced him to think, pray, rethink and re-pray. God has shaped him through silence. So now his words reflect an understanding of what God most certainly can do, has done, and will do. His faith has been amplified. His words bore witness to this transformation.

Some will say to me, "Big deal, he had John to prove what God can do. The child was born. It is easy to trust God after the miracle!" Is this what it takes? If this is true, then why do we so easily forget the miracle God performed in our life just last week? The Israelites who experienced the plagues in Egypt and who walked across the Red Sea on dry ground still wanted to return to Egypt when things seemed bad for them. Does the miracle create faith, or was it the silence that changed *Zac?*

The more pertinent question - does the miraculous really work to change us? We experience miracles all the time. What about the bill that got paid, the healing that God ushered into our relationships, the money that was found, the void that was filled, the life that was transformed, the church need that was met, the baby that was born in our family, the answer to yet another problem, the life that was extended, the sinner that found forgiveness, the marriage that was restored, and the numerous answers to countless prayers that all the children of God have witnessed over the centuries. Do we confront the next challenge with faith considering all that God has shown us? Do we really believe in the Advent Story? Do we understand that the same God who brought John the prophet child to an elderly couple is the same God Who is with us today? Do we believe that the faith *Zac* found is the same faith God instills inside each of us? An old friend use to repeat this phrase: "*God is who He says He is, and God can do what He says He can do.*" Would it not be better for us to remain silent until we can express this kind of faith to those who are listening to our words? It is time to stop talking until God gives us the words we need to speak. It has taken me over a decade to get these words right and I continue to listen and edit every new day. Throughout all these days God has never failed to speak to ears that are open to hear.

(LAUGH WITH ME...)

To encourage reflection, the monks who vow
silence are required to share one thought on the
five-year anniversary with the head Monk.

After five years, the monk meets with the head monk and he
says, "food is bland, should be spicy to engage our senses!"

Five years later, another thought, "Bed too hard, should
be softer to allow easy rest to encourage restful body."

Five years later, he meets with the head Monk. "I can't take it
anymore! I'm ending my vow and leaving the Monastery!"

"Good!" The head monk responds, "All
you've done for 15 years is complain."

Day 25

"And the child grew and became strong in spirit, and he lived in the wilderness until he appeared publicly to Israel." (Luke 1:80)

Setting the Stage: Listen...

"There are a variety of ways to listen. We can listen with our ears closed, only hearing what we choose to hear. We can listen with our ears covered, drowning voices which have something important to say. Or we can listen, truly listen, even when it is the last thing we would choose to do. "Those who have ears to hear will hear what the Spirit is speaking to the churches." (Rick Farmer)

"TALK TO YOU LATER." THIS IS AN OFT SPOKEN WAY OF SAYING goodbye. It is both an invitation and an informal contract between people, as we pledge that we will connect with our voices again. When I say "talk" I do not mean text or email or some form of social media connection. I am talking about voice connection through face-to-face meetings or a phone call. The importance of voice connection is a topic of much study in recent years. One series of experiments were performed by members of the Harvard Business Review. This research suggested that talking is superior to texting in terms of personal connection. Kumar and Epley wrote, "We recently conducted several experiments that suggest people undervalue the positive relational consequences of using voice relative to text alone, leading them to favor typing rather than talking - a potentially unwise preference."[174]

These researchers discovered that the connection level did not increase from seeing the other person as much as it increased when hearing their voice. Their voice. There is something about the voice. In a day of technological dominance in our interactions, it may seem old-fashioned to pick up the phone and connect. However, it seems that of all ways to communicate, voice to voice may be the most meaningful connection of all for most of us. I wonder if this is one reason we still read the Scriptures aloud in our worship services, as we tune ourselves to the voice of God a couple times a week. Excuse me, I think I will go call my mom now just to hear her voice............ Yes, it was Mom. She did not have much to say, but the sound of her voice was a gift. My Mom struggles to formulate her thoughts nowadays. Sometimes her words do not make sense to me. But the sound. The Beautiful sound. I struggle with my addiction to texting. I sometimes wonder what this is doing to our brains and our ability to truly connect with people. As a teenager I could sit and talk on the phone for hours at a time. (Her name does not matter, so stop asking.) The Key is that there is connection in a voice that cannot be duplicated in other ways.

The sense of sound is transforming. Listening to music, a first phone call from a new friend, the hello of a family member separated in space and time, the announcers call of a winning touchdown, the purity of church bells, the ticking of a clock, the beauty of a foreign language, the joy of certain accents. Today I can say I miss my sister's voice more than I can even express. Never mind her WV Hillbilly accent and her kind soft tones. That would be enough. But it was the wisdom that flowed like a river in the desert that came to me when needed most as she spoke in a language all her own. Did you know that tone of voice is the most

---

[174] *Research: Type Less, Talk More*, Amit Kumar and Nicholas Epley, October 5, 2020. Harvard Business Review, Analytical Department. hbr.org

accurate way of determining a person's mood? Not facial gestures or words, but tone of voice. Listen to the tone if you really want to know what is going on inside another person.

John the Baptizer listened. Intently listened. Then he spoke. And the words that poured forth from his mind were used of God to prepare the world for the coming of Messiah. And this world has never been the same since. He set the stage.......

"Until the time came for him to appear publicly to Israel." ..... Luke 1:80

I talk too much. My wife knows this, my son knows this, and all my friends know this. I have noticed that many pastors do. We believe we have so much to say. Like anyone who talks too much I often put my foot in my mouth. Once a word goes forth it works to bring life or death, builds up or tears down, and it can never be pulled back. It is out there, doing its thing for the rest of eternity. I have said things to people I love I would do anything to take back, for I know they resound in their memory in ways that cannot be erased. I am learning to cherish moments of silence, though I often am the one to break them up at the most inopportune time. (Rick, please quieten down a bit.)

When pastoring, the quietest place in my life was in my car. Every Sunday morning, I drove to church in silence. I looked forward to this time. No voices in my ear, no demands or complaints, no phone or TV. Just silence. Silence breeds prayer, and prayer breeds the presence of God. I loved Sunday mornings in my car, as silence prepared me for the worship to come. It was the one place that seemed to me an escape from the world. A quiet ride to quiet the mind. Knowing it would not last long, it was time to seize the moment before it slipped away, for each Sunday was about to get very noisy and crowded. The quiet moments of our lives seem to slip away, as the chaos of our lives awaits, and our souls are drenched in the noise and activity of our world. Silence, the forgotten vaccine for the troubled soul.

The Henry Nouwen Society exists that God's people might *"foster the spirituality of solitude, community, and compassion."* There was a period in Henry Nouwen's scholarly priestly life when God set him aside for silence. A man who often authored a book a year while teaching in various universities, found himself called to South America, where he spent six months in residence. He was looking for God's direction for a new vocation as a missionary to the third world. God called him and taught him, but not with words. It was through the silent ministry of a man named Adam; a young man Nouwen looked after. He was unable to talk, walk, or dress himself. Henri's call was to tend to this man. It took him two hours a day to prepare Adam for the day to come, bathing him, shaving him, brushing his teeth, combing his hair, and guiding his hand as he tried to eat breakfast. One who visited was left wondering – *"is this the wisest use of this honorable Priest's time?"* Henry's response: *"It is I, not Adam, who benefits most from our friendship.*[175] His time with Adam, away from fax machines and computer screen and day timers, had taught this Priest the utter joy of solitude. Silence opened Henry to voices he otherwise would not have heard. First, Adam's voice, who had so much to teach Henry. But then God's voice, which is often only heard when we quiet the world around us.

However, solitude cannot be the end of the matter. It is not enough to embrace transformative silence and never become a transformative agent who declares what we have heard to those who need to hear. *Zac* surrenders his son to a Grand Plan. Suffering can drive us to places of intense solitude. But we cannot stay there. There is a higher purpose for which we were born. What we comprehend in silence can become the message we take to the world around us. Luke relayed this truth in these words about John: "And the child grew and became strong in spirit, and he lived in the wilderness until the time came for him to appear publicly to Israel" (Luke 1:80).

---

[175] Henry J. M. Nouwen, *"Adam: God's Beloved"* (September, 1997). Orbis Books. ISBN: 1570751331 & ISBN13: 9781570751332.

Notice the progression. A father is silenced to learn to embrace a son by faith, and only did he speak when it was time to declare his son's name - "He is to be called John" (*God is gracious*) (Luke 1:60). *Zac* speaks of someone beyond himself - his son. A son born with a purpose declared through his name; a purpose ordained as he was knit together in the womb. He lived into his purpose, for meaning and purpose is what brings supreme value to life. Jordan Peterson, one of the greatest thinkers of the 21st century, says it like this: "Meaning emerges when impulses are regulated, organized, and unified. Meaning emerges from the interplay between the possibilities of the world and the value structure operating within that world. If the value structure is aimed at the betterment of Being, the meaning revealed will be life-sustaining. It will provide the antidote for chaos and suffering. It will make everything matter. It will make everything better."[176]

Suffering and chaos are without end in the world we occupy. John was born into this chaos but meaning and purpose had already brought supreme value to his life. He was the herald of *God's Gracious Gift* about to arrive on earth. *The Answer* was about to climb into the chaos. This Answer was not a political policy or a scientific equation but would be a Person. A Person who was about to change everything. And John was allowed to introduce this "Keynote Speaker into the Workshop of Life." This was to be his purpose. Where did John learn this purpose, this profound agenda taught him since birth? In Silence. In the Wilderness. A place where sounds of nature and the symphony of the land were the voices he heard. John listened in silence, just like his dad. But when he spoke, his voice became the voice of a new day on the way. John's destiny was realized, and the world was changed.

Many of us will travel through our lifetime without touching the surface of our purpose, the meaning behind our existence.

---

[176] Jordan Peterson, *12 Rules for Life: An Antidote to Chaos*, 2018. Published by Random House Canada.

We will spend our time creating noise to drown out the chaos in our lives. We will plan to deal with suffering through indulgence, activity, stimulation, money, power, or some other kind of noise. If we cannot still ourselves long enough to take inventory of the emptiness inside and the chaos around, we will settle for a way to manage our days to simply make it through the day. We will convince ourselves we manage as best we can. John, not a single time, "managed" a day. He embraced the day precisely because he understood his purpose. His life had meaning because he dove headfirst into his destiny. Only the value structure which embraces meaning, our true purpose, can conquer the voices we hear within the chaos of our lives. And once these voices are conquered, we must find new ones that lead us toward our Purpose. The voices we need most are not the ones most offered.

We are used to noise. Our computer is our companion. Our cell phone is our friend. And silence is awkward in most arenas. At this very moment I am inside a college library where people are either gathered in groups discussing whatever or looking down to their cell phones to discover whatever or typing on their computers about whatever. I am amazed at how few people read a book in this Library, how often silence is a modified silence in today's world, even in places designated for silence. Silence forces us to deal, and we do not want to deal. We want the chaos to go away, not to confront our often-meaningless existence highlighted amid chaos.

This is the heart of cancel culture so popular in our society today. If I do not like what I hear I will just shut out the noise you are making, refuse to listen, and actively work to make sure others cannot hear you as well. Some have not made it this far in this book because they simply do not agree and refuse to grapple with information that does not affirm or confirm their personal ideology. It is a vastly different time for us. We avoid chaos, believing it has nothing to teach and little to offer. Imagine if Martin Luther King, Jr. had chosen to avoid the chaos of his time? MLK is not a prophet so much for what he believed, but for what he accomplished through word and deed in the face of chaos at every turn.

I was transformed the day my grandfather died, my first real moment of chaos. I locked myself in my dorm room for hours, and just lay in silence. I could not speak, and I could not hear. I wanted to scream but nothing came from my mouth. There were no words and there were no answers. There was only silence. But in this silence, God spoke. It took a while, but at some point, between the tears and the pain and the void in my soul, God spoke. Very quietly but very powerfully. Beyond words. *"Your grandpa is ok. He's with me. You will see him again. Everything is ok. I will be his voice for you."*

This was a voice that calmed all my fear, and I heard what I needed to hear in the silence of the night. And when the silence began to fade, the meaning of his life inspired me. This inspiration did not lead to simple emulation. Rather, it was a creative explosion. Because of all he taught me, I understood my place, and my faith was rooted in the sum of a life lived with purpose. But it was not my grandfather's purpose that confronted me in this chaos. It was my purpose. A purpose introduced by my grandfather became a purpose I would live daily. He became a bridge to Christ for me. This was the whisper that drove me from my room and back out into a different kind of chaos. Though flawed, frightened, and fatigued, faith began to flow toward meaning and purpose.

I found my place as a student, which grandpa said I would. I migrated toward Seminary and Counseling, which he said I would. I learned from my mistakes, which he said I would. I excelled as a learner and eventually a teacher, as he said I would. All of this was motivated deep within my soul through the chaos of his death and my loneliness in that room without him. For the first time in my young life, I understood why I was born.

John grew quietly within the chaos, being a 1st century Jew living beneath the strong hand of Roman Rule. Like his dad, he learned through silence, until the time arrived. Calling the wilderness his home, he lifted his voice to fulfill his purpose, "make straight the pathway for our God" (Luke 1:4, a passage from my memory). Once we hear a call toward our meaning and purpose, we cannot go back without losing our way. And if we truly hear it, we have been given a gift we must not flounder.

"The Voice of God calls daily. It is impossible not to hear if we choose to listen." (Rick Farmer)

"A Day In His Kingdom"

I rise on the wings of the dawn. I hear Him. I hear Him.
He speaks so soft and yet so clear
So soft that just my heart can hear
A voice that chases all my fear

Then I stumble upon the clouds that block the noonday sun
Yet, I hear Him. I hear Him.
His voice brings light unto my path
The day becomes a joy at last
As He calls to me, "Take my hand and hold fast."

Lord, why are there moments of doubt?
Why does my heart cease to shout?
Is faith to come and then to slip away?
Is it in the way I pray?
I ask you Lord, why through the day
are there moments of doubt?

Then I listen for His whisper through the shadows of dusk
And I hear Him. I hear Him.
Sometimes as if He is so near
This is when my heart can hear
A voice that chases all my fear

But Lord, why do my doubts return?
Inside I feel my spirit burn
Return to me my Rock, My King
For in your voice my strength you bring
I ask you Lord; return this day to light my path

As the morning comes and all grows quiet
I hear Him! I hear Him!
His voice becomes an endless tree
Whose branches serve to rescue me
In love His Spirit sets me free

And doubt begins to fade away
As I praise Him for another day
A Day in the Kingdom He builds through me
I dream that I can almost see
The One who died that this might be
(Rick Farmer)

"Christmas celebrates the awesome and amazing fact
that God is grander, wiser and more mysterious than
we could have ever imagined." (Dan Schaeffer)

"We must resist the modern ill-conceived assumption that this
theological interest in any way precludes a healthy historical
interest. Rather, as Wright insists, Luke's theological story
'only means anything if it takes place within public, world
history'…. Luke tells *Theophilus* that he is seeking to write
reliable history (an orderly account, Luke 1:3) by carefully
investigating reliable sources (Luke 1:2)."[177] (Gregory Boyd)

---

[177] Gregory Boyd with help from N. T. Wright, "Cynic Sage or Son of God?", page 256

Day 26

"Caesar Augustus issued a decree that a census should be taken" … Luke 2:1

Setting the Stage: The Census that set the stage

THE CENSUS LUKE ALLUDED TO HERE DOES NOT HAVE A LOT OF historical support as an actual event during the time which Jesus was born. Certainly, historical events which we believe took place have been adopted by historians with less evidence than what Luke gave us in his Gospel, but when it comes to Scripture, scrutiny is often amplified. If Luke was reporting events truthfully and accurately, there are incredible ramifications that many in this world would rather not face. I will admit to you that I cannot appeal to other information in support of this Census, but I can ask three questions that you may ponder with me that give credence to the strong probability that Luke is telling the truth.

1. *Is there anything in the text suggesting Luke is making up the story?* Given that the early church embraced Luke's Gospel, that he had clearly discussed things with Jesus' mother, and that his Gospel was in circulation within 35 years of Jesus's death, we have a particularly good reason to trust what we read. Otherwise, protest would have been easy to lodge at the time.

2. *Are there any recently discovered fragments which give credence to Luke's version of the Census?* Yes, there are. Two of note are things which I explain to you in the Essay to follow. First, recent discoveries have led us to believe that Herod died later than 4 B.C., which opens a period that could very well have allowed *Quirinius* to be Governor at the time of Jesus's birth.

3. *Could Jesus' actual birth year be later than once thought?* We know that the Governorship changed hands in 6 B.C. Often this was done in Rome to get social circumstances under control, which can equate to a census for Tax Purposes. However, Luke was aware of two things we can say with some confidence. *Quirinius* was quite possibly in charge of two censuses, each of which would take years to accomplish. And if Luke himself seems aware of two censuses, then it is highly likely he is speaking of the first one in reference to the registration of Joseph and Mary in Bethlehem.[178] We are left to explore the evidence that the first census took place during the time of Herod's reign.

If Herod was still alive, then the fragments that were discovered verifying migration to people's hometown for a census becomes far more likely under his reign. It is possible that Herod was alive in 2 B.C. and *Quirinius* was Governor for the first time during this period. There is one fragment recently discovered that may point to two periods of Governorship for *Quirinius*.

The final question we might entertain is: *Why would Luke make up a story at the very beginning of his Gospel that could easily be disproven, thus invalidating for his audience anything which follows?* My immediate answer is - "he would not." Why bother to write a Gospel at all if you are going to begin by making up an easily disputable story about a Census that never took place, which

---

[178] Gregory A. Boyd, "Cynic Sage or Son of God?", page 258-259.

many in Luke's world would be able to prove? It seems to me he would put this Census record in writing only if he were sure about it, and only if he wanted to validate his research into the Life of Jesus by beginning with a fact that would go a long way in proving his trustworthiness as an historian.

(LAUGH WITH ME...)

-Thanksgiving is an emotional time. People travel thousands of miles to be with people they only see once a year. And then discover once a year is way too often. (Johnny Carson)

-I never believed in Santa Claus because I knew no white man would be coming into my neighborhood after dark. (Dick Gregory)

-I remember Christmas years ago when my son was a kid. I bought him a tank. It was about a hundred dollars, a lot of money in those days. It was the kind of tank you could get inside and ride. Instead, he played in the box it came in. It taught me a valuable lesson. Next year he got a box, and I got a hundred dollars for a new sand wedge. (Unknown)

-One Christmas in the good old days I got the best gift from my landlord. There was ice on the pipes in my apartment, and he fixed it without me even having to ask. He put antifreeze in the radiator. (Herb Shriner)

-Why is it when we talk to God we are said to be praying, but when God talks to us we are diagnosed as schizophrenic. (Lily Tomlin)

The Roman Census….

Although we have little historical evidence for the decree Luke spoke of, other than his record here in Luke 2:1, we do have some evidence which would lead us to believe Luke can be trusted. Let us observe the fact that he mentioned a "first Census," which took place when *Quirinius* was Governor of Syria. A "first Census" implies there is a second to follow, which Luke knew about. We are now aware of two details which Luke may have been the first to relay to us. 1. *Quirinius* had two periods of leadership in Syria. Luke is showing us that he was aware of two different periods when *Quirinius* served Rome in Syria, the last being the A. D. 6 period, preceded by a B. C. period, of which we are certain he ruled as Governor. 2. Luke mentioned a "first Census," which most certainly implies there was a second, else why did he write "first Census?" Could it be that Luke reported what he reported because he was more aware of things in that day about Syria than we can be today? He lived within 30 years of these events, and he claimed to have made a "thorough investigation" in his introduction, so why should we not give credence to his statement here? In summary, "the probability that *Quirinius* was governor of Syria on two different occasions cannot be ignored." These two periods covered 12 B. C through at least 6 A. D., with a second term beginning in 6 A. D. Luke is aware of two distinct Census times. This is a fact that must be reckoned with.

A second interesting observation is that Luke is aware of something we did not discover until recent times about life in Roman Provinces in the 1st century A. D… There was a requirement to return to one's hometown for registration during an official Roman Census. Luke seemed certain on this point, and it was the reason Joseph and Mary traveled to Bethlehem. Archeologists unearthed an actual document from the Roman province adjacent to Syria which reads: *"Gaius Vibuis Maximus, Prefect (Governor) of Egypt orders: 'Seeing that the time has come for the house to house census, it is necessary to compel all those, who for any cause whatsoever are residing outside their districts, to return to their own homes, that they may both carry out the regular order of the census, and may also diligently attend to the cultivation of their allotments."* [179]

Luke was informed as to this practice within Roman Provinces, even before other historical documents confirmed his claim. His attention to detail is fascinating. For one thing, it tied the earthly father of Jesus and his birth mother to the city and people of David. Later Jesus' Messiahship would be challenged on the grounds that he was not from Bethlehem but grew up in Nazareth. This detail was used against Him, since those who knew the Law and the Prophets would certainly be aware that Jesus was to come from the house and lineage of David, born in David's City (Bethlehem). How often do we draw faulty conclusions because we look on the surface of things? Luke took us deeper into the matter. Jesus was born in Bethlehem, just as the prophets foretold (See Micah 5:2; 1 Samuel 17:56-58).

In addition to this, God ordained the Roman Government to be the vehicle through which the Christ Child would be born within the boundary of the City of David. The Gospels gave us some incredible details surrounding Jesus' birth, which not only confirmed the historical accuracy of Luke's research, but also pointed us to the activity of God as God rules over the various aspects of human life. Rome decreed a Census, the Magi found Christ in the stars, a Priest fathered a child Prophet, and Shepherds arrived to herald the event to the least and the last in this area of the world (See Matthew 2:1,2, and Luke 2:8-20). Rome, Wise

---

[179] For a thorough discussion of this discovery please consult: *The Case for Christmas: How reliable is the New Testament in portraying the story of Christ's birth?* from BeliefNet.com This Article is about a portion of a book written by Lee Strobel (investigative journalist) and discusses his observation about Roman Census practices in the 1st Century A. D.

Men, Temple Workers, and Common Folk, all proclaiming God's Sovereignty as the Coming of Jesus unfolded. There is not a crevice in this universe where God's will be not manifest. This is the foundational Truth on which the Advent story is proclaimed. This is Metaphysical Reality which survives all generations to follow. God was at work in the 1st century precisely because God has a purpose for Human history.

Let us imagine for one brief second what the world might be like had Jesus not been born. James Kennedy and Jerry Newcombe drafted an amazing book on this topic, though I do wish they might redo this book and make it more appealing to younger Americans. Early in his book he writes: "Some people have made transformational changes in one department of human learning or in one aspect of human life, and their names are forever enshrined in the annals of human history. But Jesus Christ, the greatest man who ever lived, changed every aspect of human life—and most people do not know it. The greatest tragedy of the Christmas holiday each year is not so much its commercialization (gross as that is), but its trivialization. How tragic it is that people have forgotten Him to whom they owe so very much."[180]

In his book *A Study of History*,[181] Arnold J. Toynbee devotes more space to Jesus than any other historical figure. He writes: "What is it about this man to explain his ascendancy in the world? A multitude of sages, prophets, poets, and kings bequeathed to the world their teachings; but only one broke all human bounds. If we examine this question objectively and logically, we must ask again, why did one single soul succeed to such a place of honor? Is he the

[180] Jerry Newcombe and Dr. James Kennedy, *What if Jesus Had Never Been Born?: The Positive Impact of Christianity in History*, November 12, 1994. Thomas Nelson, Inc., Nashville, TN. Chapter 1.

[181] Reference to Toynbee's work is quoted in Arthur W. Kac, "The Messianic Hope". Page 150. He is quoting Arnold J. Toynbee, "A Study of History: Abridgment of Volumes I-VI" by D.C. Somervell, 1947, 1957. Oxford University Press, global. oup.com

only jewel in God's treasure house, and are all other souls mere broken pottery fragments?"

We cannot escape the impact Jesus has had throughout the history of our world. His teachings and his followers have been largely responsible for shaping hospitals, universities, literacy and education across the globe, capitalism, equal justice for all, the overcoming of slavery, the elevation of women, scientific inquiry, benevolence and charity, higher forms of justice, high regard for human life from all races and ethnic backgrounds, civil liberties, Alcoholics Anonymous, the separation of religion and government, the codification of languages, the development of art and music, and the transformation of countless lives for the better. These are just a few I can name off the top of my head. This world would be a far worse place to live in if not for the coming of Jesus of Nazareth, and this without mentioning the hope He gives to millions across the globe of a better world one day someday. It is impossible to blow off the impact of Jesus by pointing to the realities of the pain and mistakes "Christians" have made.

Followers of Jesus have certainly committed atrocities in his name. However, these were those who misrepresented his teachings to work for the very things Jesus willingly surrendered to become One of us – things like power and money and control and suppression of the human will and spirit. The 1st century followers of Jesus were known to be a compassionate people, inclusive to an extreme, and would never support the atrocities people choose to list when they make a modern case against Jesus Himself. It is important in our time to understand that Jesus did not teach these tendencies of mistaken followers, and certainly did not inspire them. We do not see a hint of the things some who claim to be Christian have done to harm humanity in the entire Gospel of Luke. You do not need to take my word for this. I invite you to read for yourself … Dr. Luke needs no appointment. He is waiting.

"Certainly, the modern tendency among more radical critics to prefer their own speculations over such ancient testimonies is unwarranted. The early tradition has to be seriously wrestled with, and any attempt to replace it is going to have to include a plausible alternative to their testimony as to how this tradition got started, and why it was so quickly spread, and universally accepted." (Gregory Boyd)

"In God's upside-down economy, the road to the top is from the bottom - and that lies in the face of everything our culture believes is necessary to be successful.....
In fact, almost everything Jesus said about the nature of Christian discipleship is precisely the opposite of what our culture exalts. (Tullian Tchividjian)

"Indeed, in the current climate it would seem to be a good thing if Theologians and others would cease to utter judgments about what "modern people' *can* believe and think instead more deeply about what modern human beings *should* believe." (C Stephen Evans, page 123)

Day 27

Joseph also went up from the town of
Nazareth in Galilee to Judea, to Bethlehem
the town of David, because he belonged to
the house and line of David.... Luke 2:4

Setting the Stage: A Theological Meaning for a Metaphysical Reality

DURING THE DAYS OF JESUS' BIRTH, AND FOR THE NEXT 1300 years, knowledge was dominated by the *Theological* Stage, according to the "the French social theorist Auguste Comte (1798–1857). According to Comte, human societies moved historically from a *theological* stage, in which the world and the place of humans within it were explained in terms of gods, spirits, and magic; through a transitional *metaphysical* stage, in which such explanations were based on abstract notions such as essences and final causes (*see teleology*); and finally to a modern, *"positive"* stage based on scientific knowledge."[182] According to Comte, the *theological* stage lasted until around 1300 A. D., perpetuated via the tremendous influence of the Roman Catholic Church on the knowledge people trusted as reality. From 1300 – 1800 A. D. a *metaphysical* stage dominated the human search for knowledge. This stage did not serve as a denial of the *theological*, but instead

---

[182] "History & Society: Law of three stages", written and fact checked by The Editors of Encyclopaedia Britannica. December 20, 2023. This article was most recently revised and updated by Brian Duignan. Britannica, britinnicca.com

opened the door for a new way of understanding ancient religious documents and the truths declared in them. The Bible was exposed to contextual analysis, source analysis, and philosophical discussion about age old texts during this period, especially the later centuries of this period. Smack in the middle of this stage was *The Reformation*[183], as Martin Luther began to "push back" against the Theological Truth embraced by the Catholic Church throughout the Middle Ages. Comte's identification of this Metaphysical stage is fascinating in terms of understanding how we go to where we are today.

Let us consider examples of Martin Luther taught and its impact upon our slow progression toward the rejection of the Advent event within the context of daily life in our time. Of course, this was not Martin Luther's intent, but it was the result. The three main ideas of Martin Luther were that Salvation could not be bought, that the teachings of the Church should just be from proper theological understanding of Scripture rather than Traditional Church Authority, for he believed the Pope/Priests were false authorities. He believed that all people of Faith were equal and did not need an intermediary like a Pope or a Priest to interpret the Bible, for there existed a Priesthood of all believers. It is important to understand the connection between this idea and the birth of the United States of America.

Advent is a real-life Existential event that visibly proclaims the Truths that Luther espoused. Martin Luther was proclaiming what Luke had already claimed. "God with us," *Immanuel,* is the summary of what Martin was trying to say. Consider the Advent

---

[183] The Reformation was a religious revolution in the Western church in the 16th century. Its greatest leaders undoubtedly were Martin Luther and John Calvin. Having far-reaching political, economic, and social impact, The Reformation became the basis for the founding of Protestantism, one of the three major branches of Christianity." For further research I recommend the article quoted here: Britannica, The Editors of Encyclopaedia. "Reformation". Encyclopedia Britannica, 15 Nov. 2023, https://www.britannica.com/event/Reformation.

event. First, the major players – Young Jewish peasant teenager, a carpenter, a priest and his wife, a crazed preacher in the desert, shepherds of ill repute, a tiny unknown town in Judea, Magi from the east, and a band of twelve men that covered a variety of sociological and vocational backgrounds. This is not to mention the universal nature of Luke/Acts, where we see these various groups of men and women founding a Faith that transformed the entirety of Human history. The Catholic Church had largely abandoned the very purpose for the Coming of Christ, according to Martin Luther. Only because of a shift in worldview was Martin Luther allowed to thrive.

The *Metaphysical* Stage allowed a broad search for knowledge, where human minds instead of only institutions were politically allowed to investigate creation. Think of all the changes that took place in our understanding of reality during this period – 1300-1800 A. D. Consider just a few of the changes that took place that we can document:

1400-1600: Renaissance culture (arts, science, ideas) began in Italy and spreads though Europe: freedom of thought, interest in classical Greece and Rome.

1450: The Printing Press, freeing religious people to read and interpret ancient texts.

1452–1519: Leonardo Di Vinci, need I say more?

1500-1600's: European countries established slave trade in west Africa. We cannot underestimate what the rise of human freedom from Catholic control creating opportunity for the inevitable rise of evil institutions flowing from human agency. This led to slave workers for the sugar and tobacco plantations in South America and the Caribbean, and the cotton plantations in the southern U.S.

1517: Martin Luther officially protested the Catholic Church, and the religious Reformation began. Protestant religions emerged in Europe. Eventually, these lead Europeans to flee toward a "New World" in search of religious freedoms. This passion for religious freedom would become the heart and soul for the eventual overthrow of slavery, both in the United States and Europe.

1519: Magellan sailed around the world and proved the Earth is round. This was an immeasurable breakthrough for the scientific community.

1558-1603: Period of William Shakespeare. The roots of modern media were born.

1600-1700's: Scientific Revolution began; The Scientific Method was developed: Galileo proved solar-centered solar system; Isaac Newton studied gravity; William Harvey studied human circulation; microscope was invented. All these discoveries were made possible by The Reformation.

1689: After the "Glorious Revolution" of 1688, English Parliament passed the Declaration of Rights, making Parliament stronger and protecting the rights of the people and the person.

1700's: "Age of Enlightenment" in Europe: thinkers questioned the authority of religion, believing that reason and science can solve human problems. Foundations for the *Naturalist* Worldview were in place.

1776: The United States colonies composed the *Declaration of Independence* from Britain's control; the American Revolution, war between U.S. and England, lasted until 1783. This was the natural result of a desire on the part of the people to rule themselves, to separate faith and governmental control, and to express individual autonomy, the most important consequence of The Reformation.

1789: The United States Constitution was signed, giving power to the government only as allowed by the people.

1790: Movement to abolish slavery began to grow in England and later in America. Please note the proximity of this to the signing of The Constitution. The Founders understood that religious liberty and freedom meant this institution needed to end. The fight began here and consummated in the Civil War. Without this stage of Enlightenment in this New Nation, this event is postponed for who knows how long? The Reformation was a precursor to the freeing of the Slaves.

1807: Britain abolished the slave trade. U.S. followed in 1808, but slavery was not made illegal in all states of the U.S. until 1865. The leaders of the USA knew this institution to be evil, but it took another 60 years for this *Metaphysical Truth* to conquer economic realities. At the core of this movement were those from a newly formed Christian understanding of the world (The Protestant Movement), soon to be under attack by a growing *Naturalistic* Worldview.

1825: First steam railway was built in England. Free flow of ideas and scientific inquiry became possible and readily accessible. Without this technological shift, the *Naturalist* worldview could not grow and thrive. We were a culture on the move, which increased our dependance upon science and technology, which translated foundationally into our educational institutions. No longer was the church the center of Community, for Community becomes a broader category than ever before in human history. As geographical barriers were broken, ideological domination became more possible across said culture, and change happened faster than we can intentionally analyze and assess. The result, our present *postmodern* worldview, where private truth prevails.

1889: Eiffel Tower was built in Paris as a symbol of the Industrial Revolution. A visible sign of the shift of worldview, as Science and Technology took over Western thought.[184]

2024: The release of *A Timeless Script from a 1ˢᵗ Century Doctor*, as an unknown college professor invites a New Generation of thinkers to challenge present worldview paradigms in favor of A *Timeless* Document that holds The Answers we are searching for, beginning with Luke's telling of the *Timeless Story of Advent*. This is the moment in which our lives cross paths, me and you and those we will teach and inspire in the days to come.

The Star of Bethlehem: Joseph and Mary traveled to the place marked for them in the Night Sky...

Several years ago, I began a personal investigation into the Star of Bethlehem. Something had sparked my interest, and I could not shake it. Around the same time, I got my first taste of a computer program that allowed me to look at the stars during any year in history from any vantage point on the earth. I was able to see what the Magi were looking at in the night sky around the time Jesus was born. The irony of the clash of worldviews often occurred to me as I explored this phenomenon. Matthew includes the Star in his Gospel for theological reasons. We search the skies for the Star in search of *Metaphysical* reality. And we use the tools created by science as we live in a world powerfully impacted by a *Naturalist* Worldview. The search for the Star is one way to highlight the stages of knowledge we have passed through over the last 2,000 years. My interest had been sparked, so I bought a

---

[184] These events documented in https://www.edu.gov.mb.ca/k12/cur/socstud/ foundation_gr8/blms/8-5-1b.pdf

computer program to investigate the sky, read up on the history we had about this time, grabbed my Bible to read about the event, and off I go. This must be said as we investigate: We are creatures of the 21st century, guided by a worldview which creates both opportunity and barrier. This is true for all of us.

Understanding worldview is truly relevant to our understanding of Advent. Most of us would deem our way of thinking as a given. Why deeply analyze what we do naturally - think the way we think? We would not be thinking this way if this had not served us well in some way. Is this true? What would we gain today if history had remained open to Metaphysical Realities that the Bible and other religions proclaimed. One of these events was the Star of Bethlehem, which we can now newly investigate due to the pushback against a strictly *Naturalist* worldview. Recently, philosophical agents and scientifically minded observers began to explore the truth of this event once again.

We have since entered a new stage toward the discovery of knowledge, though Comte is no longer around to identify this stage. We are now inside the *postmodern* stage of *epistemology*, the search for knowledge. As we push back on a denial of the *metaphysical* that science demanded from us, we have done so without a *Theological foundation*. This is one reason the Gospels are of primary importance in our time. We are allowed to peek inside the details of Truth espoused by people who claimed inspiration from God in these revelations, a claim which has substantial evidence of support. Our present worldview makes room for such claims, but without a proper understanding of the concept of Truth to guide us. Our ability to travel across time and hear what the Gospel writers have to say to us will be dependent upon how we answer the question of "What is Truth?" Our understanding of things like *The Star of Bethlehem and The Virgin Birth* will be determined by our worldview.

When considering the Star that shone brightly over Bethlehem sometime around the event Luke described, we need to investigate three primary players in the night sky. First, there was Regulus, the "King Star," located in the constellation Leo. Leo is the constellation connected to Judah, and the Magi would have known this. The other two characters would be Jupiter and Venus, the two brightest lights in our night sky if we exclude the Moon. So, my attention was drawn to the interaction between Regulus (King Star), Jupiter (King Planet), and Venus (Mother Planet).

Planets were called "wandering stars" in the 1st century, for the simple reason they had no nightly route the way stars do, for stars travel from east to west each night in the Eastern sky under investigation. Planets jump all over the place, determined by their relative location to earth as we all travel around the Sun. This is what made the events of 4 to 1 B. C. so interesting. Firstly, The Star of Bethlehem could not have been such a magnificent event in the sky that it was noticed by everyone. Otherwise, Herod, among others, would not have been surprised by the observation, if in fact it were obvious to everyone. Those who looked for it noticed, but most did not notice it at all. A second interesting point - Herod quite possibly died later than we once thought. Instead of forcing us to look for the Star of Bethlehem around 4 to 6 B. C., we now know that Herod possibly died in 1 B. C., allowing us to look to the sky from 3 to 1 B. C. for the Star of Bethlehem.[185]

Realizing these two possibilities makes our search most interesting. We need "wandering stars" as part of this phenomenon (planets), because Matthew told us the Star appeared to stop over Bethlehem (Matthew 2:9). We call this retrograde motion, as stars appear to stop and start in the night sky, because the orbit of every planet around the sun creates this appearance relative to

[185] *Herod's Death, Jesus' Birth and a Lunar Eclipse.* A thorough discussion of the details contained in the book **The First Christmas: The Story of Jesus' Birth in History and Tradition,** written by John A. Cramer, Professor of Physics, Oglethorpe University. Article of discussion is found on *"Bible History Daily"*, December 15, 2022. Biblical Archeology Society, BiblicalArcheology.org.

our locations around the Sun. If the Star of Bethlehem appeared to stop, as Matthew claimed, there had to be planets involved. Number 24:17 says: "I see him, but not now; I behold him, but not near. A Star will come out of Jacob, a Scepter will rise out of Israel. ....."

"I see him, but not now, I behold him, but not
near. A Star will come out of Jacob, a Scepter
will rise out of Israel..." (Number 24:17).

The Magi were looking for a Star to rise in Jacob, around the constellation Leo, close to a star called Regulus, the King star. During a ten-month period in 3 to 2 B. C. Jupiter hangs out next to Regulus in Leo for a ten-month period. Jupiter and Venus appear closely tied next to the constellation Leo on two occasions. Jupiter and Venus conjunct twice, right next to Regulus, within a period which is outlined in Luke. I believe these conjunctions, occurring 9 and half Jewish months apart, could mark the conception and the birth of Jesus. Wow! If in fact Herod died in 1 B.C., as recent evidence suggests, these events preceded his death and would most certainly qualify as Star of Bethlehem material. In the night sky

Venus stacked closely on top of Jupiter right next to Regulus on August 12 of 3 B. C. - Conjunction number one.

Saturn and Venus gathered once again around Regulus on June 17 of 2 B. C. This was Conjunction number two, 10 months after the first Conjunction of the same. Could this be our Star? It would be the brightest light these Magi had ever seen in their lifetime. And it fell within a likely window of time in which Jesus was born. It met the criteria discussed in Matthew 2, the best document we have for details about the Star. And it appeases the apparent contradictions that many have attached to the investigation of the Star. In my view, this is the Star of Bethlehem, set in the night sky billions of years before the Magi discovered it by a Creator who had an eternal plan for the Birth of Messiah (To this I will say Wow backwards - "Wow!").

The reason this event was so important within a discussion of the Gospel of Luke would be the purposeful limitation Luke placed upon himself when discussing the events inside his Gospel. Luke does not record information about this Star. It would be easy to conclude he had no way of interviewing any of the witnesses of this event, and therefore he would purposely not include that which he could not verify. Rather than point to a contradiction in the Advent events Luke and Matthew record, it points us to both authors' integrity. Luke declared that he wrote what he wrote due to his deliberate and thorough investigation. Given he did not have the Gospel of Matthew in front of him, could not text him or email him to ask what he wrote, and had no access to the witnesses of The Star, he did not include these details, though they most certainly would have fit within his Worldview. A document's accuracy is supported by the information included and the information not included when it comes to rating the integrity of the author.

However, it must be understood that Luke pointed out several details that set the stage for the events recorded in Matthew 2. First, Luke was quite clear about the Leadership in Judah at the time of

Jesus' birth. He certainly dates these events under Augustus as Caesar and Herod as supposed king of Israel, though Luke uses the proper name for his title during this time, referring to him as *tetrarch* in Luke 3:1.. It is also clear from Luke's Gospel that the census under discussion took place before the second census that took place while Quirinius was governor of Syria, beginning in 6 A. D... Luke's knowledge of a census during the B.C. years is never questioned by any historians of his time, and this would have been an extremely straightforward way to dismiss his Gospel. It never happened.

"The Gospel writers are communicating what they believe to be Objective Truth, though not in the same way that we moderns use the terms "objective/scientific truth." Throughout history we have altered the meaning of Objective Truth. I suggest to you that *Objective Truth* and *scientific truth* are not synonyms. There are ways of understanding reality objectively which do not come via the scientific method. That which is real is that which is objectively true, even if we must leave the laboratory to find it. We do not honor science with a denial of the miraculous." (Rick Farmer)

"For Science and the Bible, 'right' and 'wrong' are not arbitrary. They are based on physical or spiritual laws upheld by formidable evidence and the test of time. Law that are natural and not man-made. Law that helps us choose the right paths in life. Law every bit as dazzling as gemstones."[186] (Michael Guillen)

[186] Mechael Guillen, "Amazing Truths: How Science and the Bible Agree", 2015. Zondervan, Grand Rapids, Michigan.

Day 28

"But you, Bethlehem Ephrathah, though you are small among the clans of Judah; out of you will come for me One who will be Ruler over Israel, whose origins are from old, from ancient times" ... Micah 5:2.

Setting the Stage: The Shepherds come to the City of David.... (Luke 2:8).

MICAH WROTE AND SPOKE SHORTLY BEFORE THE ASSYRIANS attacked Judah in 701 B. C. This would mean that his prophecy is dated at least some 700 years before Jesus was born. Before there was a Roman Emperor to issue a decree for a census, before there was a Temple for the Messiah to worship within, before there was a Roman Governor to issue a decree, before there was a restoration of the tribe of Judah to the area around Jerusalem, before there were shepherds to tend to the lambs needed for Temple worship, before any of the circumstances that led to the birth of Jesus in the City of David, Micah spoke.

Bethlehem means *"House of Bread"* in Aramaic. What better place for the Bread of Life to first lay His tiny head? It was in this town David was crowned king in Israel. What better place for the Magi to come bearing gifts for the King? Rachel, the once barren mother who gives birth to Israel, was buried in Bethlehem. What better place for the Virgin mother of Jesus to give birth to a child born to die? Bethlehem is the town where Ruth gleaned the fields for food in her poverty. What better place for a peasant couple to glean the fields for a place to lay their son? The rich heritage of this tiny town in Judah pointed toward a rich heritage of a God who notices, A God who sees all and loves all. It was an unlikely son who became Israel's greatest King.

David was the smallest and youngest of his brothers. He who is chosen last by the world is often chosen first by God. This was a constant theme in the Gospel of Luke, as Luke focused on Bethlehem in the birth narrative to prepare us for the kind of King this unlikely Messiah would become. Just as David would have been our last choice for King, a babe born in a cave in a tiny, impoverished town would be the last child expected to become Ruler in Israel. God amazes and surprises!! God predicts and fulfills! God promises and accomplishes!! Pointing to such unlikely events as Truth is one of the things that gives credence to the Gospel narrative. Why make such an outlandish claim if not true?

The journey from Nazareth to Bethlehem was around eighty miles in length. It would have taken Mary and Joseph 4 to 6 days to make the journey. It was not a simple trip, up one hill then down another. Across rugged terrain with a pregnant mother in tow. As one who has hiked in WV, up and down and over and around is not an easy go of things. This is in the best of conditions. I wonder at times if this journey was not a symbolic representation of the coming of the Christ Child into our hearts and lives. The Arrival of Jesus, though longed for and anticipated, is a tumultuous event.

There are hills to climb, miles to traverse, and pains to endure. There are times of doubt and rain, hunger and pain, when we think we will never be the same. There are unwelcoming hosts, skeletons and ghosts, and narrow impassable roads. We walk for miles and seem to go nowhere, we bare our souls to those who seem not to care, and we finally arrive only to find there is no bed to share. The Journey of faith is often like our own personal journey to Bethlehem. But when the baby is born, when the Gospel begins to breathe, the trauma of the journey fades away.

Every year Christians visit Bethlehem once again. It is not that we take the journey, eighty miles, up and down, with aching legs in pouring rain. It is the birth of the Child we seek to remember, as we traverse the chaos of our lives and this world. Celebrating the coming of our Lord is the end goal. The miracle of Life celebrated in those tiny hands and feet. Bethlehem may have been their goal off in the distance, but the Child in our heart becomes the true source of Hope. We congregate in Bethlehem, the birthplace of a King, each time we light the candles, sing the songs, and revive the story. We long for the day when hope is born anew. We celebrate a time when dreams were realized precisely because so many of our dreams never were. Generations of the hopeful longed for this day, just as Generations of the hopeful have looked back to this day. If we choose, we can gather in Bethlehem, under a miracle star, understanding at last that God has entered the fray for all Generations past and future. There was never a day like this day. There was never a birth like this birth. And there is no time like the present to gather in Bethlehem once again.

The Shepherds come to the City of David…. Luke 2:8

Let us take a moment and visit the shepherds. There are differing views about the importance of shepherds being the first upon the Advent Scene. Was it as simple as - they were the ones outside at this hour of the night? Or was there more? One author suggests, "The shepherds stand for social poverty and sinful humanity and yet it was they who received the message about the birth of the Messiah (not influential politicians or priests) and it was they who 'made known' the good news. In God's Kingdom, peasants are prophets and the first shall be last (Lk 13:30)."[187] This seems, on the surface, to be quite possible. However, others suggest that shepherds held a prestigious position among the Hebrew people, as heroes of faith like Abraham and David were shepherds, and Jesus Himself was called "The Good Shepherd" in John 10. These are some facts we know about shepherds from 1st century life around Bethlehem in Judea.

"The shepherds' lives were ironic. Their job was to care for the animals sacrificed to atone for the people's sins. Yet because of their handling of these dirty creatures, they themselves were unclean and thus prevented from keeping the ceremonial law. Now this was a prime example of religious irony. Those who most need what religious institutions offer are the very people who are not invited inside. Ironic, but sad, for this is still happening in our churches today, where people are expected to clean up their act before coming to be made clean.

Because they were ceremonially unclean, they were often regarded as untrustworthy, irreligious, and poor in reputation."[188] Jesus was born "the Lamb of God," according to the prophet John the Baptizer (John 1:29). The irony of those who cared for the sacrificial lambs of this time becoming the first witnesses of the birth of "The Lamb" is a second irony. I have often understood that God has a tremendous sense of irony. This is one occasion it is on full display. Those who would soon have their job description transformed were given fair warning with their visitation to the Manger. Those who cared for the lambs sold and sacrificed in Judea were the ones The Angel sought. "The Sacrificial Lamb" to end all sacrificial lambs was to be born. The Author of Hebrews discussed this at length: "Day after day every priest stands and

---

[187] *Luke 2: 15-20 - Visit of the shepherds,* June 5, 2020. Published by Catholic Identity., catholicidentity.bne.catholic.edu.au/scripture/SitePages/Luke-2-1520
[188] *Where the Lambs Are Kept: A Narrative Retelling of Luke 2:8–15,* written by Russ Ramsey, December 23, 2015. Published by Bible Theology: TGC (U S edition). TheGospelCoalition.org

performs his religious duties; again, and again, he offers the same sacrifices, which can never take away sins. But when the Priest had offered for all time one sacrifice for sins, He sat down at the right hand of God……. For by one sacrifice, he has made perfect forever those who are being made holy" (Parts of Hebrews 10:11-14).

Given the symbolism connected to the concept of shepherd and sheep, it seems apparent that God is very intentional about choosing a vocation with an historical connection to the very purpose of Advent. They who were last in society were first with The Good News. Two details stand out when considering shepherds of this time. First, they did not take part in the life of Temple or Synagogue on a regular basis. Given the nature of their job, which involved 24/7 service to their sheep, it would leave them little time to participate in religious services or duties. They were the ones who worked to make religious observance possible in the first place, tending the sheep needed in the Temple. Like the cashiers who work weekends at Walmart, vocational choices took precedence over religious duty. This was one reason they were looked down upon by the religious elite, who most certainly would have chosen anyone to announce the Messiah before choosing shepherds.

It is easy to understand why Luke was the only author to include their arrival by the manger. Shepherds were not even allowed to testify in court in Jesus' time. Their testimony was thought invalid and not trustworthy. For Luke to highlight their witness was a risky venture if one wants to be taken seriously. Luke was more concerned about accurate representation of Truth rather than insuring acceptance with the public. Given they did not take part in religious duties, this meant they could not be trusted to give truthful testimony. Luke, following the theme that stands out throughout his entire Gospel, highlighted for us the least, the last and the lost as those who are the first recipients of God's Abundant Amazing Grace. Given that Luke wrote to a Gentile audience, he continuously highlighted the theme of God's love for the marginal and the non-religious. Luke constantly used examples that other Gospels did not include – shepherds, peasants, tax collectors, woman of ill repute, Romans, Samaritans, and a variety of well-known sinners resembling me and you. Most certainly this was one reason Luke highlighted them rather than the Magi. Equally certain is Luke's desire to make sure the world understands the amazing Love God extends to all through the birth and life of Jesus.

A second consideration is the task to which the shepherds applied themselves. Given that the time of God's visitation was early spring or late summer (sorry those December 25 advocates out there), they would have been tending the sheep for future sacrifice at the Temple. The One who was born the Lamb of God is visited by those who were tending the sheep that pointed to the need of atonement for all God's people. The symbolism found in the choice God made pertaining to shepherd witnesses was profound. The Atonement theme rang supreme as Messiah was born in Bethlehem. The men who watched over the sheep born for slaughter were the first to speak forth the Divine message of the ultimate "Lamb of God" who was born to take away the sin of the world and bring an end to all sacrifice.

Romans 8 spoke of the lambs led to slaughter, as Paul reflected on our destiny apart from Christ's intervention. The connection between the shepherd and us is obvious. The shepherds pointed us to the reality of sin, and their arrival at the manger pointed us toward God's answer for our sin. Shepherds left the flock to bow down to the one who would bring an end to religious ritual pertaining to sacrifice, who removed the legal requirements the shepherds could never meet and allowed them to kneel in adoration to the One who brought liberty to those who stood condemned by the Law. The shepherds were perfect witnesses. Luke was right to highlight them. And God speaks to us through these shepherds each Advent Season as we find ourselves a part of the least and the last and the lost, whose value before God is forever settled by the Angels' proclamation: "Glory to God in the highest heaven, and on earth peace to those on whom His favor rests" (Luke 2:14).

"A good shepherd always feeds his sheep first, even when he himself is hungry. Light is a shepherd; the blind are its sheep." (Matshona Dhliwayo)

"A higher percentage of Americans are church members today than were church members in the era of the Revolutionary War....... Deciding the reasonableness of belief in God on the basis of sociological facts is like deciding whom to vote for in an election on the basis of who is leading in the public opinion polls..........to ascertain what is true or best in favor of the anonymous authority of what existential writers like to call the crowd." (C.Stephen Evans, page 123)

Advent Eve

Christmas Eve – "They found Mary and Joseph, and
the baby, who was lying in a manger" ... Luke 2:16

Setting the Stage: The Place...

MODERN RENDERINGS OF THE BIRTH STORY OF JESUS OFTEN DO
not address an accurate view of 1st century life in Bethlehem. As
a poor city filled with peasants, we would assume there would be
no "Inn" as we think of "Inn." There was no Roman Road leading
to Bethlehem; therefore, the likelihood of a commercial Inn is
zero to none. The Greek word used is *kataluma*, which has various
translations depending upon how deeply translators go into 1st
century practices. In the New English Bible *kataluma* is translated
"house" (See Luke 2:7, New English Translation).

However, it is amazingly easy to make the case that the actual
meaning of the word in this context is "guest room." "If *kataluma*
means guest room in Mark and Luke at the end of the Lord's
life, why not at the start in Bethlehem?"[189] The likely scenario is

---

[189] E.F.F. Bishop, Jesus of Palestine, 1955. London: Lutterworth Press, p. 42. For
a thorough discussion of these issues, I found one article to be especially helpful
in terms of understanding 1st century practices in a small town like Bethlehem. It
is unthinkable that a culture built around the concept of hospitality would have
forced an expectant mother out of the town in search of animals to help her with
the birth of her child. It is more likely that Jesus was born in a peasant home, in
which animals would be kept at night by most, in the primary living area of the
home that quite possibly was built into a cave. If curious, please read this article

something like this: Joseph and Mary go to the home of someone connected to family or extended family and present themselves as Joseph and Mary from the linage of (who knows the name they use, but they used a name.) They would be greeted as family at this point, for surely someone from this clan is still in the town. They were told the guest room was occupied, which would allow for some privacy, but they would not be turned away in 1st century Jewish culture. They were placed in the communal living area, a place where animals would be kept at night. Given that many houses were built into caves, it is very possible that this home was built into a cave and the primary room was in fact a cave, given the obvious public exposure of the room when the shepherds arrived.

It is doubtful that Joseph and Mary were left to themselves to deliver their child. A manger, with a natural connection to animals, would have been in such a room described above. We do not do justice to the reality of cultural hospitality in the modern telling of this story. It is not that the people of Bethlehem would not be there to support Mary as she delivered. The amazing thing is that the Messiah is born in their midst, and they have little clue as to the amazing event they are a part of. This is the parallel to present America. There was no doubt lots of activity surrounding the birth of Jesus in the town, just truly little understanding of what this birth means for them.

Christmas Eve – "They found Mary and Joseph, and the baby, who was lying in a manger" ... Luke 2:16

For 2,000 years people have speculated the site was a cave or a stable. Having researched the background that makes the most sense when considering Luke's account, we can deduce

for further insight: Dr. Kenneth E. Bailey, Associates for Biblical Research: The Shiloh Excavations (This article was reproduced in the Fall 2007 issue of *Bible and Spade*.), bibleacrcheology.org

the following: Jesus was born where animals lived. The manger provided evidence of this, along with the belief that animals were often kept in living quarters of a person's home during the night hours.

There was no room for Mary and Joseph in the town's normal lodging accommodations. There was *"no room in the inn."* Inns in Jesus day were not the Hotels we are accustomed to, especially when speaking of a small town of fewer than 1,000 people, such as Bethlehem. Instead, there would have been lodging rooms in houses, rented by the owner for travelers to and from Jerusalem. A normal house in Bethlehem would consist of two floors. The lower level would be something like a small barn, where the animals owned by the residents would be kept. The upper level was where the people lived. So, the likely scenario was that Joseph and Mary were offered a place in the lower level of a house, with the animals belonging to said house. No matter how we choose to embrace this tradition, cave, barn, or first floor, the truth of Luke's account still is the same. The details point us to the Truth of this tradition.

First, Jesus came into this world in very humble circumstances. He was not born into wealth and earthy glory but was counted among the chickens and such. He was not celebrated by the nation, as in a Royal Birth, but by smelly shepherds. No one secured a palace for his birth, but instead he was laid among the animals. Whereas humans were clearing streets and waving banners for Herod when he passed, Inn Keepers and Homeowners were pulling their blinds upon Jesus' arrival. Angels and Shepherds were singing, but the rest of the world was getting on with the business of life, oblivious to the most important birth the world had ever known. Divine Power marks his eternal Being. Straw and hay marked his earthly arrival.

Second, Jesus lived the way he was born. He was never a man of wealth and power as this world understands such things. He owned no home, had no sons to work his fields, received no dowry from wealthy in-laws, did not marry into a royal clan, was not considered the expert in his field, worked all his life with his hands, was known to wash feet as if a servant, often avoided attention when he could easily have gotten it, turned away those who could have made him a super star, did healings behind closed doors when he could have made a spectacle of them, advised people to remain quiet about his identity, begged others to care for his mother when dying, invited himself to dinner at times not having a home of his own, did not have a keen business sense about him, relied on wealthy women to tend to his financial needs, put his little bit of wealth in the hands of a thief, angered and alienated the wealthy and powerful with his words and questions, refused to embrace political gain, and never turned away the needy though always dealing with little of the world's resources. Humility ruled his words and his actions, though he of all people had no reason to be humble. Grace governed his interactions, though many placed little value on the gifts He offered them. His birth was quiet and uneventful for most. But His life ended up changing the world!!

Third and foremost, He was fully human and fully Divine, in Luke's mind. God became Human. Mary had already been told *"He will be called the Son of God."* **The Son of The God!!** A Son is made from the same Being that the Father is made of. If God begets a Being, this Being of necessity is Divine. Just as human produces human, Divine produces Divine. Jesus is both made of the stuff of God, and at the same time made of the stuff of Humanity, having been born of both. This mystery has baffled thinkers since the birth of Jesus. How can anyone be both human and Divine? Not sure. I do not know. I cannot explain it. All I can say for certain is that Luke most certainly believed it, as did the first century Church he wrote about in Acts. It is right there in his genealogy listed in Luke Chapter

3: "Jesus......the son of Adam...the son of God." Jesus is both. Advent is the miracle of New Being. Advent is the miracle of the God-Man.[190]

"Christmas doesn't come from a store. Christmas means perhaps a little bit more." (Dr. Seuss)

---

[190] For a great discussion of the God-man, the reality of Jesus as both human and divine and its practical implications for today's world, see this article written by Martin Luther King, Jr.: "The Humanity and Divinity of Jesus", Martin Luther King, Jr., November 29, 1949, to February 15, 1950. Essay published in *The Martin Luther King, Jr. Research and Education Institute,* Stanford University, kinginstitute.stanford.edu and you might choose to read: "A Case for the Divinity of Jesus: Examining the Earliest Evidence", DEAN L. OVERMAN, 2009. Roman and Little field publishers.

The Arrival

Christmas Day

Setting the Stage: The History of Christmas Day....[191]

25 DECEMBER – THE DAY THAT THE ROMAN CATHOLIC CHURCH chose to mark Jesus' birthday. In fact, no one knows the exact date Jesus was born!

1. In countries with large populations of Orthodox Christians*, such as Russia, Ukraine and Romania, Christmas Day falls on 7 January. Some Greek Orthodox Christians celebrate Christmas on 7 January, too.

2. What about 'Xmas'? Do you get offended when people use this shortened version of Christmas? Lots of people think this is just a modern-day abbreviation – but it dates to the 16th century! The 'X' is said to represent the Greek letter *Chi*– the first letter in the Greek word for Christ, Χριστός (pronounced *Christos*).

3. You may have heard that Christmas trees originated in Germany. I searched further. Many historians think the

---

[191] The facts which follow are gathered and passed on from 3 different sources: 1- 9 comes from *"10 FACTS ABOUT CHRISTMAS!"* from National Geographic for Kids. NatGeoKids.com.; Facts 10-12 come from *"10 interesting facts about Christmas"* from Hugh Baird College. HughBaird.uk.ac ; 13 - 20 come from *"45 Amazing Christmas Facts You Need to Know"* from SHARI'S BERRIES (December 3, 2021). berries.com.

origins of this festive tradition may date back to the Romans and even the Ancient Egyptians, who used evergreen plants and garlands as symbols of everlasting life. (My favorite vision of the Christmas Tree is the explosion of fire that happened in Christmas Vacation starring Chevy Chase.)

4. Every year, Norway sends a beautiful home-grown Christmas tree to London, where it is decorated with lights in Trafalgar Square. Standing a towering 20m tall, the terrific tree is a gift to say thank you for the help the UK gave Norway during World War II. There are some traditions that have a life of their own.

5. St. Nicholas was a Christian Bishop who lived in the 4th century – known for being kind and generous, he later became the patron saint of children. This was the inspiration behind Santa Claus. So even the legend of Santa Claus originated within the environment of Church Tradition. My how things have changed with our Jolly Fellow....

6. In Iceland, children leave shoes under the window for 13 mischievous trolls called the Yule Lads. If the child has been good, they'll find sweets in their shoes – but if they have been bad, the Yule lads will leave them a rotten potato! I always wondered why my mom and dad gave me rotten potatoes during my teenage years for Christmas.

7. Jingle Bells was written as a Thanksgiving Song. You have noticed that Christmas vernacular is missing from the song, even though it is sung around Christmas time more than any other Christmas time song. This may be one reason my dad began playing Christmas music in October.

8. In 1644 Christmas celebrations were made illegal in England, and soon after, in the English Colonies in America, too! At that time, government members felt the religious meaning of Christmas had been forgotten and banned the holiday festivities. Some people still celebrated

in secret, however, until Christmas was once again legal…
almost 200 years later in some places! I'm thinking we
could use a dose of something like this today, though I'm
thinking it might be met with indifference in favor of more
capitalism.

9. Christmas in Japan is a secular holiday with less than 1%
of the Japanese population identifying as Christian. When
KFC launched their "Kentucky for Christmas" marketing
campaign in 1974, it was an instant hit and now KFC is a
popular choice for Christmas dinners in Japan. Please send
a Bible and my book to someone you know in Japan. Let us
change that 1% figure together.

10. You might be aware that Oliver Cromwell banned the
Pagan holiday of Christmas for 12 years from 1647 in
the UK, but did you know that the ban was only lifted in
Oklahoma USA in 1907? This means in some parts of the
USA Christmas was banned for over 260 years!

11. Queen Victoria was the first official person to send a
Christmas card, but the first commercial card came in 1843
when Sir Henry Cole produced 1,000 and sold them for one
shilling each. There are currently only 12 of these cards left
in the world with one going up for auction a couple of years
ago for £30,000. Can you imagine? Better check your old
Christmas Card collection.

12. One out of every three men in the USA wait until Christmas
Eve to do their Christmas Shopping (I'm hiding my face now).

13. Bing Crosby's version of *White Christmas* is the highest
selling single of all time. I must find a way to get to the
north of Florida for Christmas this year!!

14. Franklin Pierce was the first president to put up an official
White House Christmas Tree. The year was either 1853 or
1856, for both dates are claimed.

15. A Facebook survey revealed in 2010 that two weeks before Christmas is the most popular time of the year for couples to break up. I was once a part of one of those couples. Former girlfriend, if you are reading this, just know it was not much fun.

16. Vancouver, Canada, is the proud owner of the first ever ugly sweater Christmas party. I've never been to one of these, but I do have sweaters that will fit the bill if you want to invite me to one.

17. The first Christmas celebration in what would become the USA was in 1539 in Tallahassee, Florida. No presents or gift exchange. No tree. Just a religious Mass. My grandfather claimed to me he was there.

18. Ancient Greeks claimed that mistletoe was an aphrodisiac. This is probably why we still kiss under the mistletoe. I confess, I love mistletoe.

19. The reason we give gifts at Christmas developed from the tradition within the Matthew Advent Story that had the Magi presenting gifts to Jesus shortly after his birth. I know of one only child that once got 93 presents under the Christmas tree. Can you imagine?

20. Advent is an oft forgotten time in our country. Though we manage to spend more money, visit more family, throw more parties, and visit more friends than any other time of the year, we have neglected the most important Truth of this Time. God became a Human Being to declare for all time that we are not alone, we are not forgotten, we are forever loved, and we will never be abandoned by the One Who left His Eternal Throne and came to us as a Babe in a Cave. This is the message Luke left for us, each one of us. (Rick Farmer)

Christmas Day

**"The Angel of the Lord appeared to them, and the glory
of the Lord shone around them, and they were terrified.
But the Angel said to them, 'Do not be afraid. I bring
you Good News that will cause extraordinary joy for all
people. Today in the town of David a Savior has been born
to you; He is Messiah, the Lord........."** (Luke 2:9-11)

There are those who would negate this miracle by making
Christmas a Holiday, surrounding the celebration with a super
man in a red suit, countless hours of shopping, lights and trees and
pageants galore, all the while spending the season "making sure we
make enough money to buy things we don't need for people who
have everything."[192] The complications of Christmas abound, as we
argue about public nativity scenes and the words we use to describe
the event. The Truth is, although mysterious, Advent is simple.
God loves the world. There is a gulf between Humanity and The
Creator. God climbs inside a virgin mother's womb to bridge the
gap, destroy the gulf, and defeat the alienation we all experience
and feel every day of our existence. God becomes human because
there is no other way. An invisible Being of unspeakable Power and
immeasurable Glory cannot be known without first sacrificing
this Form. It is impossible to know God without God making God-
self known, and it is impossible for God to do such a thing if God
does not stoop to our level as a full-fledged Human Being. So, God
does. God does not meet us halfway. God comes the entire way.
God comes to us, as One of us, in order that the reconciliation of
Human Beings and their Creator might move from that which is
hopeless to that which is possible.

You see, **"When the time was right, God sent His Son, born of**

---

[192] I first heard this phrase used by Tony Campolo at the Jubilee Conference in
Pittsburgh, PA. It stuck.

a woman, born under the law, so that we might receive adoption as children" (Galatians 4:4). Timing is everything. God knew the day, the hour, the very second Jesus needed to arrive in this world. God set a sign in the heavens and prepared a world in need to hear and receive the impossible.

Therefore, Advent is much more than a holiday. Advent is the key to everything Human. Advent cannot be undone or forgotten. There is not enough darkness out there to diminish The Light. There are not enough presents to overshadow God's gift. There are no laws that can legislate the meaning of Advent away. This Child, this Godman, is the reason for and the Living fulfillment of Christmas past, present, and future. Might we lift our hearts and our candles, our cups and our eyes, our lives and our families, to the King of Kings and the Lord of Lords. He is the reason we sing, the reason we congregate, the reason for our laughter and celebration. Advent is the celebration of the birth of God into our world. This is the simple Truth Luke wanted us to understand. This is the simple Truth, he wanted us to ponder in our hearts and minds as we open ourselves to the possibilities that exist within a Transcendent Metaphysical Reality.

The 20th century was a transition period for Western Culture. We began to move past a strictly scientific worldview, as psychology and other social sciences began to step forward. As a society we benefited from this in our search for knowledge. However, there were disappointing aspects that now, ironically, limit our thinking. For in the movement leading to *postmodern* worldview, we lost touch with both important tradition and meaningful history. We began to deem them irrelevant to the modern, or postmodern, world. We did this to our peril, for those who lose touch with tradition will lose touch with their ancestry, and those who devalue history will repeat her mistakes (For an introductory discussion of the importance of studying history follow this footnote).[193]

We began to think as a post-Enlightenment people, as the elite ideas of universities began to trickle into the common thoughts and language of the people. Luke wrote about Advent as a *Metaphysical* Reality. In other words, the Truths he left for us are meant to be understood as ultimate, universal Truths that apply to all people of all ages. Those who celebrated Advent prior to the 20th century had some sense of this, a sense of awe and wonder about the events that transpired. It was in no way a Commercialized Event, designed to feed the Capitalist Machine as it would soon become.

This changed during the 20th century. Advent became a time where buying "stuff" for Christmas was a patriotic duty. Beginning with what we now call "Black Friday," Christmas shopping became a means of survival for many businesses. The retail arena began to explode in November and December, as the religious foundations of the Advent Season took a back seat to the ever-growing commercialization of Christmas shopping. Advent shifted from a *Metaphysical* Celebration of a history changing birth to an *Existential* Event defined by the experiences of modern culture.[194]

---

[193] "The Values of History", Museum on Main 603 Main Street Pleasanton, CA. 94566, 925.462.2766. www.museumonmain.org

[194] Metaphysics is what most of us think of traditional philosophy. It's looking at the big cosmic, fundamental questions-- God, the nature of time and space, the meaning of life.

Existentialism is an umbrella term for various philosophies that hold that existence precedes essence. Basically, there is no meaning to life, at least not one that is discoverable via rational thought. We're just here, for no discernable reason and no discernable purpose.

Therefore, existentialism connects with metaphysics when it is exploring metaphysical concepts. But on the other hand, it rejects metaphysics in the sense that it holds that there is no actual answer to metaphysical questions and therefore the endeavor might be pointless. *(This explanation is taken from a Reddit online chat discussion from a posted by ttd-76. It is one of the best answers to the question of the relationship between metaphysics and existentialism I came across in my reading.)*

This shift is not without consequence, consequences Gen Z is now pushing back in response to. For many of us Advent is in fact a *Metaphysical* Reality. For these, Advent is shaped by foundational truths which transcend human observation and experience (*Existentialism*). The true meaning of Advent is found behind the details, underneath the events, above the experiences, deeply rooted in the cultural and religious significance of the event itself. Our personal *Existential* celebration of this day will never take us far enough into the meaning of Advent. And we cannot discover the ultimate meaning of Advent on our own. We need Luke, the Angels, the prophesies, the Virgin Mother, the Star, and the myriad of miraculous events surrounding the Truth for the Purpose of this Day. I maintain, in agreement with Luke, there has never been and can never be a day to match this day.

Advent ends all speculation about how God views humanity. The True meaning of Advent overwhelms the Atheist, overcomes the plans of the Enemy, and outlasts the indifference Humanity shares. The Christ event erases all doubt when answering the question of meaning and purpose. That which we long for has been discovered. That which we strive for begins here. That which we are born to discover lies embedded within the story of Advent. We cannot gaze deeply into the manger without being changed. We cannot stand under the Star without finding hope. And we cannot hear Luke's voice without having what we believe challenged to its core. Advent is both offensive and life affirming, confrontational yet bathed in compassion, mysterious yet profoundly simple. Advent reminds humanity each year that there is no expiration date on Truth.

Last night I took my dog outside to do her thing before bed. All along my Florida driveway were ant hills – ants scurrying back and forth, busy with their lives, preparing for the next Ant holiday to arrive. They had no idea my car would soon smash into some of their homes; their existence did not allow for such understanding. They are *Existential* creatures, not able to bother with the *Metaphysical* realities of their world. I wondered to myself: "How might they be saved? How might they be warned?" It occurred to me that nothing short of becoming an Ant while retaining my understanding of all things would suffice. I would have to become a Human-Ant to help them understand. I cannot make possible such a transformation, but what if I could?

Today I walked across campus. Young people were scurrying back and forth to class, the gym, the cafeteria and wherever. They did not realize Advent was beneath them and all around them. Their *Existential* existence left little room to think about ultimate reality and universal Truth, like Advent. How might God reach them? How might God wake them to a reality which does not fit into their culturally trained Worldview? I get it now. God could become one of them. God could fit God-self into a tiny baby and grow as they grow and learn as they learn and speak as they speak, all the while retaining a deep understanding of the Ultimate, the *Metaphysical*, the Transcendent.

If God did this, some would understand and believe. Some would discover eternal meaning and purpose which can never be undone. Others would not listen. But at least meaning, purpose, hope and life are offered in a language they might understand. This is why Luke wrote what he wrote. He wrote for those of us willing to open our hearts and our minds to Ultimate Reality and Universal Truth. This is the "Timeless Prescription" we all need, and Luke offered it to us on God's behalf. The "Timeless" story of when God's Son became a Human Being to restore all people to God's Family once again is relevant for every day and all times. God desires to make things right, to so impact the world that nothing would ever be the same. This is the "vaccine" against a strictly *Existential* existence that drives us to buy stuff we do not need for people who have everything to bring meaning to our chaotic and empty lives. Luke's Advent Story is indeed "A Timeless Script From a 1st Century Doctor".

Simply put, if you are a human who desires meaning, purpose, the answer to the "Why" of our existence, you are traveling the correct route if you choose to climb into the Advent Story and find the answers you seek. Luke recorded the answers we desire in all Generations. Luke captured the essence of the Human situation. Luke presented the Key to understanding the reason we exist. Jesus is not just a Babe in a Cave who created a neat story to read together toward the end of each year. Luke introduced to us the depth of God's love, the potential for humanity, the truest reason for Joy, the cure for our depression and isolation, the glue for our relationships, the reason for our tendency to worship, the impetus behind our longing for life, the very reason this planet exists in the first place. Before there was life, there was a Star marking the day God was to visit us. Before there was a baby, there was a promise of the "Seed." Before there was a history to read, there was a pre-history of a Divine Being who desired to share Glory with God's children. Before there was a single question to be asked, there were answers provided by *A Being* who is *Being* with a desire to share *being*. Before there was death, there was Life Everlasting. Before there was Christmas, there was an unparalleled longing for His Arrival. Before humans began to surrender to the circumstances of life, there was a "Timeless Script" given as vaccine and cure for whatever we are to face. Advent is central, clear, and celebratory. Luke has written for us "A Timeless Script from a 1st Century Doctor."

Luke's Script is God's Gift - The Beautiful Jesus of Today is Coming to a Life near you………..

"Faith is to believe what you do not see; The reward of this faith is to see what you believe" (Saint Augustine)

A Final Question

Does Luke Make His Case?

"But Mary treasured all these things and pondered them in her heart. The shepherds returned, glorifying and praising God for all the things they had heard and seen, which were just as they had been told." Luke 2:19.20

Before considering the sheer magnitude of the significance of the Advent Story in our 21st century, there is a nagging question that must be addressed, that we began to explore in the preceding pages of this manuscript. *How do we discover Truth?* We find it quite surprising that Social Scientists and Theologians often agree upon an answer in principle, even though this often gets lost in translation. As noted, Social Scientist Earl Babbie asks: "Reality is tricky business. You already suspect that some of the things you 'know' may not be true, but how can you really know what is real?"[195] He further acknowledges that *Agreement Reality,* the things we claim to 'know' simply because they are embraced by the culture in which we live, are always dependent upon both Tradition and Authority. For example, Babbie acknowledges that good science is formulated by the systematic exploration of a theory. We do not base good science on philosophy or belief, so he says. However, it must be noted that every theory is based on presuppositions that, in the end, are based on unprovable assumptions. For instance, consider the *Theory of Evolution.* Assumptions are made about the fossil record, the first second of the universe, the power of natural selection in the creation of diverse species, and many other things we can point to as unproven suppositions. We simply cannot get away from *Agreement Reality* within the arena of scientific inquiry.

The Theologian finds herself in the same place. She is unable to prove her basic assumptions in the Laboratory, unable to provide sufficient evidence that might prove the premises she embraces before she ever begins declaring Truth. Though some will argue that the Scientist has more evidence for these presuppositions than the Theologian, neither of them can provide definitive proof that their version of reality is, without doubt, True. Both systems of thought leave us short in declaring *Reality with Certainty.* Have you ever imagined what it might mean for us if a race of beings from another planet came to Earth one day with recorded visual evidence of the fact that they are the ones who deposited Human DNA on our planet? In an instant both Scientific and Theological explanations for Life would need to be revised and rewritten. I am not claiming to believe in such a theory, I am simply trying to help you into the mindset of understanding that when we cannot say things with certainty, we must allow ourselves to be open to

---

[195] Earl Babbie, "The Practice of Social Research" (14th Edition), page 6.

explanations which contradict our own unproven claims to Truth. This takes us back to the two sources we rely on most – Authority and Tradition. For the Scientist, *Naturalism* Rules and Science is updated daily, regardless of Tradition. For the Theologian, Revelation is Authority and Science helps us to grow and adjust Tradition, without ever abandoning the Authority we ascribe to the Ancient Documents we embrace. Both methods of declaring Truth have limitations.

I have consistently appealed to the writings of Lesslie Newbigin, recognized as one of the most amazing minds of the 20th century by many within Theological circles. We cannot avoid important considerations he declares when considering the Truth we affirm within the writings of Luke. "All understanding of reality involves a commitment, a venture of faith. No belief system can be faulted by the fact that it rests on unproved assumptions; what can and must be faulted is the blindness of its proponents to the fact that this is so".....The Advent Narrative "is not a set of beliefs that arise, or could arise, from empirical observation of the whole of human experience. It is the announcement of a name and a fact that offer the staring points for a new and life-long enterprise of understanding and coping with experience."[196]

The reality of diversity in this human search for Truth is obvious in both disciplines. Within the realm of Social Science, we are met with several worldviews and differing scientific theories about the nature of things. Scientists cannot reach consensus on much of anything. A powerful recent illustration of this was found within the Covid Pandemic, as "the science" of Covid changed from day to day and the Scientific Community continues to debate both the origin of and the best way to deal with the Covid Phenomenon. Consensus is simply not apparent.

Within the Theological Realm, Denominationalism is a sign pointing toward the presupposition that Enlightenment

---

[196] Lesslie Newbigin, "Foolishness to the Greeks", page 148.

Ideology has won the day in the West. When the individual rules, consensus is impossible, and diverse theologies and worshipping communities emerge. Whenever a free will creature can be trusted to choose from the smorgasbord of theological options, based solely on the principle of personal preference and consumerism, it is apparent that Enlightenment thinking reigns supreme. Martin Luther sought to revive Catholicism, for he did not function within a worldview where each individual becomes the ultimate authority within The Church. The bottom line - Christian believing and behaving is always confined within the structures of our own cultures, and unless we are willing to allow other cultures to correct our shortcomings (i.e.; Luke's Culture), just as we are called to give this same gift to cultures beyond our own, Enlightenment strategy will prevail. This book is a challenge to move beyond your specific worldview, to hear the words of those who came from cultures which differed from our own and open ourselves to the possibility that Luke is giving us the Gift of "Timeless Truth" from a vastly different culture than our own.

Trusting the testimony of Luke is the door through which we enter the story. Mary and the shepherds, the primary witnesses of the birth of Jesus, are left to ponder *what* happened and *why*. The *Why* as entertained in Luke's mind through the testimony of his witnesses. Of note are two particularly vital details in these two verses that invite us toward contemplation and evaluation. First, we are not left to doubt the event itself. It is impossible to proclaim a birth that did not occur when it comes to the baby's mother. This is an experience never forgotten. We are left with little doubt that the event itself occurred, and that Luke had spoken with Mary about the significance of this birth from Mary's perspective (Luke 1:46-55). Luke had her reality in his mind as he wrote, and he recorded her song for us as insight into the Truth pondered by this amazing mother. We do her injustice not to consider her testimony.

Second, the shepherds discovered what the Angels told them (Within a *Metaphysical* Cosmos), which was exactly as they were told (*Existential* Reality). There was no reason for the Shepherds to be there if not for what the Angel told them. They set out to become a pivotal part of a story which changed their understanding of reality, and no doubt changed their entire existence. It makes perfect sense that God would ensure witnesses, and it is irony that these witnesses were the very type of witnesses the religious elite would choose to ignore. It was indeed a metaphor for today, for every day. Only those who are open to the possibility that their view of the world is important to consider can open themselves to the possibility of the Divine for today. This is true for Believer and Non-Believer alike. Those who Believe but close themselves to a New Word for a New Day are just as likely to miss the message of Advent as those who are indifferent or adversely inclined to the true meaning of the birth of God's Son. Believers will leave the "shepherds" of our time outside sanctuary doors in the name of Tradition, and Non-Believers will simply ignore the celebration, call it a holiday, and move forward with life, as if Jesus had never been born. Living in a day where vaccines are needed and *Soul Transforming Treatment* is paramount, Advent must be resurrected in our midst. Luke is a *1st Century Doctor* who needs to be heard.

Personally, Luke is my favorite Gospel. It is because my mind functions the way he writes - analytical, poetic, and philosophical all rolled into one. We have before us his grouping of material according to content and relevance; His profound insight into both Hebrew and Greek literary forms as he organizes parables according to these media formats; And his incredible insight into the psyche of the investigative and analytical mind. Luke appeals to the Greek thinking person, those of us who measure the facts to arrive at an understanding of Truth. He wrote during a prescientific time, but he most certainly had a scientific mind. He clearly believed that Truth can be validated, that investigation is necessary, and that facts need to be established. Thus, he set himself upon the task of doing so. I have read books by people who choose to critique Gospel claims about Jesus that do not exercise the same care and investigative ability as Luke does. Luke clearly knew what he was doing, why he was doing it, and what was at stake.

Matthew is a Gospel with a Jewish flavor and audience, Mark focused on eyewitness testimony of the activities of Jesus from Peter's perspective, while John was written to respond to a growing Gnostic Understanding of Jesus during the later years of the 1st century. Luke is altogether different. He desired to convince a Greek thinking and Greek speaking world under Roman Rule that a New King, The Messiah called Jesus Christ, had arrived in the land. He traced Jesus from his birth, rooting his genealogy in the birth of humanity, all the way to the Person of the Holy Spirit, who took the Good News of Jesus to Rome itself (Luke/Acts). He pulled together witness after witness after witness to tell the story of Jesus of Nazareth. He highlighted his birth, his parents, his stories, his core teachings, his activities, his relationship with the people, and of course, his death, burial, and Resurrection. He then allowed us to follow Christ through the Book of Acts as He continued His work through the Apostles, empowered by His Spirit as they go. He left no stone unturned and did not miss a trick when making his case for the Divine Being who walked this earth as the one and only God-Man.

Three *timeless truths* make up Luke's Script for our day. First, Luke brought to the forefront, with the coming of Jesus, the reality of a New Kingdom on earth which was not from earth. A Kingdom that is both around us and within us, both Transcendent and Immanent. A Kingdom that operates by a distinct set of rules with vastly different priorities. Whereas Matthew emphasized Jesus the Messiah of Judah, Luke emphasized Jesus the King of all nations. It is little wonder that this Gospel was meant for the Greek mind.

Greek thinkers often contemplated the concept of Truth, especially as it related to the question of Absolute Truth, or Truth that applies to all people in all times. Luke painted a picture of this kind of Truth, as he highlighted a Good Samaritan alongside a redeemed Tax Collector further emphasized by the story of a Prodigal Son.

There is no way we can embrace a Messiah or King for all people if He is not seeking and saving all people, even the lowest and the least. Luke presented Jesus as Messiah for all, Teacher for all, and a King above all Creation. There was no limit to His love and no condition to His contact. Jesus sought whomever, loved however, and saved whatever. Luke gave us the most vivid representation known to humanity of the depth, the breadth, and the length that God will go to restore this world into harmonious relationship with our Creator through the gift of God's Son.

A second *timeless truth* Luke left for us was his consistent appeal to the often overlooked in his culture. He highlighted the prominent role of women more than any other Gospel Writer. He referenced more marginal people in the teachings of Jesus than any other Gospel Writer. And He spent more time reflecting on the Birth of Jesus than any other Gospel Writer. Could it be that Luke, more than others, had begun to grasp the powerful impact the Gospel was having throughout the Gentile world? Could it be that Luke, as he traveled with and tended to Paul, was so profoundly affected by Paul's mission to the Gentiles that he was granted an epiphany as to why Jesus taught and lived as he did? Could it be that Luke, as he pieced together information from various sources and organized the testimonials of Jesus' friends and followers, was so profoundly impacted by the transformation of the Gentile world all around him that he saw the need to make sure those he interviewed might tell the story to the non-Jew for generations to come? What is the goal of a historian, if not to guarantee that the most momentous events of the past are told and retold till the end of time? Luke told the story well. Luke allowed us to peek into the life of Jesus Christ in a fresh new way, while preserving for us the overwhelmingly consistent content relayed to the world by other witnesses and writers. Luke trusted the voice of the outlier, and so should we.

A third striking *timeless truth* Luke gifted us was the importance of "Truth." We could spend a year discussing his style and his expertise, but none of these matter if the content is not True, if the information he placed before us cannot be trusted. Can Luke be trusted? Consider the man. Educated. Intelligent. Gifted. He was an *Existential* genius conveying *Metaphysical* reality as few ever have. There was a myriad of options open to a man of Luke's skill set. So many things in his world he could have done. For some reason, he chose to become a traveling companion and personal physician for the Apostle Paul. And as he went forth, he found it of utmost importance to retell the story of Jesus. There is little doubt he believed what he wrote. There is even less doubt that he thought the Gospel of Jesus the most valuable information he had ever encountered.

Many have tried to convince us that Objective Truth is the same as Scientific Truth. In Luke's world, this cannot be true. Luke is proposing what he claims is Objective Truth, that which is real and knowable. It is certainly not Scientific Truth, for we have no way of testing his information in the laboratory. The closest we can get is to examine the evidence to see if Luke faithfully represents the facts of his day, the reality of his time. When we do this, the results are amazing.

"At one time, it was thought that Luke had completely missed the boat concerning the events he portrayed surrounding the birth of Christ (Luke2:1-5). Critics argued that there was no census and that everyone did not have to return to the ancestral home. They also pointed out that Josephus (well-known 1st century historian) had dated the governorship of Quirinius of Syria, whom Luke mentions, as beginning in A.D 6, too late for the birth of The

Christ. In every case, however, archaeological discoveries proved the critics to be wrong. In the case of Quirinius, it was found that he served two separate terms as governor, the first beginning around 7 B. C., which fits perfectly with the time of Christ's birth. F.F. Bruce, one of the most respected of New Testament scholars, noted that where Luke has been suspected of inaccuracy by modern critics, archaeology has repeatedly proved Luke to be right and the critics wrong."[197]

It is quite clear for the open-minded truth seeker that "Luke's status as a world-class historian, accurate in even the smallest details, has been brought to light by modern archaeology. For example, Sir William Ramsay, considered one of the greatest archaeologists of all time, originally thought he would scientifically discredit Luke's accounts by visiting and examine the places mentioned in his Gospel and Acts......But after years of retracing Luke's account of Paul's travels and doing archaeological digs along the way, Ramsay completely reversed his view of the Bible and first-century history".[198]

---

[197] It is an amazing area of research, traveling back in time to investigate the origins of Luke's Gospel and the trustworthiness of his testimony. This quote can serve as a beginning for you, for those of you who might like to consider the historicity of Luke's claims. The article quoted here is easy to find and will lead you to even more references to explore. It is my hope that this book serves as a beginning point for skeptics, a challenge for those who are undecided, and an affirmation of faith for those who already believe. This course is: "Compelling Historical Evidence for the Virgin Birth of Jesus Christ," Eddie Hyatt, 9 A.M. 12/9/2015. Charisma News, charisma news.com

[198] See footnote above and see the source he used listed in this footnote. "Sir **Willian M. Ramsay** spent decades investigating the New Testament because he was initially a skeptic. However, in time he began to discover the honesty and accuracy of the authors, the truthfulness of the information, and the trustworthiness of the NT. In fact, Ramsay concluded: "Luke is a historian of the first rank: not merely are his statements of fact trustworthy, he is possessed of the true historic sense ... This author should be placed along with the very greatest of historians." In Ramsay's book Trustworthiness of the New Testament, he provides us with much valuable material showing that the NT is authentic and true. His

His research was solid, his motives were pure, and his expertise was not questioned. In most cases such evidence would make any thinking person take notice. If we were to consider Luke on his own merit, style, content, and research skills, we would realize he could certainly find work in any arena requiring an exceptional resume. Luke, in my view, is a very trustworthy witness. He was consistent throughout both of his works (Luke/Acts), he was faithful to the actual historical details of his world, and he was incredibly careful to faithfully represent those who saw the events he described. Within the Gospel of Luke itself, there is truly little reason to doubt what he writes, unless one brings a bias into the reading beforehand.

Thus, the rub. We will be inclined to gain from Luke what we set out to gain? For those of us who are of Faith, we will find a beautiful rendition of the birth, life, teachings, and passion of Jesus. For those of us who are not so inclined, we will vehemently search for inconsistencies and missing details. As always, when we approach the Gospel of Jesus Christ, we are left with something more than a scientific article or a spotless biography. We are left with the Story of Faith, the testimony of one who already believed. Some call this Propaganda. Others call it Testimony. I call it Gospel. Good News for a world in need of Good News. But not just any Good News, it is Good News that stands up to scrutiny, that passes the test of time, Good News that delivers on all that it promises. So, as we celebrate Advent, when we light our candles and sing our Christmas Songs, as we feel the depths of the "Silent Night" lyric once again, let us remember that Luke has given us most of the story we are celebrating. Because of Luke we

---

book is a faith builder for us and an apologetic tool to share with skeptics and those who may have begun to doubt." You can read this book for quality research purposes on the historicity of Luke's Gospel: William Ramsay, *The Bearing of Recent Discovery on the Trustworthiness of the New Testament, 2nd Edition,* 2021. Christian Publishing House, Cambridge, Ohio. (This information was taken from the introduction to Ramsay's book as listed on amazon.com).

know about the Shepherds, hear Mary sing to us, can rejoice with Elizabeth, and can travel to the Manger once again. Luke not only gave us *The Greatest Story Ever Told*, but Luke allows us to linger in the details of these events in a way that transforms our lives and our hearts each day.

What did Luke gain from his work? The same thing the rest of us gain – Salvation and Resurrection, as we climb inside the Gospel of Jesus, "son of Mary, son of Adam, Son of God" (Luke 3:23-38). Luke becomes our brother, as we are ushered into the family of God thriving within the Kingdom of God no matter our failures and no matter our shortcomings. All of us Gentiles, born outside the Community of Faith, are brought near by the gift of the Christ Child. **"Do not be afraid, I bring you good news that will cause extraordinary joy for all people. Today in the town of David a Savior has been born to you; He is the Messiah, The Lord" (Luke 2:11).** Thank you, brother Luke, for telling this Story so powerfully! For giving us *A Timeless Script From a 1ˢᵗ Century Doctor.*

A Closing Prayer

"The Light of the World"

Where is the birth of joy?
Is it hidden in the dawn of a yet undiscovered day?
Is it to be found in the sunshine or in the rain?
What about this day?
How long will my heart feel as though there is no life within her?

I know my Lord lives there
He exists on both sides of my weeping
He is in the midst of every tear, of every ray of sunshine,
Of every drop of rain

He hears me
As I call to Him from this land of loneliness
As I look for Him through the darkness that surrounds my soul
His light is shining
He hears me
He stretches his hand
It is a hand I cannot touch
Yet He leads me

His are arms which cannot hold me
Yet they cover me with the warmth that
Not even a summer day can bring

His are eyes which need not look at me
Yet they discover for me a path to safety,
A path to undiscovered life

At last Joy has found me
It is not the joy of a leper who has been cleansed,
But the joy of a leaf in autumn who knows he
Must die to bring new life.
It is not the joy of a newborn bride,
But the joy of a seed giving herself up for the tree.

It is not the joy found in the song of the sparrow,
But the joy of winter as she gives way to springtime.

It Is not the joy of a father holding his first-born son,
But the joy of an eagle as she forces her young from the nest.

It is joy that cannot be defined or contained
As a feeling within my soul
For it only exists through the touch of one
I have yet to see

For the moment it is only a candle
A candle which will someday burn with the
Brightness of the sun

Today it dimly shines as the Son slowly rises at dawn,
Shining ever brighter till the fullness of His Day has come.
(Poem by Rick Farmer)

**May The Christ Child find a new and more
meaningful place in our hearts and minds from
this day forward and forever more. Amen.**

Source List, Select

Babbie, Earl. *The Practice of Social Research, E 14*. Boston: Cengage Learning, 2016.

Barclay, William. *The Gospel of Luke*. Philadelphia: The Westminster Press, 1953 and 1956.

Batson, Douglas. "Missions History: Precise Timing of Advent, Douglas Batson." December 8, 2022. *Global Frontier Missions – Until All Have Heard* (Dec 8, 2022): globalfrontiermissions.org

Bausch, William J. *A World Full of Stories*. New London, CT: Twenty Third Publications, 2007.

Bloom, Paul. "Sweet Spot: The Pleasures of Suffering and the Search for Meaning." *Portion of this book developed for - The Atlantic,* "What Becoming a Parent Really Does to Your Happiness", *by Paul Bloom (Nov. 2, 2021).* TheAtlantic.com.

Bodenner, Chris. "The Breakdown of the Black Family." *The Atlantic* (Oct 11, 2015): theatlantic.com. ***Editor's Note:*** *This article previously appeared in a different format as part of The Atlantic's Notes section, retired in 2021.*

Boice, James Montgomery. *Whatever Happened to the Gospel of Grace?* Rediscovering the Doctrines That Shook the World. Wheaton, IL.: Crossway Books, 2001.

Boomershine, Thomas E. *First-Century Gospel Storytellers and Audiences: The Gospels as Performance Literature.* Eugene, OR: Cascade Books, July 2022.

Boyd, Gregory. *Cynic Sage or Son of God: Recovering the Real Jesus in an Age of Revisionist Replies.* Wheaton, IL: A Bridgepoint Book, Victor Books, 1995.

Brasseaux, Shawn. "WHO WAS THEOPHILUS?" *Christian Ambassador* (11/28/2017): forwhatsaiththescriptures.org

Card, Michael. *Immanuel: Professions on the Life of Christ: BILLY GRAHAM SPECIAL EDITION.* Nashville: THOMAS NELSON trade paperback, 1981 & 1990.

Craig, William Lane. *Reasonable Faith: Christian Truth and Apologetics (3rd Edition).* Wheaton, IL: Crossway Books, 2008.

Dawkins, Richard. *The God Delusion.* NY, NY: HarperCollins Publishers, 2006.

DeRose, Jason." The importance of religion in the lives of Americans is shrinking," *NPR, WJCT News* (May 16, 2023): npr.org.

Dobson, Geoggrey. "Wired to Doubt: Why People Fear Vaccines and Climate Change and Mistrust Science." Review published by *Frontiers* (January 28, 2022): frontiers.org.

Donegan, Devillier. "The Roman Empire in the First Century." *Devillier Donegan Enterprises* (2006): PBS.org

Dy, Glory. "How Do We Know That Angels Are Real?" *Christianity.com.* (Posted on April 8, 2022): Fact checking: Salem Web Network.

Dyvik, Elinar. "Share of global population affiliated with major religious groups in 2022." Published by Statistica (2024): Statistica.com

Easter, Michael. *The Comfort Crisis: Embrace Discomfort to Reclaim Your Wild, Happy, Healthy Self.* NY, NY: Rodale Books, Penguin Random House LLC, 2021.

Eisner, Wendy. *Very Well Family: "What Does the Name John Mean?" Very Well Family* (Updated March 8, 2023): Fact checked by Daniella Amaro. VeryWellFamily.com

Elder, John. *Prophets, Idols, and Diggers.* Indianapolis, IN: Bobbs-Merrill, Co., 1960.

Elflein, John. "Global Burden of Disease Study," *Journal of Psychiatric Research, Volume 126* (July 2020): Pages 134-140.

"Depression in the U.S. - Statistics & Facts," Aug 31, 2023. Statistica.com.

E. Earle Ellis. "History and Society: St. Luke." *Britannica* (Last updated Sep 20, 2023): britannica.com

Evans, C. Stephen. *Philosophy of Religion: Thinking About Faith.* Downers Grove, IL.: InterVarsity Press, 1982.

Eykel, Eric Vanden. *The Magi: Who Were They, How They've Been Remembered, and Why They Still Fascinate.* Minneapolis: Fortress Press, 2022,

Fitton, Tom. *A Republic Under Assault.* NY, NY: Threshold Editions, An Imprint of Simon and Schuster, Inc., 2020.

Fruchtenbaum, Arnold. "The Messianic Timetable According to Daniel the Prophet," Published by *Jews for Jesus* (April 20, 2018): JewsForJesus.org

Gitnux. "The Most Surprising Only Child Statistics and Trends in 2023." *Market Data, Parenting Statistics* (August 2, 2023): blog.gitnux.com

Guillen, Michael. *Believing is Seeing.* Coral Stream. IL: Tyndale House Publishers, 2021.

Amazing Truths: How Science and the Bible Agree. Grand Rapids, MI: Zondervan, 2015.

Hammon, Mason. "Ancient Rome and Modern America Reconsidered." *The Massachusetts Historical Society. Third Series, Vol. 73* (1961): pages 3-17 (15 pages).

Hauer, Rev. Cheryl L. "Mary: A First-century Jewish Woman." Rev. Cheryl L. Hauer International Development Director. *Bridges For Peace* (2023): BridgesForPeace.com

Hauerwas, Stanley and Willimon, William H. *Resident Aliens: Life in the Christian Colony.* Nashville: Abingdon Press, 1989.

Haught, John R. *Science and Faith: A New Introduction (Paperback)."* Mahwah, NJ: Published by Paulist Press, Jan 2, 2013.

Henneberger, Melinda. "Vatican Says Jews' Wait for Messiah Is Validated by the Old Testament." *New York Times* (Jan. 18, 2002): NYTimes.com

"History & Society: Samaritan, Judaism." Written and fact checked by *The Editors of Encyclopaedia Britannica* (Last Updated: Jan 18, 2024): https://www.britannica.com/topic/Samaritan

"History & Society: Law of three stages." Written and fact checked by *The Editors of Encyclopaedia Britannica* (December 20, 2023): This article was most recently revised and updated by Brian Duignan,britinnicca.com

Hyatt, Eddie. "Compelling Historical Evidence for the Virgin Birth of Jesus Christ," *Charisma News* (12/09/2015): charismanews.com/culture/53743

Kalfus, Sky. "Darwin's Evolution and Positivism." *Science and Society, Science Leadership Academy @ Center City* (Nov 12, 2010):, science leadership.org. and also, The Sociological Perspective, From the classes of Walsh Bedford, 2018-19. Social Science Libre Texts, socialsci.libretexts.org.

Kapelrud, Arvid S. "Aaron, biblical figure." *History and Society, Britannica* (December 20, 2023): britannica.com.

Kennedy, D. James and Jeremy Newcombe. *What if Jesus Had Never Been Born?* Nashville: Thomas Newson Publishers, 1994.

Kinnaman, David and Lyons, Gabe. *UNchristian: What a New Generation Really Thinks About Christianity.* Grand Rapids, MI: Baker Books, 2007.

Kotselas, Vangelis. "The Top Ten Facts About Greek Culture." *Social Media Manager for Study in Greece* (November 7, 2021): StudyInGreece.edu.gr

Kumar, Amit & Epley, Nicholas. "Research: Type Less, Talk More." *Harvard Business Review, Analytical Department* (Oct 5, 2020): hbr.org

Lagercrantz, Hugo & Changeux, Jean-Pierre. "The Emergence of Human Consciousness: From Fetal to Neonatal Life." *Pediatric Research* (March, 2009): nature.com

Lenten, Liza. "How Was the Bible Written," *Engaged Media, Inc.,* Yorba Linda, CA. (2015): Page 66. www.engagedmediamags.com

Levan, Dr. Kevin. *The New Birth Order Book: Why are you the way you are?* Grand Rapids MI: Fleming H. Revell and Division of Baker Book House, 1998.

Lindsley, Art. *True Truth: Defending Absolute Truth in a Relativistic Age.* Downers Grove, IL: INterVarsity Press, 2004.

Luckman, Jim and Elizabeth. "The Five Gifts from Aristotle for Living a Meaningful Life." Jim Luckman and Elizabeth Luckman, July 3, 2020. Published by *LinkedIn Corporation* (July 3, 2020): LinkedIn.com.

MacArthur, John F., Jr. *God With Us: The Miracle of Christmas.* Grand Rapids, MI: Zondervan Books, Zondervan Publishing House, 1989.

The Jesus You Can't Ignore: What You Must Learn from the Bold Confrontations of Christ. Detriot/NY/San Franciso/New

Haven, Conn/Waterville, Maine/London: Gale Cengage Learning, 2008.

McNeal, Reggie. *The Present Future: Six Tough Questions for the CHURCH.* San Francisco: Published by Jossey-Bass, A Wiley Imprint, 2003

Morgan, Robert J. *Come Let Us Adore Him.* Nashville, TN: Published by J. Countryman, a division of Thomas Nelson, Inc., 20005.

Morley, Brian. *"Western Concepts of God". Internet Encyclopedia of Philosophy:* This is a Peer Reviewed Site. https://iep.utm.edu/god-west

Mundell, Ernie. "U.S. Birth Rates Continue to Fall". *U. S. News and World Report, HealthDay Reporter,* (Jan 10, 2023): USNews.com

Myers, Alicia D. "Motherhood in the Greco-Roman World." Bible Odyssey (2023): BibleOdyssey.org

Newbigin, Lesslie. *Foolishness to Greeks: The Gospel and Western Culture.* Grand Rapids, Michigan: William B. Eerdmans Pub. Co., 1986, 1988.

The Open Secret: An Introduction to the Theology of Mission. Grand Rapids, MI: William B. Eerdmans Publishing Pub. Co., 1995.

The Gospel in a Pluralistic Society. Grand Rapids, MI: William B. Eerdmans Pub. Co., 1989.

Nolan, Beatrice, "US Happiness Ranking Plummets as One Group Struggles Most." *Science Alert, Health (March 21, 2024):* www.sciencealert.com

Nouwen, Henry J. M. *Adam: God's Beloved.* Ossining, NY: Orbis Books, Sep 1997. (ISBN: 1570751331 & ISBN13: 9781570751332).

O' Neil, Conner. "Why are millennials and Gen Z shying away from religion?" Published by *KARE 11* (July 28, 2022): KARE11.com

Peck, M. Scott. *The Road Less Traveled: A New Psychology of Love, Traditional Values, and Spiritual Growth*. NY: Simon & Schuster, 2003. (25th Anniversary Edition, first published in 1978).

Platt, David. *A Compassionate Call to Counterculture*. Carol Stream, Il., Tyndale House Publishers, Inc., 2015.

Poplin, Mary. *Is Reality Secular? Testing The Assumptions of Four Global Worldviews*. Downers Grove, IL: IVP Books, InterVarsity Press, 2014.

Ramsey, Russ. "Where the Lambs are Kept: A Narrative Retelling of Luke 2:8-15." Published by *Bible Theology* (Dec 23, 2015): TGC (U S Edition). TheGospelCoalition.org

Ramsay, William, *The Bearing of Recent Discovery on the Trustworthiness of the New Testament, 2nd Edition*. Cambridge, Ohio: Christian Publishing House, 2021.

Ross, Hugh. *The Improbable Planet: How Earth Became Humanity's Home*. Grand Rapids, MI: Baker Books, Baker Publishing Group, 2016.

Ruggeri, Amanda. "The rise of 'one-and-done' parenting." *B B C* (January 11, 2023): bbc.com/Worklife.

Sanders, James A., "Jubilee in the Bible." *Sage Journals, Biblical Theology Bulletin* (Feb 2, 2020): Journals.sagepub.com

Scott, William (1955). "The practice of medication in Ancient Rome". *Canadian Anesthetists Society Journal*. 2: 281–290. doi:10.1007/BF03016172. S2CID 71952217

Sheen, Fulton J. *Life of Christ*. Garden City NY: Image Books, 1977.

Sproul, R. C. *Not a Chance: The Myth of Chance in Modern Science and Cosmology*. Grand Rapids, Michigan: Baker Academics, 1994, Chap.1

"R.C. Sproul Proves that God Does Not Exist," *Ligonier Updates (May 29, 2014)*.

Stoner, Winebrenner (Author), Newman, Robert C. (Collaborator). *Science Speaks: Scientific Proof of the Accuracy of Prophecy and the Bible (Paperback, 3rd Revised Edition)*. Chicago: MOODY BOOKS PRESS, 1969

Tarnas, Richard. *The Passion of the Western Mind: Understanding the Ideas that have Shaped our World View*. NY, NY: Ballentine Books, 1991.

Tchividjian, Tullian. *Unfashionable: making a difference in the world by being different*. Colorado Springs, Colorado: Multnomah Books, 2009.

Van Dyke, Henry. *Keeping Christmas. Six Days of the Week*. NY: Charles Scribner's Sons, 1924 and 1952.

Whitbourne, Susan, Drauss. "The Truth about Only Children: More evidence that birth order is not destiny." *Psychology Today* (April 9, 2022): PsychologyToday.com.

Yancey, Philip and Brand, Dr. Paul. *In His Image*. Grand Rapids, MI: Zondervan Books, Zondervan Publishing House, 1987.

Yancey, Philip. *What's So Amazing About Grace?* Grand Rapids, MI: Zondervan Publishing House, 1997.

Appendix A

Luke speaks directly to Gen Z

What do you need to know about the kids and young adults of Generation Z? Here are some of the most important things.

1. They're everywhere. "Gen Z—those born between 1996 and 2014—makes up 21 percent of the U.S. population, according to U.S. Census estimates. That's slightly less than millennials (21.6 percent), more than Gen X (19 percent), and more than baby boomers (20.5 percent). By 2020, *The Washington Post* reported, Z's had about $3 trillion (about $9,200 per person in the US) in purchasing power." Recent publications indicate that by 2021 the Gen Z Cohort had $360 billion (about $1,100 per person in the US) in buying/spending power, a number which has most certainly grown as more Gen Zers join the workforce. [199]

A Timeless Word from Luke: "Do not be afraid. *I bring you good news that will cause great joy for all people.* Today in the town of David a Savior has been born to you; he is Messiah, the Lord" (Luke 2:10,11).

Good News is commodity for Gen Z, largely because commodities reflect supply and demand demographics. Gen Zers do not feel optimistic about the future of this country. There are good reasons for this tendency. However, Luke offers Good News that was introduced during a time when the future of the Jewish people and the poor and oppressed faced a similarly pessimistic time. For these people, Good News prevailed throughout the century. This was not in terms of political conquest, wealth, or power. The reign of Rome was at its peak. But the Good News Luke delivered had more to do with a fulfilling life, meaningful daily existence, and a growing sense of empowerment for what was once deemed a hopeless and helpless people.

Followers of Jesus numbered 70 to 100 the day he died, around 500 during the time of His Resurrection visitations, grew to around 1,000 by 40 A.D., became as many as 10,000 by the end of the 1st century, and amazingly grew to 3 million by the end of the 2nd century. It is not exaggeration to say that the Christian faith took over the Roman Empire in less than 300 years. Today Christianity is the largest religion in the world, with estimates numbering over 2.5 billion people worldwide. This is a little over 30% of the world population. Though these numbers are slowing to some degree in the United States and the West, countries in which we think we can create our own Good News (It doesn't seem to be working,

---

[199] According to Statistica: https://www.statista.com/statistics/296974/us-population-share-by-generation/

as this Manuscript highlights), the Numbers are geometrically climbing in areas like the African Continent (from 10 million in 1900 to 718 million today), Asia (growth rate of about 2.11% per year of identifying Christians), and the Global South (home to more than 1.1 billion Christians.) These are all places where "Good News" is once again a commodity, just as it was in the 1st century for Jesus' early followers. Those looking for "Good News" tend to migrate toward Jesus. I predict Gen Z will follow this flow.

2. They've always been wired. Gen Z has never known a world without the internet or cell phones; younger Z's have never known a world without smartphones. Google has always existed. They take Wi-Fi for granted. They spend between six and nine hours a day absorbing media, according to a survey from Common Sense Media. Among teens, 92 percent go online daily, Pew Research reports. Their preferred mode of communication is digital, primarily through social media and texting. Drew Wike, director of student ministries at Greenwood Baptist Church in Florence, South Carolina, recently noticed some of his students sitting together in a restaurant. "They weren't talking to each other," he says. "They were *texting* each other."

A Timeless Word from Luke: "The shepherds said *one to another.* Let's go to Bethlehem and see this thing that has happened, which the Lord has told us about... When they had seen him, they spread the word concerning what had been told them about this child, and all who heard it were amazed at the what the shepherds said to them... The shepherds returned home, glorifying and praising God for all the things they had heard and seen, which were just as they had been told." (Luke 2:15, 17, 18, 20).

Can you imagine their social media accounts, had they had them? Luke understood the power and influence of social interaction. He knew that it was from the "grass roots" that a movement is born, as a planet-transforming event is left in the hands of a group of shepherds to take to the world. Why would such a group make up a story that made their own life more difficult than it already was, damaging their reputation even further, and pushing them further outside the religious culture of the time? Why? Because this was not a religious movement, this was a Cosmic Event which needed to be shared to all who had ears to hear. They could not help themselves any more than My Gen Z students can be without their phones in class. These Shepherds became the social media mechanism of this time. The Word got around.

3. They've seen porn. And maybe lots of it. No other generation has had pornography so readily available, literally at their fingertips. A survey of college students in New England found 73 percent had seen porn online before they turned 18. "Sexting"—sending and receiving sexually explicit text messages—starts early for many Z's. A survey of middle-school-aged students in Los Angeles found 25 percent said they'd received a sext. A smaller study of college students by professors at Drexel University found more than half (54 percent) reported sending a sext before they turned 18, often as a form of flirting. Gen Z is growing up in a sex saturated environment and never lived in a day which had any resemblance to a time of sexual restraint or taboo.

A Timeless Word from Luke: "The Lord answered him: 'Doesn't each of you on the Sabbath untie your ox and donkey from the stall and lead it out to water? Then should not this woman, a daughter of Abraham, whom Satan has kept bound for eighteen long years, be set free on the Sabbath day from what bound her?'" (Luke 13:15, 16)

Luke understood the power of cultural trends to capture and define human behavior. He identified this power and influence as transcendent, often a sign of something more powerful than simple cultural trends, but a sign of spiritual warfare at a cultural level. Luke understood the transcendent influence upon human behavior, a *postmodern* trend. Communication is key to understanding, and understanding is key to a search for Truth. And connection between people far outweighs the limits placed on our communication by outdated traditional practices. In Luke's Gospel people became creative communicators of need and response. Luke's Gospel remains a roadmap toward understanding a Generation seeking answers to new questions.

4. They're more accepting of sexual fluidity. Gen Zers mostly support gay marriage and transgender rights. For them, such things are part of everyday life. This is not a moral issue; this is a human rights issue for them. For the Gen Z Generation, not embracing the lifestyle choice of a marginalized human being is the ultimate insult, and this regardless of religious ideology or personal preference. People deserve to be heard and accepted. It would be rare for a Z to *not* have a friend from the LGBTQ+ community. Additionally, a 2016 survey of gender and sexuality by J. Walter Thompson Company, a New York-based marketing firm, found only 48 percent of those 13 to 20 years old described themselves as "completely heterosexual," compared to 65 percent of those 21 to 34. In his book, James White describes the Gen Z attitude as "an increasing sexual fluidity that refuses either the homosexual or heterosexual label. The idea is that both labels are repressive." [200]

A Timeless Word from Luke: "What shall I compare the Kingdom of God to? It is like yeast that a woman took and mixed into about sixty pounds of flour until it worked all through the dough." (Luke 13:20, 21)

Luke was fully aware of the power of social trends, the need to understand these trends, and to address people with worth and dignity as we explore the powerful influences which impact generational human behavior. We cannot create dialogue with

---

[200] James Emory White, Meet Generation Z: Understanding and reaching the new post-Christian world, 2017. Baker Books, Grand Rapids, MI.

a people group if we do not recognize the power and impact of worldview and ideology. Ideas are "yeast," so we cannot entertain Truth dialogue without recognizing and understanding the "dough." Luke emphasized parables because he knew wisdom is a more powerful weapon than political debate. There are reasons people believe what they believe. Wisdom, as Luke emphasized, demands that we speak to the heart of a cultural trend, rather than go on the offensive against individual persons. Luke wrote a Gospel which allowed the narrative to speak for itself, without pointing fingers of condemnation toward those with whom we may disagree. It is little wonder Gen Z is turned off by the political debate of today. Luke was not into politics, but instead into a search for real answers to very real problems, just like Gen Z.

5. They're racially diverse . . . and multiracial. Z's have friends from a variety of ethnicities. About half of kids under 5 in the U.S. are ethnic minorities, according to the U.S. Census. Six of the 15 most common last names in the United States were of Hispanic origin in 2010, compared to none of the top 15 in 1990, the Census Bureau says. If your church's congregation is not diverse, Z's will wonder why. And when Z's get married, they're more likely than their forebears to wed someone of another ethnic group. About 1 in 6 marriages today are of an interracial couple, according to Pew Research. In 1980, the rate was less than 1 in 10.

A Timeless Word from Luke: "People will come from east and west and north and south and will take their places at the feast of the Kingdom of God. Indeed, there are those who are last who will be first, and first who will be last." (Luke13: 29, 30)

Luke understood that the movement which began with the birth of Jesus was not a Jewish Phenomenon, A Roman Event, or the birth of a new Greek god. He understood this was a Universal Happening, in which all peoples in all areas of the world would be challenged with the Reality of a New Kingdom open to everyone.

Luke recognized that the barriers often created by religious movements were dismantled and destroyed with the coming of Messiah, the very design Gen Z embraces.

6. They're independent. Gen Xers repeatedly warned about "helicopter parenting," having reacted by giving their kids—Z's—plenty of space. This hands-off parenting has yielded both pros and cons. On the pro side, Zs are self-directed and confident. On the con side, they're not necessarily equipped with much real-life wisdom or many boundaries. In an age of cyber-bullying, sexting, internet porn, and hooking up—not to mention hacking, scams, and identity theft—the consequences can be dangerous.

A Timeless Word from Luke: "When you are invited, take the lowest place, so that when your host comes, he will say to you, 'Friend, move up to a better place.' Then you wil be honored in the presence of all the other guests. For all those who exalt themselves will be humbled, and those who humble themselves will be exalted." (Luke 14:10, 11)

Gen Z participants would find Luke appealing, in that Luke believed the lowest among us are those in the most need of elevation. As self-directed confident individuals, they proclaim with a loud voice that people from all categories are to be held in high esteem. They have the courage to speak this "nontraditional view" precisely because of their self-directed confidence, a trait which Luke displays with his countercultural voice. Luke and Z's are both countercultural entities to be reckoned with.

7. They're aware of a troubled planet. Most Z's have grown up after 9/11 and have only known a world where terrorist attacks are the norm. Additionally, they've lived through the Great Recession, and they've seen their parents, or many of their friends' parents, struggle through job losses, foreclosures, and more. "They're a hopeful generation, but realistic," says Josh Branum, family pastor at Faith Bridge Church in

Jacksonville, Florida. "They see the world for what it is. They are not afraid, but they are going into it with their eyes wide open."

A Timeless Word from Luke: "'Sir,' the servant said, 'what you ordered has been done, but there is sitll room.' Then the master told his servant, 'Go out to the roads and country lanes and compel them to come in, so that my house will be full." and "My son, the father said, 'you are always with me, and everything I have is yours. But we had to celebrate and be glad, because this brother of yours was dead and is alive again; he was lost and is found." (Luke 14:22, 23 and Luke 15:31, 32)

Luke understood he lived in a world where something was not right, where cultural trends were harming human life, a world in which answers were needed from a place beyond Roman Authority, Greek Ideology, or Jewish Faith. Gen Zers recognize we live in just such a time as this and they are open to exploring new possibilities in order to find real answers.

8. They're justice minded. Partly because of No. 7 above, Z's want to make a difference in the world. Like millennials before them, they're keenly aware of justice issues concerning poverty, human trafficking, refugees, racism, and more. They want opportunities to have an impact, and they're likely to become generous givers to charitable organizations as adults. "They're kids who volunteer, who have a heart for mission and justice, who sign up for things that previous generations didn't," says Burns. "It's part of their DNA."

A Timeless Word from Luke: "He has scattered those who are proud in their inmost thoughts. He has brought down rulers from their thrones but has lifted the humble. He has filled the hungry with good things but has sent the rich away empty." (Luke 1:51-53)

Mary's song is full of a poetic cry for justice, not just for her people, but for all people whom God so passionately cared for. She wrote this song at a Gen Z age when compared with our time. Despite her youthfulness, she wrote this song for everyone, especially the lowly and the forgotten. Luke's Gospel was a powerful participant in the cries for mercy and justice for the forgotten peoples of this world. Luke did not accept a surrender to silently watching as people suffered. Neither does Gen Z.

9. They are post-Christian. Almost a quarter (23 percent) of America's adults—and a third of millennials—are "nones," claiming no religious identity at all, according to Pew Research. Many Z's are growing up in homes where there is no religion whatsoever, and they may have no experience of religion. "Gen Z is very secularized," says Rick Eubanks, student minister at Oak Grove Baptist Church in Burleson, Texas. "Previous generations grew up with some Judeo-Christian values of the past, at least as a reference point. Today's generation has little to no acquaintance with the Gospel.

A Timeless Word from Luke: "With this in mind, since I myself have carefully investigated everything from the beginning, I too decided to write and orderly account for you, most excellent Theophilus, so that you may know the certainly of the things you have been taught." (Luke 1: 3, 4)

Luke would never have us embrace faith blindly, but instead was meticulous in his research and his reasoning. He understood the need for a connection between faith and reality. Just as Zs need to understand church as a meaningful activity, which offers value in day-to-day life, Luke understood that a *Messiah from Above means little to People Living Below.* This was his reason for relating a *shepherd/Angel Event,* whereby The One Who is Eternal comes to us as a Child who will now endure the daily events of human life. This was not the arrival a God separated from the events human beings endure. But this was a *Divine Being* who voluntarily entered poverty, suffering, and the heartache of death, just like so many of us. Luke emphasized that Jesus was (and is) someone who understood - *"He gets us."*

10. They're Open To faith. Although only 4 in 10 Gen Zers attend religious services weekly, 78 percent of older Zs say they believe in

God, according to a survey by Northeastern University. They view religious leaders as better role models than celebrities, professional athletes, or political leaders. "They're hungry for spiritual things," says Eubanks. "They're seeking something outside of themselves, which can be a good thing." This may be why they are more open to a college professor than they are open to a famous actor propagandizing outside a courtroom in New York.

A Timeless Word from Luke: "The Spirit of the Lord is on me (Jesus speaking in his hometown), because he has anointed me to proclaim good news to the poor. He has sent me to proclaim freedom for the prisoners and recovery of sight for the blind, to set the oppressed free, to proclaim the year of the Lord's favor." (Luke 4:18, 19)

Luke understood the connection between Faith and Life. He understood that a faith that does not connect with the day-to-day issues we face is really no faith at all. Luke highlighted the fact that the coming of Jesus was indeed "Good News", the type of "News" that has transforming impact within the lives of individuals and communities. Luke highlighted the rejection of Jesus in his hometown so that we might understand that what Jesus offered people was a challenge to the status quo, and that Jesus would rather risk rejection than offer a politically correct version of Truth. Jesus offered His Life, not just an idea or a concept to live by. For Jesus, faith was all encompassing in that it could not be an expression of morality or simply a cultural trend, but instead becomes a direction in which we live all of life. Gen Zer's get this.

(Information gathered from: "Ten Traits of Generation Z." Lifeway Research, Sep 29, 2017. And "Guide to Gen Z: What matters to this Generation and what it means for marketers." Arielle Feger, February 23, 2024. EMarketer: https://www.emarketer.com/insights/generation-z-facts/#:~:text=Born%20between%201997%20and%202012,Gen%20Zers%20join%20the%20workforce.)

Appendix B

Timeless Truths Embraced by Luke:
An Essay for the Modern World (Rick Farmer)

**"America tells you that the only things worth knowing
are those that can be known. America is wrong."**
(From a billboard seen in season two, episode one of
the TV series called "Outer Range" on Prime.)

I am extremely passionate about the Gospel of Luke as a *Word for
today*. Behind my Passion for Luke's Gospel and my belief in the
value of this Gospel for our time is a commitment to the concept of
Objective Truth for all. Under the umbrella of this commitment lies
a major assumption - *There are some objectively true suppositions
that matter for all of Humanity*. Luke identified some of these,
which are important in our time, just as they were in the time he
wrote. What follows in this brief Essay is my case for why truth
matters in our time, followed by a concise list of suppositions of
Truth from Luke's perspective. I will make this case briefly, and
then list for you the Truths Luke would have had us embrace
moving forward. We might think of these as important religious
truths for our time, but we must understand this was a non-
existent category in Luke's mind. He simply believed these things
to be True, to be evident, to be trustworthy fundamental concepts

through which we gaze to gain a more accurate understanding of Reality itself. The idea that we refer to them as "religious truths" was not a Lukian concept, but rather a method modern people use to place restrictions upon the scope and influence of some ideas. Flowing from a *Postmodern Worldview,* bathed in the *Humanistic* and *Naturalistic* paradigms of our time, labeling a thing "religious" simply gives us opportunity to relegate what follows to the realm of "subjective experience" and "private truth,"" which need not be taken seriously in the realms of fact or reality. Luke did not limit himself in such a fashion and I stand in agreement with Luke as I think and write.

Many *postmodern* thinkers identify the fact there is no valid reason to dismiss all subjective experience (or private truth) from the realm of the objectively true or that which is Real. This dismissal is simply assumed by *Naturalists, Humanists,* and surprisingly, some *Postmodernists,* without needing to make a case for why they are doing so. In other words, many contemporary thinkers assume they know more about Reality just because they claim they know more about Reality. Evidence is not a requirement when it comes to these presuppositions, though evidence seems to be the very mechanism relied upon after these assumptions are set in place. Holding a view which is not dated is the priority. However, it is likely the modern thinker knows less than they could know, given their propensity to exclude lots of information from realms they choose not to explore before ever commencing their investigation.

Epistemology is supposed to be an investigation of what distinguishes "justified belief" from opinion. If we assume this to be an accurate description, how can we justify some presuppositions over other presuppositions simply because of the source of the supposition being presented? We play this game in politics and family discussions every day. However, should we not arrive at "justified belief" based on the evidence for the supposition, not the source thereof, if we are serious about epistemological investigation?

If the goal is to arrive at a "justified belief" of that which is True, why would we limit any idea, no matter how ancient it might be, if the idea helps us toward the process of discovering *True Knowledge?* Almost any psychosocial theory I can name can be found in some form in the writings of ancient Greek Philosophers. Should we give them credit for their foundational reflections which helped build Western Culture, or should we simply dismiss them out of hand since their writings were part of antiquity? Honestly, we have no choice but to embrace and learn, for their ideas are still with us. Why do so many *postmodern* thinking people choose to do the opposite? Many in the *postmodern* community choose to dismiss Luke, and writers like him, before ever giving him a chance to join the conversation. This is a bit like dismissing my wife's viewpoint about men because she is not a man.

There is a huge share of blame to go around when considering the limits placed upon Truth discovery. I believe The Church is largely responsible for this plight. Theology took a wrong turn sometime after the Enlightenment. Theologians became consumed with making a Biblical Worldview credible to the world. The dismissal of Theological Truth from the Public Discussion of Truth was primarily because we were asking the wrong questions. Theology was so consumed with asking "how can we make the Gospel relevant in the modern world?" that we stopped asking *"Who is Jesus?"* and "Why is this important for our time?" Simply put, we imposed questions upon Gospel writers like Luke that they did not deem important to ask, to which they never offered an answer. We get it wrong in the *postmodern* world when we limit the questions which can be asked, for wrong answers run amuck when we ask the wrong questions.

Consider one example. Let us suppose we want to address the issue of our social need for thriving families. Being that we are *postmoderns*, we have decided beforehand that there is no "right" answer, only possibilities to be discovered. Based on this unproven presupposition, my sociological question becomes: "How might we better equip single moms to create opportunities for their children as they grow into adulthood?" Most of us would affirm the need and the value of such a question. The question slips through without a considerable amount of debate or push back. After this pattern is set by *the postmodern* context, along comes the "enlightened theologian," desiring to make the Gospel relevant to the world, so they ask a different question: "How might the Church respond toward enabling single parents to thrive in the modern world so that their children might have boundless opportunity to thrive as they grow into adulthood?" (We Theologians tend to be verbally verbose). From this we develop some church programs to empower some single parents and off we go answering the *postmodern* question in a "Christian way." Both theology (in this case applying to those who are church people) and the *postmodern worldview* (which shapes the question and therefore the answer) survive and thrive in our post-truth world. As long as we know our place, we are left alone to do our theological thing. But what if the question we should be asking about single parent families never gets addressed because our presuppositions will not allow it? This is a huge *postmodern* problem. We are afraid to ask the "right" questions for fear of offending the "wrong" people.

We are seldom encouraged to explore a third possibility because The Church has been unable to articulate the "right" question and simultaneously remain relevant? As a result, the Theologian ends up asking the wrong question, and the *postmodern worldview* controls which questioned can be asked. Because theologians are often so hellbent on remaining relevant within the discussion presented, they miss the boat entirely, having the parameters of their question confined within the realm of "the religious community." Yes, they are part of the modern conversation, but only as an offering for those who privately embrace faith in the raising of their children.

What if the real question for the Theologian is something like: "What is happening to the family Unit and is this good for our future as a nation?" For the unchurched, this question and its answer, and the programs the Church offers society to answer such a question, are largely irrelevant, since artificial parameters have been set up which determine who the relevant listeners are to any given question/answer under discussion. In the post – truth world, theologians are confined to an arena of subjective experience of truth when it comes to family structure. My line of questioning comes with a presupposition that some family structures are better than other family structures, the very thing we are not allowed to assume. It becomes a question we are not allowed to ask in the public spheres of life. We are not told or given evidence as to why we can't ask such questions, only that it is "wrong" to do so. Never mind that social research reveals a drastic drop off in the success of raising our children into thriving adulthood when the father is absent. Never mind the fact that two-parent homes are objectively superior to single parent homes when it comes to opportunities and the future of our children. Never mind that kids who attend church have better grades, are more productive, commit less crime, and are more likely to thrive in the real world. We make this issue about DEI in society and about relevancy in the Church, thus we limit the importance of Truth in both arenas.

We cannot escape the unspoken truth that being "wrong" feels the same as being "right," so relying on subjective experience to determine right and wrong is dangerous in the same way that using opiates to cover up necessary warnings connected to pain is dangerous. We need true knowledge about the consequences of relying on opiates. We cannot make our judgments based on the subjective experiences resulting from heroin use without risking health, future and even our lives. Society at large is harmed when we ignore the objective realities associated with opiate addiction. So, if we need something beyond personal subjective reality to make right choices about drugs and parenting and a whole myriad of other important things, why do we somehow convince ourselves that issues like sexual identity or single parenting are entirely subjective experiences to be decided by "how I feel about such things?"

Honestly, I was not searching for relevancy in the research or content of this book. I was searching for something different, which Luke understood to be "Timeless Truth" for each person in every generation. Christians reading please understand - Gen Z does not care how relevant you are. They care about something more important than this. They care about things that matter to human beings at a deeper level than moral condemnation or acceptable behavior. They do not seek relevancy, but rather they seek meaningful connection. They are struggling to heal the isolation environment we have created for them, inside and outside The Church.

Luke never engaged in such a relevancy quest. His approach was a Transcendent Journey. He first established the Authority of the Christ with his narrative. He built this case based upon meticulous research into the world in which he lived, the power of tradition and prophecy, the circumstances of the world in which all people live, the role of parents in the lives of all children, the beauty of faith in the midst of suffering and oppression, and the sheer raw power of Jesus in the face of the political powers of his time. The difference in this approach is astounding. Luke never settled for a cultural assumption about family, other than the family of origin provided by Tradition and Authority. Luke does not acknowledge Roman families and Greek families and Jewish families as equally valid expressions of Family in his time. Luke proclaimed the Creator's intent for Family, painted a vivid picture of what this looks like, and applied this vivid concept of Family to his discussion of that which is True – for everyone. He did not spend time apologizing, rationalizing, compromising, or politically correcting his message. He simply declared the event itself and what this event meant for the world. Luke transcended a *Postmodern Worldview* and a *Relevant Theological Strategy* and simply proclaimed Truth. This is precisely why his Gospel is *Timeless*. No catering, no compromising, just Cosmic Communication. For Luke, the question being posed is something more like: "For what purpose did God create Family and how does Jesus fit into this concept of Family?"

I am suggesting that to understand such a question from Luke's perspective we must be able to discern the suppositions which guided his thinking. I wrote this Manuscript with these in mind. Listed below are the things Luke believed to be objectively true, though he in no way assumed we could embrace any of these without evidence. Luke meticulously investigated the evidence, and his Gospel was his attempt to share what he found. (I plan to write more about this in my next book, God willing.)

What follows is the beginning of a list of the Truths Luke embraced. As you read this list, remember, Luke traveled many miles and many roads through a variety of witnesses recording a considerable amount of evidence to present his findings to the Jury – you and me in the 21st century. None of us were there. We are all relying on testimony and historical evidence. But as we deliberate, it is of utmost importance to deliberate wisely before we discard the evidence Luke presented. Allow yourself to transcend the *postmodern worldview* as you read and consider.

This is what Luke believed to be Truth, in his time and in ours:
(Remember this is Luke through the filter of my 21st century baby boomer postmodern mind. I cannot escape my world entirely, no matter how much I might desire it. Nor can you….)

Tradition is of tremendous value and Authority must be affirmed and acknowledged.

Reality is both Visible and Invisible; That which is invisible can be made visible in at least two ways – Revelation from the Invisible, Impact of the Invisible on the Visible world.

Prophetic utterances are of tremendous value when they are honored, understood, proclaimed, and fulfilled.

Some Truths are for all people in all times.

Metaphysical Truth can also be Objective Truth; Reality can be understood and defined beyond what can be revealed through the Scientific Method.

The Ideas and Beliefs of pre-scientific people are valid, reliable, and valuable.

History matters - We cannot survive or thrive as a people at any time without a profound commitment to the value of History. Those who choose to ignore our past are both doomed to repeat it and inviting peril upon themselves.

The birth of Jesus changed the Future and the Reality of this world, both at a personal level and a community level.

Facts matter when establishing Truth. However, facts can exist apart from their discovery in the scientific laboratory.

Jesus displayed a genuine love for all sorts of people from a variety of cultures and social classes. Jesus was a Self-Actualized Leader born during a time of tremendous need. Jesus and his family were well acquainted with suffering and oppression - There are no life experiences he does not understand, then or now.

Luke invited all readers to investigate his claims - He was noticeably confident in the outcome if a person chooses to do so.

Luke was not interested in claims of Truth without validation of these claims; To ignore the Gospel of Luke is an unwise choice, both for the individual and the community.

Luke believed the coming of Christ is both a fact in history, a promise made before recorded history began, and the most important existential event that ever occurred for all people in all nations in every time.

(As time passes, I have no doubt I will add to this list. For now, these are places to begin as we grapple with the Truth found in the Gospel of Luke, if indeed we choose to do so. I extend this invitation. Blessings, Rick Farmer)

Printed in the United States
by Baker & Taylor Publisher Services